Proofreading & Editing PRECISION

5th Edition

Larry G. Pagel
Associate Professor
Walker L. Cisler College of Business
Northern Michigan University
Marquette, Michigan

Contributing Author

Robyn R. Hart
Business Instructor
Fresno City College
Fresno, California

THOMSON

SOUTH-WESTERN

Australia · Brazil · Canada · Mexico · Singapore · Spain · United Kingdom · United States

THOMSON

SOUTH-WESTERN

Proofreading & Editing Precision, Fifth Edition

Larry G. Pagel

VP/Editorial Director:
Jack W. Calhoun

VP/Editor-in-Chief:
Karen Schmohe

Acquisitions Editor:
Jane Phelan

Project Manager:
Penny Shank

Consulting Editor:
Marianne Miller

Production Project Manager:
Cami Cacciatore

Marketing Manager:
Mike Cloran

Marketing Coordinator:
Georgianna Wright

Manufacturing Coordinator:
Charlene Taylor

Production House:
GGS Book Services

Printer:
Globus Printing Company
Minster, Ohio

Art Director:
Stacy Jenkins Shirley

Internal Designer:
Beckmeyer Design, Inc.

Cover Designer:
Beckmeyer Design, Inc.

Cover Images:
© Getty Images

Photo Researcher:
Darren Wright

For more information about our products, contact us at:

Thomson Higher Education
5191 Natorp Boulevard
Mason, Ohio 45040
USA

Preface

For any businessperson whose daily activities involve working with written or printed communications, the ability to proofread and edit is most important. Proofreading and editing skills are critical for students, office workers, originators of documents, and other professional businesspeople who strive for excellence in their communications. Excellence is an attitude that must be developed. Excellence is accuracy, which is the most important standard in business.

Proofreading & Editing Precision, 5th edition, is a comprehensive activity-oriented text-workbook designed to sharpen proofreading and editing skills using hard copy (handwritten or printed) and computerized activities. It provides a thorough review of the rules governing language arts and document preparation and applies them in realistic business documents.

This text-workbook may be used effectively in any course that requires the production of written communications. It may be used in courses including keyboarding, word/information processing, office procedures, business communications, and business English.

SPECIAL FEATURES

Some of the special features in *Proofreading & Editing Precision,* 5th edition, include the following:

- An engaging layout

- A pretest and a posttest

- A Spotlight on Accuracy feature at the beginning of each chapter to highlight the importance of precision in written communications

- Activities that make use of a variety of documents, including letters, memos, e-mails, reports, resumes, minutes, and news releases

- A list of commonly confused and misused words

- Teamwork exercises to build peer editing skills and to foster collaborative learning

- Foreign language proofreading exercises provided in International Vocabulary activities

- Proofreading at the Computer documents

- Spelling and word usage reviews included in each chapter

- A complete index

- A list of proofreaders' marks provided at the end of the text-workbook for easy reference

Teamwork

The Computerized Minisimulation provides practical hands-on experience in proofreading, editing, and formatting. This optional activity consists of six business documents that are typically found in a business that utilizes Internet technologies. As an "employee," the student's responsibility is to proofread, edit, and format printed and online documents. The Minisimulation is divided into three parts, which gives students the option of completing the Minisimulation all at once or in three stages.

CHAPTER PROFILE

Each chapter contains brief reviews of proofreading concepts in order of increasing difficulty. Concepts include spelling; word division; capitalization; abbreviations; number expression; sentence construction; punctuation; formatting of business documents; and editing for errors in content, clarity, and conciseness. The last chapter is devoted exclusively to on-screen proofreading. This chapter includes information processing tools (spreadsheet, database, and voice recognition software) and e-mail.

To provide several opportunities for applying the principles reviewed in the chapter, each chapter includes the following:

- **Proofread and Mark.** These exercises apply one rule or a short series of rules just presented.

- **Spelling and Word Usage Check.** This exercise provides a list of frequently misspelled words and three sets of commonly confused and misused words for students to identify and correct.

- **International Vocabulary.** This exercise is made up of a list of Spanish words for students to proofread. Students do not need to understand Spanish to complete these activities. Students compare a list of correctly spelled Spanish words in the first column to a list of Spanish words that contain spelling errors in the second column. This is an excellent activity for building foreign language awareness as well as a means to focus students on the task of proofreading.

- **Proofreading Applications.** The Proofreading Applications begin with a single exercise in which students must apply the concepts they learned in the chapter. That exercise is followed by a series of business documents that contain the same types of errors.

- **Proofreading at the Computer.** This optional exercise consists of business documents (on the Student CD) that provide extensive practice in proofreading, formatting, and editing documents that occur in everyday business situations. Students already proofread and marked the first document in a previous Proofreading Application. The other documents are new.

- **Cumulative Application.** The final application in Chapters 3–13 is a review exercise that encompasses all of the concepts presented in the chapter and in previous chapters.

STUDENT CD

A Student CD comes packaged with the text-workbook. The CD contains word processing files that students use to proofread and format the documents in Proofreading at the Computer. By using the CD, students gain realistic experience in proofreading, editing, formatting and printing, revising, and saving stored files of business documents. Use of the CD is optional.

SUPPLEMENTARY TEACHING AIDS

The following supplement is available to instructors for classroom use:

Annotated Instructor's Edition

The Annotated Instructor's Edition (ISBN: 0-538-44249-2) provides the student edition with answers overprinted to aid instruction and evaluation. Each chapter begins with a suggested completion time to aid in planning, and teaching suggestions are provided throughout the text as margin annotations.

In addition, the Annotated Instructor's Edition includes a suggested class schedule, evaluation and grading plans for quizzes, quizzes for each chapter, a pretest and a posttest, and transparency masters. Solutions for all Student CD activities, chapter quizzes, pretest, posttest, and the Computerized Minisimulation are also included.

Contents

Errors! Errors! Errors!

Spotlight on ACCURACY

In an e-mail message, a writer forgets to include the room number for a meeting. The error of omission may cause confusion, or it may inconvenience the recipients. What is the impact when errors are published in thousands of copies of books? Yes, even professionals in the textbook industry make errors. Some are simple typographical errors. Others are more serious content errors. In one textbook review, a state review committee discovered that Christopher Columbus sailed for the New World in 1942. In another book the Statue of Liberty was said to be made of bronze, rather than copper. And one world history text omitted an entire Chinese dynasty.

Of course, anyone can make an error—and everyone does at one time or another. The point of proofreading, though, is to eliminate errors—or at least to minimize them. Whereas mechanical or format errors may cloud a message, content errors may completely obscure it.

Adapted for use from Dona Orr, Carol W. Henson, and H. Frances Daniels, *Proofreading: A Programmed Approach,* 4th edition, Cincinnati, South-Western/Thomson Learning, 2003, p. 213.

Objectives

- Understand the importance of proofreading.

- Identify the most common types of errors when proofreading.

- Explain and apply the various methods of proofreading documents.

- Use reference sources to verify information when proofreading.

Y ou receive a letter in the mail. You look at the envelope. What do you find? Errors! Your name is misspelled. Your house number is incorrect. Even your street name is misspelled. As if all of that were not enough, your ZIP Code is wrong too. Wait! You still have to read the letter. You take a quick glance and think to yourself, "Looks pretty good." Then you notice that *January* is spelled J-a-n-a-r-y and that the letter address is incorrect, just as it was on the envelope.

You wonder: "Why didn't someone proofread this letter? Who wrote this letter? Who signed the letter without first checking it for accuracy? What kind of employees does this company hire? Do I want to do business with this company?"

IMPORTANCE OF PROOFREADING

Documents that are error-free create a favorable impression. Letters that look attractive, contain no misspelled words, and use correct grammar and punctuation indicate to the reader that the sender is a competent person who is concerned about quality. The reader of such quality documents judges the individual to be a good person with whom he or she can conduct business.

On the other hand, errors reflect carelessness and incompetence. Most people are annoyed when their names are misspelled, even though they may not say so. Grammar errors, too, are distracting; and the reader may assume that the sender is uneducated.

People expect letters, memos, reports, and tables to have a certain "look." Readers expect documents to be prepared in a standard format, making them easy to read. Irregular formats are distracting because they cause the reader to think about how the letter looks rather than what it says.

Errors are inevitable. Everyone makes them. Errors can be found in all types of handwritten, keyed, and printed materials. Errors occur in business letters, faxes, e-mail, memorandums, reports, and other kinds of documents. Errors also occur in newspapers and in magazine headings, articles, and captions. Uncorrected errors are embarrassing; they may cause misunderstandings and confusion, and they may become expensive. Why? Errors cause delays in the delivery of goods or services. Apologies must be made when an incorrect price is quoted or an invoice total is wrong. Sometimes a phone call or follow-up message must be sent to explain how the error was made and how it will be corrected. All of these steps mean more time, more effort, and more expense. How the sender might wish he or she had taken the time to check for accuracy in the first place!

Today computers, high-speed printers, and other electronic equipment enable documents to be produced faster than ever before. Form letters can be prepared for many people in an amazingly short period of time. If documents are not prepared correctly, however, this same equipment can produce errors just as quickly.

Accuracy is the most important standard in the business world. Businesses constantly seek qualified employees who pay attention to detail. Therefore, the ability to produce accurate documents is a necessity.

As a person who will soon be working in the business world, you must develop an attitude of excellence. You must not be satisfied until what you have produced is error-free. This means carefully checking names, numbers, dates, content, spelling, grammar, and punctuation. After all, you are responsible for the work that leaves your desk. Your image and that of the company depend on your ability to proofread well.

WHAT IS PROOFREADING?

Proofreading is the process of reading handwritten, keyed, or printed material and marking errors to indicate corrections. Thus, proofreading is essential to ensure the accuracy of your work.

As errors are identified, they are marked with special symbols called **proofreaders' marks.** Each symbol not only highlights the error, but also indicates the correction to be made. Proofreaders' marks are standard symbols. They should be used by executives, managers, document specialists, and all other office workers who proofread and make corrections on an original document. The person who makes the corrections will then be able to interpret them accurately. The chapters in this text present the most common proofreaders' marks. A list of these also appears at the back of this text.

People hired primarily to proofread are known as **proofreaders.** Proofreaders may also be responsible for setting format standards and training other office workers to follow the same standards.

Proofreading requires both knowledge and concentration. It demands patience and attention to detail. Information cannot be proofread by skimming. You may think that when you have finished composing or keying a document, it is correct. You might say, "Well, I'll read it through quickly just in case I missed something." Or you might say, "I used the spelling checker to search for errors, so I don't have to worry." Your task is not done, however, until you have carefully reread the document. Instead, you should say, "I know there is at least one error here; I just have to find it." In other words, you must develop the attitude that proofreading is vitally important in the preparation of documents.

Proofreading is an essential task that you need to take seriously. The more important the document, the more time you need to devote to proofreading to ensure accuracy. The best proofreaders are effective because they:

- Pay attention to detail.
- Take time to proofread carefully.
- Recognize frequent types of errors.
- Use a variety of proofreading methods.
- Are good spellers.
- Know and apply the basics of good grammar and punctuation.
- Use appropriate reference materials to guarantee accuracy.

WHAT KINDS OF ERRORS ARE MOST COMMON?

Errors may be classified as either mechanical or content. Because these are two different kinds of errors, it is important to read the material once for mechanical errors and a second time for content errors. If the material is long and complex and has many numbers or other details, proofread the material a third time to ensure that all of the errors are found.

Mechanical Errors

Mechanical errors are those that can be recognized when looking at the material without having to reference the meaning. These errors include transposition (the reversing of letters or words), capitalization, spacing, punctuation, and spelling errors. Can you find the mechanical errors in these three sentences?

1. Place thier agenda the in folder.

2. The color choices are red, blue and green

3. please send this to your assitant.

Proofreading for mechanical errors involves slow and careful reading.

Concentrate on each detail. Carefully check each punctuation mark to be sure it is correct. Check capitalization and spelling. Check for correct number usage and word division.

© GETTY IMAGES/PHOTODISC

In sentence 1 *their* is misspelled and the words *the* and *in* are reversed. Sentence 2 should have a comma after *blue* and a period at the end of the sentence. In sentence 3 the first word should be capitalized and the last word should be spelled *assistant*.

When proofreading for mechanical errors, slow your reading rate to "low gear." Read the copy letter by letter, word by word, phrase by phrase, or line by line, pronouncing each word as you read. Pronouncing each word forces you to slow your reading. It is the most effective way to proofread.

Another proofreading technique is to read from right to left. This focuses your attention on each word, letting you check for mechanical errors.

Content Errors

Content errors are errors of information or fact. They are more difficult to locate than mechanical errors because once information is in print, you tend to think of it as being correct. Content errors cause confusion and misunderstanding.

To locate content errors, read the material more slowly than your normal rate. Read complete sentences. Instead of reading word for word, concentrate on the meaning of what you are reading. Ask yourself questions such as these:

- Does the content make sense?

- Are the facts accurate?

- Do I understand what the writer is trying to tell me?

- Do the subject and verb agree?

- Is there number agreement (singular versus plural)?

When proofreading for content errors, particularly when dates, numbers, names, or other details or important facts are included in the copy, check the accuracy of the information against the original source. Be prepared to check references, such as those listed in the next section. Proofreading for content errors should be done at least twice—once for grammar errors and once for other content errors.

Can you find the content errors in the following sentences?

1. The summer meeting in Des Moines will be on February 1.
2. On April 31 the tour will stop at Denver.
3. The flyers can be sent to the members which are orange.

In sentence 1 a summer meeting in Des Moines would be in June or July. In sentence 2 the date is wrong because April has only 30 days, not 31. Sentence 3 needs a shifting of words because it sounds as if the members, not the flyers, are orange.

WHERE CAN A PROOFREADER GET HELP?

A skillful proofreader does not rely simply on memory. Competent proof-readers verify facts and rules in a variety of sources. The first source should be the copy from which the information was taken—the *original* source. The original source might include address files, price lists, sales receipts, vouchers, checkbook records, purchase orders, or invoices.

Use references such as these when you proofread:

- Atlases
- Calendars
- Dictionaries
- Office reference manuals
- Online reference works
- Spelling/word lists
- Statistical sources
- Thesauruses

References are an invaluable aid to proofreaders.

METHODS OF PROOFREADING

You can improve your proofreading by applying the methods described in this section. Use the first two methods when you read the material by yourself. Use the third method when you proofread with another person. Other helpful hints for proofreading are included in each chapter under the heading PEP (*P*roofreading and *E*diting *P*recision) Tip. **PEP Tip**

Comparative Proofreading Method

The comparative proofreading method involves comparing one document with another. Follow these steps when using this method:

Step 1 Place the document to be proofread next to the original copy.

Step 2 Place the documents being compared as close to each other as possible. This decreases unnecessary eye and/or neck movement and allows for more accurate proofreading.

This method is especially useful when you proofread statistical or technical material that contains many numbers or specialized vocabulary, such as that found in medical, legal, and scientific material. This method can also be combined with the team method, which is explained later in the chapter.

On-Screen Method

When preparing documents on a computer, you need to proofread the documents before and after you print them. Follow these steps:

Step 1 Proofread on-screen once for mechanical errors and once for content errors. (Proofread sections of the document or one full screen at a time.)

Step 2 When proofreading for mechanical errors, move your cursor and carefully pronounce each word as you read.

Step 3 Check for words that may have been omitted or added when copy was revised.

Step 4 Although most word processing software hyphenates words according to its built-in dictionary, check all of the line endings for inaccuracies. Words are sometimes hyphenated in odd places. Also check to make sure that large gaps do not occur at the ends of lines because words have not been divided. Also check words that were hyphenated originally at the ends of lines but are now in the middle of lines because of lengthy revisions that caused different word-wrapped paragraphs.

Step 5 Use the spelling checker to check the spelling in the entire document. (This procedure is discussed further in Chapter 2.)

Step 6 Print the document after you have proofread it.

Team Method

As the name implies, the team method involves two people. One person reads the draft or original copy aloud while another person follows along, reading and marking the other copy. When the copy is quite long or complex, the two people take turns reading aloud and checking the copy. The team method is especially effective when checking the accuracy of technical or statistical copy or copy that has long lists, many names, or numbers. When using this method on lists of names, the readers *must* verify accuracy of spelling. The team method ensures that copy has been proofread carefully because two people have checked it.

The team method of proofreading is effective for technical documents.

© GETTY IMAGES/PHOTODISC

• **When proofreading for mechanical errors, read the material from right to left instead of the usual left-to-right method.**

PEP**!**Tip

WHAT'S AHEAD?

Beginning with Chapter 2, you will learn how to find specific kinds of errors and how to mark the errors using correct proofreaders' marks. Errors will occur in spelling, word division, capitalization, number usage, punctuation, format, and content. You will also learn how to make editing corrections.

Within each chapter you will be introduced to several basic rules. You will then have an opportunity to test your understanding of the rules and to apply them in several ways.

- In *Proofread and Mark* activities, which immediately follow the introduction of specific rules, you will be asked to proofread in the context of short sentences.

- The *Proofreading Applications* begin with activities that concentrate on the types of errors introduced in the current chapter.

- The *Spelling and Word Usage Check* is next. This section includes several words that are commonly misspelled. You will be asked to identify those words that are spelled incorrectly and use appropriate proofreaders' marks to make corrections. A listing of misspelled words is located in the Appendix.

- The Spelling and Word Usage Check is followed by *International Vocabulary.* This activity includes a list of five Spanish words. While you may not recognize the words or understand their meaning, this exercise will help you increase your ability to find words that are misspelled.

- More Proofreading Applications follow in which you proofread two or more realistic business documents that contain errors discussed in the chapter. Some of these documents will be computerized applications (*Proofreading at the Computer*) available on a Student CD. (Your instructor can tell you if you will be completing these exercises.) The purpose of these exercises is to provide additional proofreading and editing practice.

- Each chapter concludes with a *Cumulative Application* that includes one document focusing on all proofreading topics covered up to that point.

As you complete the assignments in this text, keep in mind the importance of proofreading. With the proper attitude, you will succeed in developing good proofreading skills; you will also become a valuable, efficient, and productive employee.

Keyboarding Errors

Spotlight on **ACCURACY**

If you are a bad speller, you may think you will always be a bad speller. There seems to be an exception to every rule, and the rules are not easy to remember. George Bernard Shaw demonstrated how ridiculous some spelling rules really are. By following these rules, he said *fish* could be spelled *ghoti*. Pronouncing the *gh* as it sounds in *enough*, the *o* as it sounds in *women,* and the *ti* as it sounds in *fiction* would yield *fish*. With such rules to follow, no one should feel foolish for being a bad speller. The good news is that approximately 90 percent of all writing consists of 1,000 basic words, and that is a manageable number to learn.

Objectives

- Recognize transposition errors, added copy errors, omitted copy errors, incorrect letters, and numerical errors.

- Use appropriate proofreaders' marks to correct these errors.

- Spell correctly 12 frequently misspelled words.

- Use correctly three sets of commonly confused and mis-used words.

SPELLING ERRORS

The most frequent types of errors found in business documents are spelling errors. These errors result from striking the wrong character on the keyboard or actually misspelling the word. Regardless of the cause, the proofreader's task is to locate the errors and indicate exactly what corrections are needed. In Chapter 2, you will learn to identify spelling errors that result from transpositions, additions of extra letters or spaces, omitted letters, and misstrokes.

To locate spelling errors, read very slowly, letter by letter. If the material has been keyed from another source, such as a handwritten document or a rough draft, check the final printed copy against the original copy.

If you are using a word processing program equipped with a **spelling checker**, use it to check for spelling errors. The spelling checker compares each word in the document to the words in the program's electronic dictionary. Words that do not match the dictionary of the spelling checker are clearly marked on the screen. Although the spelling checker will identify errors such as *bisiness* or *oppertunity,* it does not read for context. Therefore, it will not recognize errors such as *form* for *from* or *short* for *shirt.* The spelling checker does not recognize **homophones**, words that are pronounced alike but are spelled differently, such as "when he through the ball" (should be *threw*) or "the third addition of the textbook" (should be *edition*). To locate misused or inappropriate words, you must read the copy carefully.

TRANSPOSITION ERRORS

Letters, numbers, punctuation marks, words, or even sentences keyed out of order are called **transpositions**. Transpositions frequently occur in vowels (rec*ie*ve), short words (*adn*), and word endings (availab*el*). Letters that are adjacent on the keyboard, such as *r* and *t, v* and *b, n* and *m,* and *s* and *d,* are frequently transposed.

Sometimes transpositions result in words that look familiar. However, when the entire sentence is read for meaning, it becomes obvious that the word is used incorrectly. Careful proofreading is required to find transposition errors such as *form* for *from, board* for *broad, trail* for *trial, sacred* for *scared, sued* for *used, untied* for *united,* and *dairy* for *diary.*

To show any copy that is not in the correct sequence, use the transposition symbol. You should also write this symbol in the left or right margin of the document to alert the reader to an error in the line. Notice how the transposition symbol is used to mark errors in the following examples:

	MARKED COPY	CORRECTED COPY
Transpose (reverse order).	The handel is broken.	The handle is broken.
	"Start the meeting by noon"	"Start the meeting by noon."
	The report due is on Monday.	The report is due on Monday.

Exercise 2-1 PROOFREAD AND MARK

Proofread these phrases for transposition errors. Use the transposition symbol to show corrections. If the phrase is correct, write **C** to the left of the number.

1. on Wedensday morning

2. quick answer is necesasry

3. the real prolbem

4. to be aware of the

5. frequent fylers

6. needless say to

7. a copy of the reciept

8. to cross street the

Exercise 2-2 PROOFREAD AND MARK

Proofread the keyed copy for transposition errors by comparing it to the correct handwritten copy. Use the transposition symbol to show corrections. If the sentence is correct, write **C** to the left of the number.

1. *Thank you for your response.*   **1.** Thank you your for response.

2. *The next meeting is in September.*   **2.** The next meeting is ni September.

3. *Call us before noon.*   **3.** Call su before noon.

4. *Our motto is "Friendly Service for All."*   **4.** Our motto is "Freindly Service for All."

5. *The committee meeting will be held on Tuesday.*   **5.** The committee meeting will be held on Tuesday.

ADDED COPY ERRORS

Another common spelling error is adding extra letters, spaces, numbers, or punctuation marks. Additions can be caused by faulty keying or by incorrect copying from the source document. Unnecessary words, phrases, and even sentences often occur in documents that have been composed and edited using a word processing software program. Writers may insert new text but fail to delete the old text. Similarly, when making changes in documents that have been printed on paper, writers often fail to cross out unwanted text.

As you proofread, be alert for the following added copy errors:

© GETTY IMAGES/PHOTODISC

- Words repeated at the beginning of a line (particularly small words such as *in, for, that, with,* and *as*).

- Extra letters added in long words and words with double letters (*schedualed, immmediately, reccommend, tommorow*).

- Words that may appear correct (singular versus plural; homonyms) but are not because of an extra letter (offices for office, please for pleas, timer for time).

- Numbers repeated in a list.

- Phrases or an entire line of text repeated.

When proofreading, use the delete symbol to show that extra copy should be deleted and the close-up symbol to indicate that extra space should be omitted. Use both the delete and close-up symbols when letters or characters should be deleted within a word.

	MARKED COPY	CORRECTED COPY
Delete or omit copy.	Purchase yourr supplies in Boston.	Purchase your supplies in Boston.
Close up space.	Hire four new employees.	Hire four new employees.

▶ Exercise 2-3 PROOFREAD AND MARK

Proofread the following phrases for added copy errors. Use the delete and close-up symbols to show corrections. If the phrase is correct, write **C** to the left of the number.

1. an approppriate response

2. take a morning nap

3. some requirred reading

4. provided some an swers

5. discusssed the situation
6. a completed application
7. during our bussiness meeting

8. work with with the manager
9. lack of preparattion
10. one problems to settle

Exercise 2-4 PROOFREAD AND MARK

Proofread the keyed copy for added copy errors by comparing it with the correct handwritten copy. Use the delete and close-up symbols to show corrections. If the sentence is correct, write **C** to the left of the number.

1. *Your tax return is due.*
2. *Answer the customer's request.*
3. *The decision made by the faculty was final.*
4. *Preside over the meeting.*
5. *Clean the conference room.*

1. Your tax return is due.
2. Answer the cusstomer's request.
3. The decicsision made by the faculty was final.
4. Preside over the the meeting.
5. Clean the conferrence room.

INCORRECT LETTERS

Keying an incorrect letter results in a misstroke. Misstrokes are easy to overlook in long words or in such words as *quarantee* (incorrectly spelled with a *q*) for *guarantee* (correctly spelled with a *g*). It would be easy to miss *change* for *chance* because both of the words are spelled correctly. The meaning of the sentence determines which of the two words is correct. Proofread carefully for misstrokes in short words such as these:

o*f*, o*n*, o*r*	the*n*, the*m*, the*y*	tha*n*, the*n*
no*t*, no*w*, ne*w*	th*e*se, th*o*se	

Use the straight diagonal line to mark a misstroke, and write the correct letter above the misstroke.

	MARKED COPY	CORRECTED COPY
Change letter.	It was a good opp*o*rtunity.	It was a good opportunity.

> ### Exercise 2-5 PROOFREAD AND MARK

Proofread the keyed copy for incorrect letters by comparing it with the correct handwritten copy. Use the straight diagonal line and proper letter to show corrections. If the sentence is correct, write **C** to the left of the number.

1. *Her name was added to the list.*	**1.** Her name was added to the last.
2. *She is our new manager.*	**2.** She is our now manager.
3. *Your help is sincerely appreciated.*	**3.** Your help is sincerely apprediated.
4. *Pay the insurance premium.*	**4.** Pay the insurance primium.
5. *They have increased their services.*	**5.** They have increased their services.

OMITTED COPY ERRORS

Another common error is the omission of copy. Omissions occur whenever a space, character, or word is left out of a document. Entire lines and even entire sentences may also be omitted. Paired punctuation marks, such as brackets, parentheses, and quotation marks, are also common errors of omission.

Omissions of letters are common in long words, in words with silent letters (knowledg*e*able and temper*a*ment), and in words with double letters (o*cc*urrence and a*cc*ommodate). Sometimes when you are scanning a document, the copy may appear to make sense, even though something has been omitted. An omission can change the meaning of copy—sometimes drastically. Note the differenc e an omission makes in the following examples:

OMISSION ERROR	CORRECT
under doctor's car	under doctor's care
send you response	send your response
sprig into action	spring into action
check their backround	check their background

To mark omission of spaces, use the space symbol (#).

To mark errors in omitted copy, use the caret symbol (^).

If space is limited, add the caret in the exact spot in the text where the omission occurs and write the insertion in the side margin. If several words must be added and insufficient space is available in the side margin, write the copy in the top or bottom margin of the page and extend a line from the copy to the caret.

		MARKED COPY	CORRECTED COPY
Insert space.	#	mail to#this address	mail to this address
Insert copy.	∧	premium is du^e^ soon	premium is due soon
		Be sure ^*the*^ coverage *is*^ extensive.	Be sure the coverage is extensive.
		Your ^*job*^ application is being reviewed.	Your job application is being reviewed.

Exercise 2-6 PROOFREAD AND MARK

Some of the following phrases have omitted copy errors. Use the appropriate proofreaders' marks to identify the corrections. If the phrase is correct, write **C** to the left of the number.

1. the eletion results

2. when you message arrives

3. the resulting conseqences

4. soon to be released

5. an interestng person

Exercise 2-7 PROOFREAD AND MARK

Proofread the keyed copy for omitted copy errors by comparing it with the correct handwritten copy. Use the appropriate insert mark to identify the corrections that should be made. If the sentence is correct, write **C** to the left of the number.

1. *Your evaluation has been scheduled for next month.*

1. Your evaluation has been schedule for next month.

2. *You will be recognized for your achievements on Friday.*

2. You will be recognized for you achievements on Friday.

3. *The advertisement will appear in Thursday's newspaper.*

3. The advertment will appear in Thusday's newspaper.

4. *If you are able to attend, please let me know.*

4. If you are able to attend, please let me know.

5. *Factory orders will be increasing.*

5. Factory ordrs will be incrasing.

NUMERICAL ERRORS

Accuracy of numbers is extremely important because many decisions are based on numerical data. Errors in dates, amounts of money, percentages, telephone numbers, social security numbers, and statistical copy can be very costly as well as embarrassing. Transposition of numbers is a common numerical error. Similarly, errors within listed items occur frequently, particularly as items are added to or omitted from a list.

Do not assume that a number is correct. In fact, check all numbers twice. If a number has been copied from another source, make sure it has been copied correctly. Verify all extensions and totals. Proofread numbers digit by digit. For example, read the number *1994* as "one-nine-nine-four" instead of "nineteen ninety-four." If numbers are to be spelled out and also written as figures, as required in many legal documents, make sure both numbers are the same; for example, six months (6 months). Finally, check your calendar to make sure the day agrees with the date listed. Is the correct date Friday, May 5, or Thursday, May 5?

Exercise 2-8 PROOFREAD AND MARK

Proofread the keyed copy for numerical errors by comparing it with the correct handwritten copy. Use the appropriate proofreaders' marks to show corrections. If the sentence is correct, write **C** to the left of the number.

1. *The exam will have 35 questions.*

1. The exam will have 53 questions.

2. *Send a check for $139.52 with your order.*

2. Send a check for $39.52 with your order.

3. *His office telephone number is 555-0174.*	**3.** His office telephone number is 555-0147.
4. *Only 9 percent volunteered immediately.*	**4.** Only 29 percent volunteered immediately.
5. *Her address is P.O. Box 1327.*	**5.** Her address is P.O. Box 1327.

> **Exercise 2-9** PROOFREAD AND MARK

Mark any errors in the keyed list by comparing it with the correct handwritten list. Use the appropriate proofreaders' marks to show corrections. If the list is correct, write **C** to the left of the number.

1. *Carrie C. Wilson, No. 53118*	**1.** Carriee C. Wilson, No. 531188
2. *Doug E. Johnsson, No. 873241*	**2.** Doug E. Johnsson, No. 873241
3. *Michael Watermann, No. 318661*	**3.** Michail Waterman, No. 381661
4. *Kris R. Braun, No. 9733332*	**4.** Kriss R. Braun, No. 973332
5. *Roger C. Galvez, No. 35826*	**5.** Rogre C. Galvez, No. 358362

SPELLING AND WORD USAGE

Misspellings are a distraction to the reader. They are embarrassing to the writer and reflect negatively on the company. Learning to recognize these errors is critical to being a good proofreader. Develop the habit of checking a dictionary or spelling guide whenever you are unsure of a word. If you are using word processing software, use the spelling checker provided with your software. Remember, the spelling checker will miss words that are spelled correctly but used improperly. To find these errors, you need to use the spelling checker in addition to carefully reading your document.

The Appendix of this text contains a list of frequently misspelled words and another list of commonly confused words. To strengthen your ability to spell these words correctly, 12 spelling words and 3 confusing words will be included in the Spelling and Word Usage Check of each chapter. In addition, these words will be applied in the Proofreading Applications at the end of each chapter.

CONFUSED AND MISUSED WORDS

addition   *n.* process of summing; an added part

edition   *n.* copies of a published book

The **addition** of new workers helped us complete the project on time.

Our class is using the third **edition** of that textbook.

affect   *v.* to influence

effect   *v.* to bring about; *n.* result

How will the downsizing **affect** morale?

Smoking has a negative **effect** on your health.

all right   *adj.* (two words) all correct or appropriate

alright   unacceptable spelling of *all right*

Mia's answers were **all right.**

The terms of the contract seemed **all right** to Sean.

PEP Tip

- Check short words such as *of*, *on*, *or*, *an*, and *at* for possible misstrokes.

- Proofread numbers carefully for transposition errors.

- Check for repetition of words and/or repetition of numbers in a list.

- Check separately for errors in numbers, dates, technical information, and names of people.

- When using word processing software, take advantage of the spelling checker. Remember, using your spelling checker is only one step in proofreading. You must also read each word carefully to make sure you intended to use that specific word.

PROOFREADING APPLICATIONS

Exercise 2-10 PARAGRAPHS

Proofread the following paragraphs to locate spelling and word usage errors. Use the appropriate proofreaders' marks to show the corrections.

Among the many profesional organizations is the Associated Writers of America (AWA). This is an organization for people who are keenly interested in writting as a profession and as a hobby. Two major events for the AWA are its annual national convention and its special fall conference, which features presentations of information for both current and potential writers.

The confrence is held in a different city each year with arrangements worked out by the AWA conference manager. He or she will work out details to quarantee that everyone attending the conference will have the opportunity to participate in a number of meetings.

At the last conference, the participants were addressed by a writer whose major occupation is serving as president of an electricle company. His talk on the struggled to perfect his writing style helped many in the audience apppreciate the challenge of good writing.

If you are interested in becoming a part of this group and in attending any of its regional or national conferences, simply watch your newspaper for informaiton on where to join.

Exercise 2-11 SPELLING AND WORD USAGE CHECK

Compare the words in Column A with the corresponding words in Column B. One of the words is spelled or used incorrectly. Use the appropriate proofreaders' marks to correct the misspelled or misused words. If both columns are correct, write **C** to the left of the number.

Column A	Column B
Ex. a(d)n	and
1. writing	writting
2. potencial	potential
3. addressed	adressed
4. participate	participate
5. oppertunity	opportunity
6. electrical	electricle
7. participants	particpants
8. confrence	conference
9. appreciate	apperciate
10. guarantee	quarantee
11. institutoin	institution
12. responsibel	responsible
13. Xiong is excellent at addition.	This is the first addition of the book.
14. This movie effected me.	The call affected her.
15. Alright, she can go.	The answers are all right.

Exercise 2-12 INTERNATIONAL VOCABULARY

Compare the Spanish words in Column A with the corresponding words in Column B. If the word in Column B is different from the word in Column A, use the appropriate proofreaders' marks to correct Column B. If the words in both columns are the same, write **C** to the left of the number.

Column A	Column B
1. adicional	aditional
2. aeropuerto	areopuerto
3. borrador	borrador
4. comercial	commercial
5. cuaderno	cuadereno

Exercise 2-13 BUSINESS LETTER

Proofread the letter for spelling errors. Correct the errors using the
appropriate proofreaders' marks.

Writers Supplies, Inc.
Suite 47—Hibbard Building
349 West Grandview Drive
Des Moines, Iowa 50313-1298
Phone: 515/555-0100 • Fax: 515/555-0101

September 23, 200-

Ms. Janet R. Jameson, Chair
National Convention Commitee
Associated Writers of America
3462 West Grant Avenue
Omaha, NE 68111-1742

Dear Ms. Jameson:

Yes, we except your invitation to particpate as an exhibitor at the June convention. We have
been strong believers in the work of the AWA and its many proffessional activities.

Thank you for sending a copy if the layout for the exhibits area. We prefer to have the two
booths numbered 32 and and 34 by the north entrance to the hall, with the edition of one double
electrical outlet.

Please send us a price list of boothe supplies so that we can place our order as soon as possible.
The list should be sent by fax or regular mail to the office address given above. Also, would you
let us know to whom our payment should be snet? An adressed envelope is enclosed for your
convenience.

Sincerely,

Calvin Brown, Manger
Sales and Marketing

tbe
Enclosure

Exercise 2-14 MEMO

Proofread and mark the spelling errors in the following memo.

Writers Supplies, Inc., Memorandum

TO: Department Heads

FROM: Calvin Brown, Sales and Marketing

DATE: September 23, 200-

SUBJECT: BOOTH EXHIBIT AT AWA CONVENITON

Janet Jameson, chair of the AWA Convention Committee, has invited us to display some of are products next summer at its national convention. It will be held on June 21, 22, and 23 in the Civic Center. Attendance is expected to exceed 1,000 participants.

Please prepare a breif e-mail outlining what items you would like to see on display. It will be a great oppertunity to meet potential customers and to display the items we have available.

Let us plan to meet on October 8 at 10 a.m. in Confrence Room Room 32 to talk over our plans.

tbe

PROOFREADING AT THE COMPUTER

Exercise 2-15 BUSINESS LETTER

1. Open 02-15 from the Chapter 02 folder on the Student CD. (This is a computer copy of Application 2-13.)

2. Proofread the letter on the screen. Correct all errors on the screen copy that you indicated with proofreaders' marks in Application 2-13.

3. Format the letter using default left and right margins and a 2″ top margin.

4. Save the letter to your hard drive or to a separate diskette as 02-15R.

5. Print the letter.

6. Proofread the printed document. If you find any additional mistakes, correct the errors on both the hard copy and the screen.

7. Save and print the revised document.

Exercise 2-16 BUSINESS LETTER

1. Open 02-16 from the Chapter 02 folder on the Student CD.

2. Proofread the letter on the screen by comparing it with the correct handwritten letter on page 24.

3. Correct all mistakes.

4. Format the letter using default left and right margins and a 2″ top margin.

5. Save the letter as 02-16R, and print it.

6. Proofread the hard copy. If you find any additional mistakes, correct the errors on both the hard copy and the screen.

7. Save and print the revised document.

November 8, 200-

Mr. Luis Villa, Sales
Acme Computers, Inc.
372 North Washington Road
St. Louis, MD 63102-4772

Dear Mr. Villa:

Associated Writers of America has asked us to have an exhibit at its national convention next summer. We have accepted the invitation and now are putting together a list of items that we will be using for the booth.

Because of the popularity and increasingly widespread use of the new version of Grammaretics 4U, we would like your assistance with part of the display. We want to have information about that software program available for those who might stop at our booth.

Would you please send me a list of what you can have for us. An addressed envelope is enclosed for your reply.

Sincerely,
Calvin Brown, Manager
Sales and Marketing

tbe
Enclosure

Word Division Errors

Spotlight on ACCURACY

Y ou may have seen headlines similar to the following in your newspaper. How would you rewrite these headlines to make them correct?

- Plane Too Close to Ground, Crash Probe Told

- Miners Refuse to Work After Death

- Stolen Painting Found by Tree

Source: HumorMatters™, Newspaper Bloopers and Funnies (http://www.humormatters.com/newspaper.htm)

Objectives

- Apply word division rules.

- Recognize hyphenation errors.

- Use appropriate proofreaders' marks to correct hyphenation errors.

- Spell correctly 12 frequently misspelled words.

- Use correctly three sets of commonly confused and misused words.

THE NATURE OF WORD DIVISION

© COMSTOCK IMAGES

Why divide words at the end of a line? Since a whole word is easier to recognize and to read, why not leave it whole? Words are often divided at the end of a line to keep the right margin as even as possible. An even right margin makes the page appear balanced and attractive. Care must be taken, however, not to divide too many words; otherwise, the document will be difficult to read.

The use of word processing software has made the task of word division easier and faster. Word processing software has a special feature called **automatic hyphenation**. This feature automatically finds words that break at the end of a line and hyphenates them between syllables. However, automatic hyphenation may result in undesirable breaks. Thus, even when using this feature, word divisions must be checked carefully to ensure accuracy.

If text has been entered with the automatic hyphenation feature turned off, words that do not fit completely on one line are **wrapped**, or moved, to the next line. But the **wraparound mode** may result in an extremely ragged and unattractive right margin. To fix this, the operator may manually divide end words in appropriate places or use the justification method, which adjusts each line to meet the right margin. Regardless of the software used, an efficient proofreader should carefully check each document for the following:

- Errors in word division

- Excessive word division

- Extremely ragged right margin (indicating insufficient word division)

GUIDELINES FOR WORD DIVISION

Every office worker who is responsible for producing business documents should know and apply the basic rules of word division. While studying the specific word division rules, keep in mind these simple guidelines:

1. Use a hyphen to show where a word should be divided.

2. Divide words between syllables.

3. If necessary, use a dictionary to determine the correct syllabication.

4. Leave as much of the word as possible at the end of a line before dividing. This makes the word easy to identify.

5. Do not divide words at the end of more than two consecutive lines.

6. Do not divide the last word of a paragraph or the last word of a page.

As you review the word division rules in this chapter, note that some rules state "avoid dividing." This means that though it may be permissible to divide a word at a certain point, it is not recommended. Such words have both acceptable and preferred division points. For example, it is acceptable to divide *external* after *ex-*; however, the preferred division point is *exter-*, which allows the reader to more easily identify the word.

While proofreading, use the insert hyphen symbol to indicate the division of a word. If a word has been incorrectly divided, use the delete and close-up symbols as shown here.

	MARKED WORD	HYPHENATED WORD
Insert hyphen.	production	pro- duc- tion
	critical	crit- ical
	quarter	quar- ter

Note: The examples given in each of the rules in this chapter appear in three columns. In the first column the correct syllabication of the word is given. The appropriate proofreaders' mark(s) is used to divide the word in the second column. The third column shows the correct division according to the rule being applied.

Rule 1 Divide a word only between syllables. A one-syllable word cannot be divided.

SYLLABICATION	MARKED WORD	HYPHENATED WORD
mem o ry	mem/o/ry	mem- o- ry
pho to graph	pho/to/graph	pho- to- graph
called	—	called
thought	—	thought

Rule 2 Do not divide a word with five or fewer letters. Avoid dividing a word with six letters.

SYLLABICATION	MARKED WORD	HYPHENATED WORD
pow er	—	power
cit y	—	city
lo cate	—	locate
of fice	—	office

> ### Exercise 3-1 PROOFREAD AND MARK

If a word is divided correctly, write **C** to the left of the number. If a word is divided incorrectly or in a manner that is not preferred, use the appropriate proofreaders' marks to correct the division.

1. inspec- tion

2. pro- mise

3. de- vice

4. fly- ing

5. con- struct- ion

6. laugh

7. fer- ry

8. fam- i- liar

9. pro- minent

10. later

Rule 3 At least two letters must appear at the *end* of a line (*in*- crease), and at least three letters must appear at the *beginning* of the next line (*larg*- est, but not larg-*er*).

Note: Although it is acceptable to divide after a two-letter syllable at the beginning of a word (*re*- pairing), it is better to avoid doing so (*repair*- ing).

SYLLABICATION	MARKED WORD	HYPHENATED WORD
in ter cept	inter/c̄ept	inter- cept
sym pho ny	sym/p̄hony	sym- phony
a bid ed	—	abided
cen ter	—	center

Rule 4 Generally, divide between double consonants. However, when the root word ends in double consonants and a suffix is added to the word, divide between the root word and the suffix.

Note: A consonant is any letter of the alphabet other than a vowel. A root word is the base word. A suffix, usually of one syllable, is the ending that is added to the base word.

SYLLABICATION	MARKED WORD	HYPHENATED WORD
ha rass ment	harass/m̄ent	harass- ment
suc cess ful	success/f̄ul	success- ful
call ing	call/īng	call- ing
con fess ing	confess/īng	confess- ing

Rule 5 Divide between double consonants when the final consonant of the root word is doubled before adding a suffix.

SYLLABICATION	MARKED WORD	HYPHENATED WORD
ad mit tance	admit/=tance	admit- tance
pro gram ming	program/=ming	program- ming
con trol ling	control/=ling	control- ling

> ### Exercise 3-2 PROOFREAD AND MARK

If a word is divided correctly, write **C** to the left of the number. If a word is divided incorrectly or in a manner that is not preferred, use the appropriate proofreaders' marks to correct the division.

1. ambi- tious

2. en- forcement

3. en- during

4. garden- er

5. guard- ed

6. i- magine

7. dres- sing

8. profes- sional

9. suppres- sing

10. ball- oon

Rule 6 Divide after a single-vowel syllable except when the single-vowel syllable is followed by the ending *ble*, *bly*, *cle*, or *cal*.

SYLLABICATION	MARKED WORD	HYPHENATED WORD
pos i tive	posi/=tive	posi- tive
res o nance	reso/=nance	reso- nance
log i cal	log/=ical	log- ical
lov a ble	lov/=able	lov- able

Rule 7 Divide between two single-vowel syllables when each of the two vowels is pronounced separately.

SYLLABICATION	MARKED WORD	HYPHENATED WORD
sit u a tion	situ/=ation	situ- ation
e val u a tion	evalu/=ation	evalu- ation
hu mil i a tion	humili/=ation	humili- ation

Rule 8 Divide compound words between the words. If the compound word is hyphenated, the only acceptable point of division is *after* the hyphen. In such cases, use the diagonal mark without the hyphen symbol.

		MARKED WORD	HYPHENATED WORD
Insert diagonal mark.	/	self/control	self- control
Insert diagonal mark and hyphen.	/=	tax/free	tax- free
		senator/elect	senator- elect

Note: A **compound word** is made up of at least two words and may be written as one word (*somewhere*) or as a hyphenated word (*self-concept*). Check a dictionary if you are unsure about the correct spelling.

COMPOUND WORD	MARKED WORD	HYPHENATED WORD
side line	side/line	side- line
steam roll er	steam/roller	steam- roller
chair per son	chair/person	chair- person

> ### Exercise 3-3   PROOFREAD AND MARK

If a word is divided correctly, write **C** to the left of the number. If a word is divided incorrectly or in a manner that is not preferred, use the appropriate proofreaders' marks to correct the division.

1. grad- uate
2. ad- amant
3. legit- imate
4. exten- uating
5. criti- cal

6. remark- able
7. hand- icap
8. horserad- ish
9. self- rule
10. affilia- tion

Rule 9 Do not divide abbreviations, numbers, contractions, acronymns (initials that represent words), times, or units of measure (a number with a descriptive word). Units of measure must always be written together.

mdse.	UNICEF	15-ft. board
9.25 percent	7 1/2 lb.	6 min.
couldn't	8 kg	C.A.R.E.
Flight 12	10:15 a.m.	No. 10

Rule 10 Avoid dividing proper names, titles, addresses, or dates. If it is necessary to divide these elements, choose a logical point that will give the best readability.

RULE	EXAMPLE
Divide before a surname (or after the middle initial if it is used).	**Carl T. Santos**
Divide between the city and state, not between the state and the ZIP Code.	**Green Bay, Wisconsin**
	San Diego, CA 92110-2134
Divide dates between the day and the year.	**April 15, 200–**
Divide between parts of a city name.	**Santa Barbara**

> ## Exercise 3-4 PROOFREAD AND MARK

Divide each of the following elements at the most logical point. Use only the diagonal mark to show the divisions. If an element cannot be divided, write **C** to the left of the number.

1. Dr. Clarence R. Dolby

2. hasn't

3. 18 lb.

4. Michiko Yoshikawa

5. SADD

6. September 19, 200–

7. Whitewater, Wisconsin

8. $379,390.92

9. Carbondale, IL 62901-2464

10. Colin DeLoye

CONFUSED AND MISUSED WORDS

accept   *v.* to agree to; to receive
except   *prep.* but; other than

Please **accept** my congratulations!
Everyone **except** Dusty arrived on time.

advice   *n.* recommendation
advise   *v.* to give advice; to inform

My **advice** is to arrive ten minutes before your interview.
I **advise** you to double-check your computations.

all ready   *adj.* (two words) completely ready
already   *adv.* before now or a specified time

Your order is **all ready** to be sent.
You have **already** received the shipment.

- As a final step in proofreading a page, read down the right margin to check the hyphenation of all divided words.

- Use word division sparingly. Some companies and individuals prefer that certain business documents not be hyphenated.

- Double-check to ensure that certain words, phrases, numbers, and abbreviations are not separated at the end of a line.

- If appropriate, use the team method of proofreading when proofreading highly technical or complicated documents. See Chapter 1 for proofreading methods.

PROOFREADING APPLICATIONS

Exercise 3-5 WORD DIVISION LIST

Proofread the words in each line. If one or more words are divided incorrectly, correct the word(s) using the appropriate proofreaders' marks. Then write the word(s) on the blank line using hyphen(s) to show **all preferred points of division**. If all three words in a line are correct, write **C** on the blank line.

Ex.	lit⌒tle	repre– sent	admis– sible	*little*
1.	stop– ping	corp– oration	worth– while	
2.	mort– gage	collect– ible	infat– uation	
3.	sep– arate	protec– tion	they'll	
4.	prefer– ence	curric– ulum	cooper– ated	
5.	posses– sing	prepa– ration	gas– oline	
6.	bro–therhood	immedi– ately	pros– ecute	
7.	compari– son	sister– in–law	mainten– ance	
8.	suf– ficient	assim– ilate	cons– cious	
9.	commit– tee	elec– trical	pharm– acy	
10.	practi– cal	trespas– sed	typ– ical	
11.	height	referr– ed	bull– etin	
12.	desira– ble	bene– factor	cler– ical	
13.	bil– lion	im– itation	custo– mary	
14.	extenu– ating	clarif– ication	reason– able	
15.	cross– filing	pass– ing	chron– icle	

Exercise 3-6 SPELLING AND WORD USAGE CHECK

Compare the words in Column A with the corresponding words in Column B. Use the appropriate proofreaders' marks to correct the misspelled or misused words. If both columns are correct, write **C** to the left of the number.

Column A	Column B
Ex. calendar	calend*a*r
1. substancial	substantial
2. desirable	desireable
3. hesatate	hesitate
4. received	recieved
5. offerred	offered
6. design	designe
7. separate	separate
8. enclosed	inclosed
9. maintanance	maintenance
10. mortgage	moregage
11. industriel	industrial
12. transportation	transportacion
13. Everyone except Billy attended.	You should except the gift.
14. Her advise was excellent.	Your advice was well received.
15. Are you already for today?	My application has already been accepted.

Exercise 3-7 INTERNATIONAL VOCABULARY

Compare the Spanish words in Column A with the corresponding words in Column B. If the word in Column B is different from the word in Column A, use the appropriate proofreaders' marks to correct Column B. If the words in both columns are the same, write **C** to the left of the number.

Column A	Column B
1. goleta	goletta
2. equilibrar	equilebrar
3. costurero	costurero
4. reemplazo	remplazo
5. vivero	vivero

Using the appropriate proofreaders' marks, proofread and correct all errors in spelling and word division.

ONCE UPON A TIME ...
THEY LIVED HAPPILY EVERY AFTER.

Make your dream come true.

You have a change to own your dream house at Paradise Valley with sensational close-out prices offerred.

So . . . let us help you make your dream come true. And we'll guarantee that you live happily ever after. Come see these custom-desinged homes today!

Purchase one of the last available homes now; and we'll give you a $5,000 SPECIAL BONUS for you to use in any way you choose, such as upgrades in flooring, appliances, decorative options, or closeing costs.

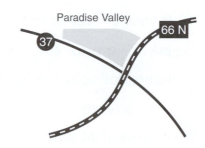

Paradise Valley

37

66 N

Exercise 3-9 BUSINESS FLYER

Using the appropriate proofreaders' marks, proofread and correct all errors in spelling and word division.

ADVISE TO TENANTS . . . DON'T BE SHY.

If you are looking for an apartment to rent, don't be afraid too approach the property managers or landlords and ask some hard questions. Their answers may effect not only your pocketbook but also your happiness. In other words, if you want to be happy where you live, demand what you want. You'll be pleasantly surprised how much you can receive. After all, you have everything to gain and nothing to lose. Right?

Here are a few tips that property managers use to advise today's renter.

✳ Ask how long the unit has been vacant. If the unit has been vacant longer than 30 days, you might lower the rent if you bargain with your landlord.

✳ Ask how long the former tenants were their and how much they paid in rent. If they rented for more than a year, you may be able to negotiate and recieve a reduction in rent.

✳ Don't hesitate to ask for upgrades such as new carpet, new drapes, or blinds. Offer to paint if is it provided.

✳ If your'e already renting and would like to stay where you are, ask for a price cut or some upgrades. It's much more profitable for your landlord to lower your rent than to look for a new tennant.

✳ Be sure that whoever is giving away the most is offering you the best deal.

Exercise 3-10 BUSINESS LETTER

Using the appropriate proofreaders' marks, proofread and correct all errors in spelling and word division.

HJ Properties
101 North Fountain Parkway
Davison, MI 48423-1015
(810) 555-0179 Fax (810) 555-0189

July 17, 200–

Mr. and Mrs. Bradley Foster III
6593 Rosebud Aveneu
Davison, MI 48423-0039

Dear Mr. and Mrs. Foster

Thank you for stopping at HJ Properties and giving us the opportunity to show you some of the available properties in Paradise Valley.

I have contacted the owners of the property you are interested in purchasing and have offered them your price quotation of $242,500. They were pleased and said they will call tomorrow to let me know whether they will accept your price or make a coun-teroffer. If they do not call me, I will call them for a defanite commitment.

In the meantime, you may be interested in looking at other attractive properties listed on the inclosed flyer. Call me if you wish to see some of these homes. We can set up appointments to veiw them.

Sincerely

Clayton R. Sierra
Residencial Properties Specialist

kj
Encolsure

PROOFREADING AT THE COMPUTER

Exercise 3-11 BUSINESS FLYER

1. Open 03-11 from the Chapter 03 folder on the Student CD. (This is a computer copy of Application 3-9.)

2. Proofread the flyer on the screen. Correct all errors on the screen copy that you indicated with proofreaders' marks in Application 3-9. Use the spelling checker.

3. Format the flyer using default left and right margins.

4. Save the document as 03-11R, and print it.

5. Proofread the printed document. If you find any additional mistakes, correct the errors on both the hard copy and the screen.

6. Save and print the revised document.

Exercise 3-12 BUSINESS LETTER WITH TABLE

1. Open 03-12 from the Chapter 03 folder on the Student CD.

2. Proofread the letter, and make all necessary corrections using the appropriate proofreaders' marks.

3. Format the letter using default left and right margins and a 2″ top margin.

4. Save the document as 03-12R, and print it.

5. Proofread the hard copy, and mark any additional errors.

6. Correct the errors on the screen copy.

7. Save and print the revised document.

Exercise 3-13 E-MAIL MESSAGE

1. Open 03-13 from the Chapter 03 folder on the Student CD.

2. Proofread the e-mail message, and make all necessary corrections.

3. Save the document as 03-13R, and print it.

4. Proofread the printed document. Did you find errors on the printout that you did not find when you proofread the e-mail onscreen? Correct any additional errors you found in file 03-13.

5. Save and print the revised document.

CUMULATIVE APPLICATION

Exercise 3-14 TWO-PAGE MANUSCRIPT

Proofread and correct all errors using the appropriate proofreaders' marks.

CHECKLISTS FOR FIRST-TIME HOME BUYERS:

WISE PLANNING PAYS!

Your first home will very likely be the single most important and largest dollar investment you will ever make in your lifetime. Therefore, you should do your homework before you see your bank loan officer to obtain home financing.

Buying your first home is especially exciting and satisfying. But it can also be stressful, confusing, overwhelming, and frust– rating; that is, if your are not ready and prepared with relevant and important information. You must have all of the necessary documents and records at your finger tips when you see the loan officer at the bank. All banks are sincerely interested in providing home loans to potential borrowers, but only if you are qualified, responsable, and (most important of all) prepared!

Preparing for a first-time home purchase is a financial challenge. Do you spend more than you make? Increase your savings plan at every opportunity. Get rid of most of your credit cards. All you need is one—perhaps too at the most. Pay cash when you buy, and avoid paying interest on the installment plan. Pay off ba– lances in full each time you recieve a statement. To spend more as you see your savings grow can be tempting—so can a new car, a television, clothing, or jewelry. Resist the temptation to buy more.

Here is one useful checklist covering those things that are most important to first-time home buyers. Your bank will, in all probability, ask you questions pertaining to these items.

CHECKLIST FOR FIRST-TIME FINANCING

1. *Income Sources* — Include regular pay, overtime, bonuses, commissions, tips, and any other sources of income.

2. *Liabilities* — Make a list of all money you owe—outstan– ding personal and business loans and credit card account balances.

3. *Pay Records* — Keep all of your recent pay stubs and other kinds of records to show salary and wages received.

4. *Tax Returns* — Keep W-2 forms and tax return papers for the past three years.

5. *Down Payment* — Be ready to answer the big question in home purchase: How much down payment do you have too apply toward the purchase of your new home? Obviously, the larger the down payment, the smaller the monthly mortgage payments.

6. *Other Assets* — Prepare a summery of liquid assets—things you own free and clear of outstanding balances—that can bring cash quickly. Keep at least three months of bank statements for savings and checking accounts. Keep documents for stocks and bonds; life insurance policies with cash surrender values; real estate holdings; and receipts for personal properties such as cars, furniture, jewelry, antiques, and other items of monetary value.

AIRLINE

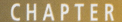

Capitalization Errors

Spotlight on ACCURACY

Word power, the ability to use the correct word, is critical in business writing. Note these differences in the use and abuse of language:

- **Differ and disagree.** *Differ* refers to things that are unlike others. Her purse *differs* from mine. *Disagree* refers to people who have different opinions. He *disagreed* with me about the value of the class.

- **Appraise and apprise.** *Appraise* means "to assess," while *apprise* means "to inform." Kwame will have the house *appraised*. Keep me *apprised* of your progress.

- **Imply and infer.** *Imply* indicates that the speaker is suggesting something, though not making an explicit statement. Harry implied that the man was a thief. *Infer* indicates that something in the speaker's words enabled the listeners to deduce that the man was a thief. We *inferred* from his words that the man was a thief.

Objectives

- Understand the basic rules for capitalization.

- Recognize and mark errors in capitalization using the appropriate proofreaders' marks.

- Spell correctly 12 frequently misspelled words.

- Use correctly three sets of commonly confused and misused words.

CAPITALIZATION

Capital letters show the importance of words. For example, the first word in a sentence, proper nouns, names, and the pronoun *I* are always capitalized. Although the trend is to use fewer capital letters, several basic rules must be followed.

The proofreaders' marks that indicate the corrections for capitalization errors are shown here:

	MARKED COPY	CORRECTED COPY
Capitalize ≡	to san Diego	to San Diego
Lowercase /	the new Member	the new member

Rule 1 Capitalize the first word of every sentence and the first word after a colon if that word begins a complete sentence.

Example: The new semester will begin next week.

Example: The memorandum to parents included the following notation: the new bus schedule will begin the first Monday in October.

Rule 2 Capitalize the first word of every complete quotation. Do not capitalize the first word of an interrupted quote.

Example: "The team," said the coach, "will practice this afternoon."

Example: Miss Wakui announced, "all assignments are due on Friday."

Rule 3 Capitalize the first word of each item in a list when each item is a complete sentence. Capitalize the first word of each item in an outline.

Example: At the end of the class period, follow these steps:

1. Print and turn in a final copy of your assignment.
2. Turn off your computer.
3. Put away your textbook.

Example: I. Varieties of vegetation

    A. Western hill country
    B. northern plains area

Exercise 4-1 PROOFREAD AND MARK

Mark all capitalization errors using the correct proofreaders' marks. If the sentence is correct, write **C** to the left of the number.

1. "We will have lunch," he said, "at the central high school cafeteria."

2. ms. Jordan said, "check your locker in the south hallway."

3. "When the team is on stage," the adviser said, "all of us should stand and cheer."

4. Each person should have the following items in a bag:

   1. sport Shirt

   2. Clean socks

   3. black tie

5. The special meeting is for the following students: freshmen, sophomores, and Juniors.

Rule 4 Capitalize all proper nouns (the names of specific persons, places, and things) and any adjective derived from a proper noun.

CATEGORY	PROPER NOUNS
Brand names	Ford, Kellogg's, Tide, Ore-Ida, Bic
Buildings	the Sears Tower, Trump Tower
Clubs	Boys and Girls Club
Company names	Midwest Express, Mobile, General Electric
Specific courses	English I, Advanced Chemistry
Geographic regions and places	Africa, Middle East, Wales, Frankfurt, the Missouri River, the Smoky Mountains, Lake Superior, Washington Avenue, Sixth Street
Governmental terms	Department of Health and Human Services, Federal Reserve Board, United Nations, Supreme Court, Detroit City Council (*but not* federal *or* state *unless part of an official agency name*)
Historic events	VE Day, Battle of Gettysburg, the Great Depression
Organizations	National Honor Society, Business Professionals of America, Future Business Leaders of America
Organizational terms within one's own firm	the Economics Department, the Education Division, the Board of Trustees, the Safety Committee
Religious groups	Lutheran, Jewish, Catholic, Protestant
References to the deity	God, Allah, Yahweh, Holy Spirit

Rule 5 Capitalize days of the week, months of the year, and holidays. Do not capitalize seasons of the year.

> *Example:* The exam is scheduled for November 29, the first Monday after Thanksgiving.

> *Example:* We will have a new schedule for the Winter season by november 1.

> *Example:* Our school will hold a special program on president's day.

Rule 6 Capitalize both parts of hyphenated words if they are proper nouns or proper adjectives. Do not capitalize prefixes or suffixes added to proper nouns.

> *Example:* The name of the new student is Esteban Perez-Vadillo.

> *Example:* The special film is for German-speaking students.

> *Example:* The Mellville High School-north High School rivalry can be quite intense.

> *Example:* The retirement party was for ex-principal Jefferson.

Rule 7 Capitalize words that show a family relationship when they appear alone or are followed by a personal name. Do not capitalize family relations preceded by a possessive pronoun.

> *Example:* The class reunion was for Uncle George and Dad.

> *Example:* The team manager is cousin Susan.

> *Example:* My Brother got me the interview.

Exercise 4-2 PROOFREAD AND MARK

Mark all capitalization errors using the correct proofreaders' marks. If the sentence is correct, write **C** to the left of the number.

1. The doctor called Aunt Phyllis about her test results.

2. The leader of the field trip is Judith A. Sutton-smith.

3. The first car in the homecoming parade will be a chevrolet.

4. Classes will Begin on the wednesday after labor day.

5. The federal Reserve Board will meet in the State of Washington.

Rule 8 Capitalize a title that comes before a name. However, do not capitalize a title that follows a name or is used in place of a name unless it is the title of a high-ranking national, state, or international official (such as the President, the Secretary of State, or the Governor).

Example: Dairy Princess Sherry Maki

Example: Ellery Preston, the president of Beacon Inc.

Example: Cameron Schmidt, Artist in Residence

Example: He was elected president of the United States.

© GETTY IMAGES/PHOTODISC

The President lives in the White House.

Rule 9 Capitalize titles in letter addresses and closings. Capitalize the first word, all nouns, and titles in a salutation of a letter; but capitalize only the first word of a complimentary close. Capitalize both letters of state abbreviations.

Example:

Ms. Clara Mendez, Head	Yours truly,
Counseling Center	
Northwest High School	Bruce Karlstad
321 North Lincoln Way	Department Head
Chicago, IL 60614-4321	
Dear Ms. Mendez:	

Example:

Mr. Philip Leron	Sincerely Yours,
Student senate president	
Southwest College	Marian Thomlinson
337 East College Street	Assistant principal
Albuquerque, NM 87109-3233	
Dear Mr. Leron:	

Rule 10 Capitalize the titles of officers in constitutions, bylaws, and minutes of meetings. Titles of company officials are not capitalized when they follow or replace a personal name.

> *Example:* The constitution states that "the President shall appoint a three-person Credentials Committee."

> *Example:* The minutes were taken by Bryan Victorson, Secretary.

Capitalize academic titles that precede or follow a name. However, do not capitalize academic degrees used as general classifications.

> *Example:* She announced that Dean Antonio Gomez will speak on February 26.

> *Example:* Each of the teachers has a Master's degree.

Exercise 4-3 PROOFREAD AND MARK

Mark all capitalization errors using the correct proofreaders' marks. If the sentence is correct, write **C** to the left of the number.

1. The constitution states that "the treasurer shall be responsible for an annual report."

2. Ben has received his bachelor's degree in education.

3. The win was coach O'Neil's 150th victory.

4. The English IV class will be taught by professor Karjala.

5. The title in the closing of the letter should be "high school principal."

Rule 11 Capitalize points of the compass when they refer to specific regions or are used as proper nouns. Do not capitalize points of the compass to indicate directions or general locations.

> *Example:* Next month the choir will tour the West.

> *Example:* All 18 teams will compete in the Southern Region tournament.

> *Example:* The summer school course includes visits to the midwest.

> *Example:* The team will travel East on the first day of the trip.

Rule 12 Capitalize the first word and all important words in titles of literary and artistic works and in displayed headings. Do not capitalize articles (*a, an, the*), conjunctions (*and, as, but, or, nor*), and prepositions containing four or fewer letters (*at, by, for, in, of, on, to, with*) unless they are the first word of a title.

> *Example:* The winning theme was entitled "Searching for the Lost Dream."

> *Example:* Please purchase the paperback book *Your Guide to Correct Punctuation.*

Example: We are to study the chapter "The Era Øf Ťhe Ethnic Groups."

Example: The library subscribes to the *Daily Mirror*.

Rule 13 Capitalize a noun that precedes a figure or letter *except* for common nouns such as *line, page, sentence,* and *size.*

Example: Place the instructions in Appendix G.

Example: The assignment begins on page 37.

Example: The sweatshirts should be Šize 14.

Exercise 4-4 PROOFREAD AND MARK

Mark all capitalization errors using the correct proofreaders' marks. If the sentence is correct, write **C** to the left of the number.

1. The choir will sing "The Sweet Song of Spring" in the concert.

2. All saturday classes are scheduled for towns East of here.

3. Proofread the material starting on Line 8.

4. The new headline should read "Bond Issue Is defeated."

5. the new chapter begins on page 42.

During our tour of the West last summer, we stopped to see Old Faithful at Yellowstone National Park.

CONFUSED AND MISUSED WORDS

allot	*v.* to allocate or distribute
a lot	*n.* (two words) a large amount; many
alot	unacceptable spelling of *a lot*

Please **allot** two hours for our meeting.

Your help made the job **a lot** easier.

among	*prep.* comparison of three or more persons or things
between	*prep.* comparison of only two persons or things

Distribute the work **among** your staff.

The goals will be divided **between** Paul and Christa.

assistance	*n.* help
assistants	*n.* helpers

Your **assistance** helped us meet our deadline.

The **assistants** are meeting at 3 p.m. to discuss the project.

PEP!Tip

- When checking for capitalization errors, skim the material to locate words with capital letters and decide if they are capitalized correctly.

- Check to ensure that each sentence begins with a capital letter.

- Review the word processing function that changes letters from upper- to lowercase and from lower- to uppercase.

PROOFREADING APPLICATIONS

Exercise 4-5 PARAGRAPHS

Proofread the following material, and mark all errors using the appropriate proofreaders' marks.

Plans for the publication of the pamphlet entitled *Schools and the Future of our City* are complete. The draft copy was approved by the Citizens Committee for Future Plans. The Chairperson was principal Roosevelt-Grant. A meeting to discuss the pamphlet has been scheduled in the Northeast part of the district on Tuesday, October 1. Questions to be discussed include the following:

1. what are the plans for the new school buildings?
2. should school activities be curtailed?
3. Do taxes have to be increased?

The meeting will be in Room 102 of east High School. Arrangements for additional meetings will be made by Dr. Andrea glivem. The meetings must be concluded in November because voting on the school bond issue will take place a week after thanksgiving.

Exercise 4-6 SPELLING AND WORD USAGE CHECK

Compare the words in Column A with the corresponding words in Column B. Use the appropriate proofreaders' marks to correct the misspelled or misused words. If both columns are correct, write **C** to the left of the number.

Column A	Column B
1. access	acess
2. resently	recently
3. schedual	schedule
4. committee	committtee
5. matterial	material
6. audet	audit
7. situation	sitaution
8. appropriate	apporpriate
9. analysis	analysis
10. communication	communiction
11. maximum	maximum
12. specsial	special
13. They did not alot the money.	Please allot the quotas.
14. divide among Jo and me	between the two of us
15. Your assistance is required.	Kiko has two assistance.

Exercise 4-7 INTERNATIONAL VOCABULARY

Compare the Spanish words in Column A with the corresponding words in Column B. If the word in Column B is different from the word in Column A, use the appropriate proofreaders' marks to correct Column B. If the words in both columns are the same, write **C** to the left of the number.

Column A	Column B
1. comprender	comprender
2. comida	comidia
3. curso	courso
4. depositar	depositer
5. diario	dairio

Exercise 4-8 LETTER

Proofread the following letter, and mark all capitalization and other mechanical errors using the appropriate proofreaders' marks.

Central Community High School
372 North Street, St. Louis, MO 63122-2731
(314) 555-0138 • Fax (314) 555-0148

october 1, 200-

Ms. Carlota Silva, President
Northern Fences Corporation
327 Witherspoon Drive
St. Louis, Mo 63138-4422

Dear Ms. Silva:

The Citizens Commitee for Future Plans recently published a booklet about planning for our future schools. This assistants was provided to help the Citizens of our community better understand the effect that our schools have on the life of the community.

As a member of the committee, I would be pleased to meet with your westside Business Culb to reveiw the contents of the pamphlet and to help the members understand the importance of the facts that the commitee has assembled. Would there be time during your October 15 meeting for such a presention?

Sincerely,

Marilyn Roosevelt-Grant
Principal

tcm

Exercise 4-9 MEMORANDUM

Proofread the following memo, and mark all errors using the appropriate proofreaders' marks.

Central Community High School Memorandum

TO: Citizens Committee for Future Plans

FROM: Marilyn Roosevelt-grant, Principal

DATE: October 25, 200-

SUBJECT: SCHEDULE FOR COMMUNITY MEETINGS

The final printed copies of our report, Schools and the Future of our City, were delivered to my office late yesterday afternoon. A copy is enclosed for you. Your assistance in preparing this comprehensive document is appreciated.

As we discussed in our last meeting, the next step is to distribute copies throughout the community and to have meetings with various clubs and organizations. Based on our discussions, I have perpared the following schedule for several committee members to meet with six community groups:

Group	Committee Members
Westside business Club	Marilyn Roosevelt-Grant and Carleton Rivera
Northenders	Daylon Olson And Diane Porozny
Central City founders	Ila Mary Jackson and Fred Flanery
Area 12 Council	Jose Velez and Elsa Greenberg
Suburban Grants Committee	Dorothy Evans and Jim Pugh
Southland commercial Club	Earl Just and Kathryn Soo

The first person listed should contact the president of the group and request the oppertunity to meet at the next meeting. Be sure to let me know when you will be meeting with your group. My phone umber is 555-0125.

Enclosure

PROOFREADING AT THE COMPUTER

Exercise 4-10   LETTER

1. Open 04-10 from the Chapter 04 folder on the Student CD. (This is a computer copy of Application 4-8.)

2. Proofread the letter on the screen. Correct all errors on the screen copy that you marked with proofreaders' marks in Application 4-8.

3. Format the letter using default left and right margins and a 2" top margin.

4. Save the letter as 04-10R, and print it.

5. Proofread the printed document. If you find any additional mistakes, correct the errors on both the hard copy and the screen.

6. Save and print the revised document.

Exercise 4-11   MINUTES

1. Open 04-11 from the Chapter 04 folder on the Student CD.

2. Proofread the copy on the screen by comparing it with the correct handwritten copy on pages 54 and 55.

3. Correct all mistakes.

4. Format the minutes using default left and right margins and a 2" top margin.

5. Save the minutes as 04-11R, and print it.

6. Proofread the printed document. If you find any additional mistakes, correct the errors on both the hard copy and the screen.

7. Save and print the revised document.

Exercise 4-12   E-MAIL MESSAGE

1. Open 04-12 from the Chapter 04 folder on the Student CD.

2. Proofread the e-mail message, and make all necessary corrections.

3 Save the document as 04-12R, and print it.

4. Proofread the printed document. If you find any additional mistakes, correct the errors on both the hard copy and the screen.

5. Save and print the revised document.

CENTRAL HIGH SCHOOL STUDENT COUNCIL
ST. LOUIS, MISSOURI
October 25, 200-

The regular meeting of the Central High School Student Council was held on Thursday, October 25, 200-, in Room 205. Members present:

Eric Ashcroft, Grade 10	Haru Tokuda, Treasurer
Marla Staloch, Grade 10	Carol Goudge, Secretary
Tony Tiese, Grade 11	Ken Baertsch, Vice President
Chih Liang, Grade 12	Colleen Seifer, President
Janice Ludwig, Grade 12	Ms. Adrian, Adviser
Steve Hovland, Grade 11	Mr. LuCuyen, Adviser

Recorder of minutes: Carol Goudge

1. The meeting was called to order at 1:45 p.m. by President Seifer. All members were present for roll call.

2. The October 18 minutes were read by Secretary Goudge and approved as read.

3. Treasurer Tokuda reported the balance in the treasury as $405.12.

4. Janice Ludwig reported the following:

   A. The homecoming buttons have arrived and can be sold starting October 28. Each council member is to sell at least 25 buttons.

B. Seven floats plus the marching band have already signed up for the homecoming parade.

5. New business included the following:

A. Mr. LuCuyen asked if the Student Council wanted to participate in the preparation of a booklet entitled <u>Student Guide for New Students</u>. After discussion, it was agreed that they did.

B. Chih Liang moved that the Student Council assist with fall cleanup activities on November 12. The motion was seconded and adopted.

6. Vice President Baertsch announced that the Homecoming Parade Planning Committee would meet during fourth period on Tuesday.

7. Tony Tiese moved to adjourn. The motion was seconded and adopted. The meeting was adjourned at 2:35 p.m.

CUMULATIVE APPLICATION

Exercise 4-13   MEMO

Proofread and correct all errors using the appropriate proofreaders' marks.

TO:	Julian Delgado, Infomaiton Systems Technician
FROM:	Mary Hopalian, Business division Dean
DATE:	June 27, 200-
SUBJECT:	REPORT ON INTERNATIONAL BUSINESS CONFERENCE

On June 17, 18, and 19, I attended the Fifteenth Annual Conference for International Business Programs held in Indianpalis, Indiana. This was a most informative conference. Following are some highlights from the conference that apply to information systems setup.

On Monday, June 17, the conference opened in a lecture room that was set up in horseshoe fashion. Tables and chairs were placed around the curve on elevated levels, with a large screen and whiteboards in front for the lecterer to use. In addition to the big screen, a computer screen was set up near the center of the room. With this setup, the lecturer cold walk around and continue talking without having to look over his or her shoulder.

Perhaps the most interesting part of the setup was a tall, narrow closet up font. This closet contained the computer hardware needed to run the equipment in the room, as well as a telephone. The lecturer had instant access to a telephone in the event of a hardware problem. The back of the closet opened to the outside hallway, allowing the computer technitian to fix any computer problems without interrupting the classroom presentation.

As our department considers expansion, I believe we can incorporate several ideas from this layout. I have requested pictures of the layout from Tracey Buroker, the building Supervisor; and I will share them with you when they arrive.

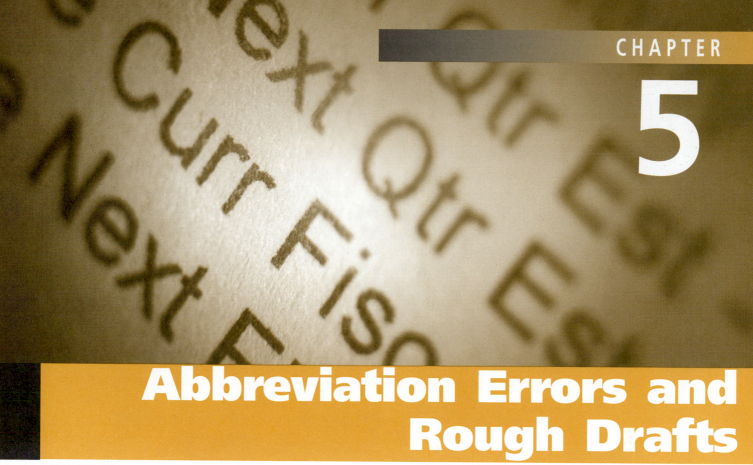

Abbreviation Errors and Rough Drafts

BRAND X PICTURES

Spotlight on ACCURACY

To be effective, an abbreviation must have the same meaning for both the writer and the reader. If confusion results, the wrong message may be conveyed. Which word or phrase is correct for the following abbreviations?

- AA (administrative assistant, Alcoholics Anonymous, associate in arts)

- ABA (Amateur Boxing Association, American Bankers Association, American Bar Association)

- RR (railroad, rural route)

Objectives

- Apply common abbreviation rules.

- Proofread revisions made from rough drafts.

- Spell correctly 12 frequently misspelled words.

- Use correctly three sets of commonly confused and mis-used words.

ABBREVIATIONS

An **abbreviation** is a shortened form of a word or phrase. Only standard abbreviations should be used. Consult a dictionary if you are in doubt about the correctness of an abbreviation.

Abbreviations may be important space savers in business writing, especially in short documents. Because the reader may not be familiar with an abbreviation, spell it out the first time and place the abbreviation in parentheses; for example, *Certified Professional Secretary* (*CPS*). Thereafter, use only the abbreviation. **Note:** Use an abbreviation only when you know the reader will understand it as you intended.

Some abbreviations are acceptable with or without periods (for example, *ft.* or *ft*; *mi.* or *mi*). Use one style consistently within a document. One space follows a period used after an abbreviation (*Mr. Luft*), and no space follows a period within an abbreviation (*p.m.*).

Use the following proofreaders' marks to make corrections in abbreviations.

	MARKED COPY	CORRECTED COPY
Spell out. *sp*	Send by (Dec) *sp* 20.	Send by December 20.
Insert period. ⊙	Mrs⊙Pahl is here.	Mrs. Pahl is here.
Close up space.	U. S. Post Office	U.S. Post Office
Delete period.	Radio Station K.V.G.N.	Radio Station KVGN

General Style

Some abbreviations may be used with formal and informal writing. The following guidelines are appropriate for most business communication (letters, memos, reports, and e-mail messages) as well as for general usage. Consult a good reference manual for more detailed rules.

◆ Personal and Professional Titles

Personal titles are used as a mark of courtesy. Generally, they include *Mr.*, *Mrs.*, *Miss*, *Ms.*, or *Dr.* Professional titles may also indicate one's military, religious, or educational status. Apply these rules for abbreviating titles:

Rule 1 Abbreviate personal and courtesy titles that come before personal names.

Examples:

Mr. Zehnder	Messrs. Zehnder and Hanson (plural of *Mr.*)
Mrs. Vogelsberg	Mmes. Vogelsberg and Connor (plural of *Mrs.*)
Ms. Hackbart	Dr. Deven Wieland

Note: *Ms.* is appropriate when the marital status of a woman is unknown or when the woman prefers this title. *Miss* is not an abbreviation.

Rule 2 Abbreviate personal titles following names. Titles such as *Jr.*, *Sr.*, *2d*, or *III* are generally not set off by commas; however, academic and professional titles are.

Examples:

Jack Ellison Jr.	Randall Markum 2d
Elizabeth Arnneski, CPS	William Lin III
Stuart Altman, Esq.	Emily Stinson, Ph.D.

Rule 3 Do not abbreviate titles appearing with surnames.

Example:

Doctor Karjala   *but*   Dr. Betty Karjala

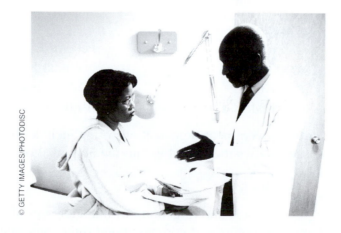

© GETTY IMAGES/PHOTODISC

Doctor Mann answered Mrs. Morgan's questions.

Rule 4 Write out professional titles whenever possible.

Examples:

Professor Camille Thoms   the Reverend Carlos Cruz

◆ Company Names

Words such as *Bros.* (Brothers), *Co.* (Company), *Inc.* (Incorporated), *Ltd.* (Limited), and *Mfg.* (Manufacturing) are often abbreviated in official company names. Check the company letterhead for the appropriate style.

Examples:
> Rounded Seeds, Inc.
> Canadian Coins, Ltd.
> Rangers Mfg.

Exercise 5-1 PROOFREAD AND MARK

Use the appropriate proofreaders' marks to identify the corrections that should be made. If the sentence is correct, write **C** to the left of the number.

1. The defendant is Mister Jones.

2. All we know is that some one named Dr. Huston answered.

3. Tell Miss. Jennings that her company is the first respondent.

4. Norman Steins, Ph.D., will forward the signed contract.

5. Prof. Houdeck will be in charge of the session.

◆ Organizations

Abbreviate names of government and private agencies, organizations and associations, radio and television broadcasting stations, and other groups when appropriate. These abbreviations are generally written in all capital letters without periods.

Examples:

FBI	Federal Bureau of Investigation
NBC	National Broadcasting Company
KRBI	(Call letters for a radio station)
KMSP-TV	(Call letters for a television station)

Note: Government organizations often include the abbreviation *U.S.* No space follows the period within the abbreviation.

◆ Addresses

Rule 1 Words and directions within addresses should not be abbreviated. However, compound compass point directions, such as *NW, NE, SW,* and *SE,* are abbreviated when used after street addresses.

Examples:

Avenue	Drive	Road
Boulevard	Lane	Square
Building	Parkway	Street
Court	Place	

469 Broadway Square West

2639 Foshay Place SE

Rule 2 Two-letter state abbreviations are appropriate only when they appear with a ZIP Code in an address. The Appendix lists the two-letter state abbreviations.

Examples:

800 College Avenue	She lives in
Saint Peter, MN 56082-1498	Saint Peter, Minnesota.

Rule 3 Do not abbreviate the name of a city, state, or country or prefixes to most geographic names except when space is a problem. Periods are used with these abbreviations.

Examples:

Saint Clair   *or*   St. Clair

Fort Madison   *or*   Ft. Madison

Mount Saint Helens   *or*   Mt. St. Helens

United States   *or*   U.S. (no space after the internal period)

South Africa   *or*   S. Africa

California   *not*   Calif.

> **Exercise 5-2** PROOFREAD AND MARK

Use the appropriate proofreaders' marks to identify the corrections that should be made. If the sentence is correct, write **C** to the left of the number.

1. We cannot send the report to the U. S. Department of the Treasury.

2. The road crosses the corner of the state of ND.

3. The ABC Radio Network was able to achieve its goal.

4. Omaha, Neb., will eliminate the surcharge.

5. Send the list of addresses to Tatiana Sonamaran at 4903 E. Alberta St.

Mount Saint Helens erupted on May 18, 1980.

◆ **Time**

Abbreviate the standard time zones and expressions of time. Note the use of periods in the following examples.

> *Examples:*
> CDT (Central Daylight Time)
> PST (Pacific Standard Time)
> a.m. and p.m. (no space after the internal period)

Note: The abbreviation *a.m.* stands for *ante meridiem* (before noon), while *p.m.* stands for *post meridiem* (after noon).

Informal or Technical Style

Some abbreviations are appropriate for use in technical documents such as lists, business forms, and informal documents or when space is a problem. Such abbreviations are not appropriate in formal reports or business correspondence.

Days and Months:

Sun.	Thurs.	Jan.	May	Sept.
Mon.	Fri.	Feb.	June	Oct.
Tues.	Sat.	Mar.	July	Nov.
Wed.		Apr.	Aug.	Dec.

Measurements:

in *or* in.	yd *or* yd.	oz *or* oz.
ft *or* ft.	sq *or* sq.	lb *or* lb.

Expressions:

acct.	*for*	account
bal.	*for*	balance
dept.	*for*	department
ea.	*for*	each
EOM	*for*	end of month
PO	*for*	purchase order
P.O.	*for*	post office
No.	*for*	number (used when a number follows the abbreviation; e.g., The new order is No. 4406.)
vs.	*for*	versus

Exercise 5-3 PROOFREAD AND MARK

Use the appropriate proofreaders' marks to identify the corrections that should be made. If the sentence is correct, write **C** to the left of the number. Use the "general style" (not the "informal" or "technical style") in proofreading this exercise and all exercises that follow.

1. The hockey game will begin at 8 p. m.

2. This decision will benefit the people who register before the deadline on Sat.

3. The enthusiasm of employees in the Acctg. Dept. is appreciated.

4. You should arrive at 8:05 a. m. E.D.T. on Wed.

5. Please notify KXLM-TV that the reception on Feb. 28 will be held at the U. S. Department of the Interior.

6. Saint George, Ut., is where our consultant lives

7. The lawsuit in general court will be titled *Good vs. Erickson.*

8. Gloves, Inc., has opened a branch store near the K.X.T.Y. transmitter.

9. Have Prof. Stoney forward the survey results to the Ind. graduate school.

10. Will Ms. Anderson have the schedule ready by Jan. 18?

ROUGH DRAFTS

Newly composed documents are usually not in final form. They may contain keying and formatting errors. Sometimes word originators simply jot down ideas and instruct a copy editor to finish composing, keying, formatting, and printing the document.

The copy editor, using a pen and proofreaders' marks, makes corrections and revisions to the printed document. The result is a rough draft. On the basis of this rough draft, the copy editor completes the final editing, formatting, and printing of the document. Both the word originator and the copy editor need to use proofreaders' marks correctly. Then revisions will be marked consistently, and fewer errors will result.

When revising text, originators may move copy, change spacing, or return copy to its original form. Proofreaders must learn to recognize and apply the following proofreaders' marks when revising text:

Both the writer and copy editor must use proofreaders' marks correctly. Then revisions will be marked consistently, and few errors will result.

	MARKED COPY	CORRECTED COPY
Move.	your (letter) of May 1	your May 1 letter
Stet (keep as is). *stet* or	the ~~spacious~~ room *stet* the ~~spacious~~ room	the spacious room the spacious room
Single-space. *SS*	products were ready *ss* to be sold through the	products were ready to to be sold through the
Double-space. *DS*	$12,087 + 3,724 *DS* $15,811	$12,087 + 3,724 $15,811

Exercise 5-4 PROOFREAD AND MARK

In the following sentences, mark the corrections according to the information given in the "Changes" line.

1. The benefits cannot be changed before the is approved.

   Changes: Add "contract" between "the" and "is."

2. The bush should be planted by May 15.

   Changes: Move "by May 15" to the beginning of the sentence; capitalize "by"; lowercase "The"; add "currant" between "the" and "bush."

3. Three youths the Council meeting on October 12.

   Changes: Move "on October 12" to the beginning of the sentence; capitalize "on"; lowercase "Three"; add "spoke at" between "youths" and "the."

4. By working extra hours and putting in more time, we will be able to achieve the goals set at teh beginning of the year.

   Changes: Move "By working extra hours and putting in more time" to the end of the sentence; delete the comma after the word "time"; lowercase "By"; capitalize "we"; spell "the" correctly.

5. the motion was seconded after a long discussion

   Changes: Capitalize "the"; insert "and approved" between "seconded" and "after"; insert a period at the end of the sentence.

6. on February 28 the constitution was approved by members at our regular meeting.

   Changes: Move "on February 28" to the end of the sentence; capitalize "the"; add "revised" between "the" and "constitution."

7. Marlys celebrated her birthday by having lunch with friends at her favorite establishment.

   Changes: Add "eighteenth" between "her" and "birthday"; delete "lunch" and insert "dinner"; delete "establishment" and insert "restaurant."

CONFUSED AND MISUSED WORDS

all together   *adv.* (two words) gathered into a single unit or group; collected in one place

altogether   *adv.* entirely, completely, utterly

The reference books are **all together** on the shelf.

She is **altogether** too busy to take on another responsibility.

allude   *v.* to make an indirect reference to something

elude   *v.* to avoid or escape notice

He **alluded** to the fact that Mary Beth was correct.

The criminal **eluded** capture.

any one   *adj./pro.* (two words) certain person; use when the pronoun is followed by an *of* phrase

anyone   *pron.* anybody; any person at all

Any one of us can go.

Has **anyone** talked with Josey?

PEP Tip

- **Use only those abbreviations that your audience will understand.**

- **Be selective when using abbreviations in business letters, memos, reports, and e-mail messages.**

- **Depending on the software program you use, your spelling checker may recognize abbreviations differently. However, you can add commonly used abbreviations to your word processing dictionary so those abbreviations are not flagged as possible errors.**

PROOFREADING APPLICATIONS

Exercise 5-5 SENTENCES

Proofread the following sentences, and mark all abbreviation errors using the appropriate proofreaders' marks. If the sentence is correct, write **C** to the left of the number.

1. Mrs Zumbro showed her commitment to her profession by volunteering her time.

2. Radio Station K.N.M.U. went on the air in Jan. 1966.

3. James Edward Tanner, III married Jennifer Courtney Postmann in Manly, IA.

4. The consultant lived at 38893 Craig Ave.

5. We cannot meet on Mon., Wed., or Fri.

6. I believe the best time to meet tomorrow is at 3:30 pm C.D.T.

7. Did you know that Thelma works for the FBI?

8. Send your resume to the manager of our Acct. Dept.

9. The U.S. Post Office in Muncie is located on Nelson Lane.

10. Doctor Jonathan Petrak is the new department adviser.

11. The new pastor at our church is Rev. Nancy Bernardino.

12. Alice Carrasco was elected to the U. S. Senate by a wide margin.

13. What did they hope to achieve by driving to 39904 West Ave.?

14. We plan to arrive by 8:45 am on Tues.

15. Miss. Jacqlyn Arneson was hired by Wisconsin Energy.

16. Edward and Emma enjoy vacationing in Mich.

17. Professor Newsome will speak at our convention in Minneapolis in March.

18. What is the bal. for our dept.?

19. Mr Westman is very particular about where he stays.

20. Kenard Thieland, Ph.D., visited San Francisco, CA.

Exercise 5-6 SPELLING AND WORD USAGE CHECK

Compare the words in Column A with the corresponding words in Column B. Use the appropriate proofreaders' marks to correct the misspelled or misused words. If both columns are correct, write **C** to the left of the number.

Column A	Column B
1. benefit	benefit
2. particular	particlar
3. committment	commitment
4. enthusiasm	enthusiasam
5. consultent	consultant
6. defendent	defendant
7. achieve	achieve
8. can not	cannot
9. believe	beleive
10. eliminate	elimanate
11. congratulations	congradulations
12. corporate	corporite
13. Derek is all together too successful.	We are in this all together.
14. Were you able to allude detection?	Jasmine alluded to her judicial appointment.
15. Is anyone able to attend?	Can any one of you participate?

Exercise 5-7 INTERNATIONAL VOCABULARY

Compare the Spanish words in Column A with the corresponding words in Column B. If the word in Column B is different from the word in Column A, use the appropriate proofreaders' marks to correct Column B. If the words in both columns are the same, write **C** to the left of the number.

Column A	Column B
1. desfile	desfile
2. arroyada	aroyada
3. incumbencia	incumbencai
4. ruborizarse	ruborizarce
5. legumbre	legunbre

Exercise 5-8 MEMORANDUM

Proofread the following memo, and mark all errors using the appropriate
proofreaders' marks.

Acme Insurance Company, Inc., Memorandum

TO: Jason Realstad, Editor *Acme Notes*

FROM: Marguerite Lorenz, Chairperson Awards Committee

DATE: Sep. 5, 200-

SUBJECT: ITEMS FOR NEWSLETTER

Here are two items for the Dec. issue of *Acme Notes*. Please modify them to fit the available
space.

Item 1. <u>Year End Awards Program Scheduled</u>. The annual Awards Program will be held in
Swift Auditorium on January 11. The auditorium is located at 9550 Prince Blvd. here in
Manhattan.

An important part of the program will be the presentation of special awards for outstanding
achievement during the current year. In addition, recognition will be given to employees who
have been with the company for 25, 30, 35, and 40 years.

The speaker for the program will be Antoine Paez, corporate consultant for Maxon Industries,
Chicago, Ill. His enthusiasm in working with companies like ours will be of particular benefit to
us as we embark upon next year's sales campaign. Mr Paez has shown a tremendously large no.
of people how to achieve the goals they have set. His message will be currant and direct. He
will give us many usable suggestions.

Please attend the annual Awards Program and extend your personal congradulations to the award
winners. More information will be distributed in December.

Item 2. <u>Manager's Meeting Scheduled</u>. Juliana Keltgen, legal council, has asked to meet with
supervisors on Thursday, January 10. The company was a defendent in a recent court case that
we won. Ms. Keltgen believes that a meeting is needed to summarize the results of the case and
to help eliminate misunderstandings in the company's hiring process. We believe you will find
this meeting well worth your time.

Exercise 5-9 LETTER

Proofread the following letter, and mark all errors using the appropriate proofreaders' marks.

ACME INSURANCE COMPANY, INC.
3842 West Grand Avenue • St. Paul, MN 55110-2910
612/555/0155 • Fax: 612/555/0156

Dec. 3, 200-

Ms. Floragene Adams, President
Southern Armstrong, Ltd.
728 Imperial Drive South
Nashville, TN 37210-4217

Dear Ms. Adams:

It is a pleasure to confirm our invitation to you to be the speaker at our Apr. 22 seminar in Wichita. You were recommended to us by Candace Okano, president of Midwest Travel Company in Kansas City, Kans.

The in-service meeting will be held in Suite 332 in the Grand Central Ins. Bldg. The seminar will begin at 10 a. m.

Two other speakers who will also be meeting with our managers are Josefina Ramos, chairperson, Board of Directors, Littleton, Inc., and Arthur Proehl, legal counsel for Juniper County.

We have also invited Ray Symthe, president, Toledo Consulting. Unfortunately, he can not be with us for this meeting.

Additional information will be sent to you concerning travel and housing arrangements. If you have any questions, please let me know.

We look forward to your being with us in Apr.

Sincerely,

Louis Roe
Seminar Coordinator

tfd

PROOFREADING AT THE COMPUTER

Exercise 5-10 LETTER

1. Open 05-10 from the Chapter 05 folder on the Student CD. (This is a computer copy of Application 5-9.)

2. Proofread the letter on the screen. Correct all errors on the screen copy that you indicated with proofreaders' marks in Application 5-9.

3. Format the letter using default left and right margins and a 2″ top margin.

4. Save the letter as 05-10R, and print it.

5. Proofread the printed document. If you find any additional mistakes, correct the errors on both the hard copy and the screen.

6. Save and print the revised document.

Exercise 5-11 MEMORANDUM

1. On the handwritten memo on pages 72 and 73, mark the changes requested (shown in the box on page 73) using the appropriate proofreaders' marks.

2. Open 05-11 from the Chapter 05 folder on the Student CD.

3. Proofread the copy on the screen by comparing it with the corrected handwritten rough draft.

4. Correct all mistakes.

5. Format the memo using default left and right margins and a 2″ top margin.

6. Save the memo as 05-11R, and print it.

7. Proofread the printed document. If you find any additional mistakes, correct the errors on both the hard copy and the screen.

8. Save and print the revised document.

Exercise 5-12 E-MAIL MESSAGE

1. Open 05-12 from the Chapter 05 folder on the Student CD.

2. Proofread the e-mail message, and make all necessary corrections.

3. Save the document as 05-12R, and print it.

4. Proofread the printed document. If you find any additional mistakes, correct the errors on both the hard copy and the screen.

5. Save and print the revised document.

MEMO

TO: Ramon Schroader, Manager
                Human Resources Department

FROM: Marguerite Lorenz, Awards Cmte.

DATE: November 23, 200-

SUBJECT: PRELIMINARY LIST FOR AWARDS

As you know, our annual Awards Program will be held on Feb. 3 with the dinner starting at 6 pm. We anticipate that the program will last from 6:45 p.m. to 8:15 p.m.

A major part of the program will be the presentation of awards to various individuals and several departments. One category of individual awards is for those who have worked at the company for 25 or more years.

Please review the records of all employees and prepare a list according to the following categories:

    1. employed for 25 years
    2. employed for 30 years
    3. employed for 35 or more years

Our plan is to give a wristwatch to those employees with 25 years. Those with 30 years will receive a piece of crystal glass, and those with 35 years will receive a miniature sculpture.

In addition to identifying ea. person, we need a brief biographical sketch that can be printed in the program. Please contact each awardee to help you prepare a brief paragraph or two about his or her years here at ACME.

Finally, will you arrange for the no. of awards to be given in each category? Each watch should be engraved with a suitable inscription.

Could I please have a preliminary report on the no. of awards and the names of the awardees by Dec. 15.

PARAGRAPH	CHANGES TO BE MADE IN MEMO
Paragraph 1	Delete "As you know." Capitalize "our."
Paragraph 2	Insert "major" between "one" and "category."
Paragraph 3	In Item 3, delete "or more."
Paragraph 4	Replace "piece" with the word "vase."
Paragraph 5	Delete "that can be printed."
Paragraph 5	Move "in the program" to appear after "person."
Paragraph 6	Replace "watch" with "award."
Paragraph 7	Change date to December 1.

CUMULATIVE APPLICATION

Exercise 5-13 EDITORIAL

Proofread and correct all errors using the appropriate proofreaders' marks.

EDITORIAL FOR ACME NOTES

As we approach the end of another year, in the spirit of the Holiday season, we want to extend our appreciation to the many people who have made this a successful year. We sincerely appreciate your strong committment to our company.

First, to the members of the Sales Dept., we salute you for your tremendous effort and enthusiasm throughout the year. Even during the recent economic recession, you were able to help our customers meet their needs in a very positive way. We can not tell you how much we appreciate your efforts.

Second, to all employees, we salute you for your excellent community service activities. Because we have been a longtime member ofthe Central City community, it is important that we show our support as a company for Central City's many activities and projects. Improvements in our community will result in improvements for us.

Finally, we salute our U. S. and European customers for their loyalty and particularily for their response to our request for assistance in the product improvement program. Preliminary results from the midyear survey show that over 50 percent of our customers provided reactions to our line of products, many offering suggestions for expanding the products and service that we have available.

have a happy holiday season! Thanks again for helping us acheive great success during the year!

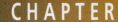

Number Expression Errors

Spotlight on ACCURACY

It should be obvious why the use of exact numbers is critical when working with business documents. Documents with incorrect numbers can cost a company thousands, even millions, of dollars. Imagine ordering 10,000 widgets with the specifications of 2″ × 12″. When the widgets arrive, you realize that each widget should have been 2″ × 21″ (not 2″ × 12″). These widgets are of no value to your company because they are not long enough for the product you make. If each widget cost your company $10, your company just paid $100,000 for 10,000 items it cannot use. Not only are you out that much money, you do not have the exact item needed to begin construction.

Objectives

- Recognize errors in the expression of numbers.

- Spell correctly 12 frequently misspelled words.

- Use correctly three sets of commonly confused and mis-used words.

The frequent use of numbers in business correspondence has created an increased need for accurate proofreading. Financial reports, telephone/fax numbers, ZIP Codes, and credit card identifications are just a few of the ways in which numbers are being used.

Often numbers must be checked against a source document for accuracy. For example, amounts listed on an expense summary are checked against receipts. Many of the decisions you make regarding numbers, however, will be related to whether the numbers should be expressed as figures or as words. The guidelines presented here will apply to most of the situations you encounter.

When you locate an incorrectly expressed number, use the same proofreaders' marks you have already learned for identifying the errors.

	MARKED COPY	CORRECTED COPY
Spell out. *sp* ◯	There were ③ cars in *sp* the holiday race.	There were three cars in the holiday race.
Express as figures. *15* ~~fifteen~~	Invite ~~eighteen~~ *18* colleagues to dinner.	Invite 18 colleagues to dinner.

NUMBERS EXPRESSED AS WORDS

Follow these general guidelines for expressing numbers as words.

Rule 1 Spell out numbers from one to ten. Express numbers above ten in figures. When a sentence contains a series of numbers, some of which are over ten and some of which are under ten, use figures for consistency.

Example: Our agent will describe the terms of five different policies.

Example: The teacher brought 6 tablets, 20 diskettes, and 4 textbooks.

Example: This group insurance policy will cover all ~~fifteen~~ *15* employees.

Example: Please include 5 apples, 18 oranges, and ~~eight~~ *8* lemons on the list.

If numbers can be grouped into different categories within a sentence, examine each category separately. Use the same style for all numbers within a related category.

Example: From the new book list for the seven library branches, we have ordered 21 hard copy versions, 33 paperback copies, 5 cassette recordings, and 9 CDs.

Example: The Sports Complex, which is open eight hours on Sundays, has 8 tennis courts, ~~four~~ *4* weight rooms, and 16 racquetball courts.

Rule 2 Spell out numbers that begin a sentence even if figures are used later in the sentence. When numbers from 21 to 99 are spelled out, key them with a hyphen.

Example: Twenty-seven children went on the trip 11 months ago.

Example: (14) _sp_ people were selected for the jury, even though only eight were needed.

When a large number begins a sentence, rewrite the sentence so that it does not begin with a number.

Example: Twenty-one thousand one hundred fifty-two people live in that town.

Rewritten: There are 21,152 people living in that town.

Rule 3 Spell out approximate amounts and isolated fractions. Mixed numbers (a figure and a fraction) are expressed as figures. (Use a hyphen to join the numerator and denominator of a fraction written in words, unless either element already contains a hyphen.)

Example: The group drank almost fifteen gallons of lemonade at the picnic.

Example: The builder will need pipe that is 2 1/8″ in diameter.

Example: The gasoline gauge showed the tank to be 3/4 _three-fourths_ full.

Example: His shoe size is ~~nine and one half~~ _9 1/2_.

Rule 4 Spell out street numbers through ten as ordinals (first, second, etc.). Use figures for house and building numbers. An exception is house or building number One, which is written as a word.

Example: The business has moved to 297 Sixth Street.

Example: The tennis courts are located near the corner of Trent Avenue and ~~7th~~ _Seventh_ Street.

Example: MFC National Bank is located at One Gateway Drive.

Rule 5 Spell out ages ten and under unless stated specifically in years, months, and days. Use figures for ages 11 and over.

Example: His daughter is six years old.

Example: On April 16, he will be ~~seven~~ _7_ years, ~~five~~ _5_ months, and ~~eight~~ _8_ days old.

Rule 6 When two numbers are used together, spell out one of the two—preferably the one that is the shortest word.

Example: At the sale, she found 6 ten-gallon cans.

Example: The inventory includes ~~twenty-four~~ _24_ (2) _sp_ roll packs of paper towels.

Exercise 6-1 PROOFREAD AND MARK

Use the appropriate proofreaders' marks to correct the errors in number expression. If the sentence is correct, write **C** to the left of the number.

1. The colors of the copies in the 3 categories should be
   30 red, ten white, and 36 blue.

2. 16 new windows will be sent to your address at
   9054 6th Avenue.

3. For the program booklet to fit into the six and
   three-fourths envelope, the booklet must be one-eighth
   inch shorter.

4. We received five hundred eight-page brochures.

5. The instructor distributed almost fifty copies.

NUMBERS AS FIGURES

Follow these general guidelines for expressing numbers as figures.

Use figures to express time except when used alone or with the contraction *o'clock*. Use *a.m.* or *p.m.* with figures. Zeros are not required for on-the-hour times of day.

    Example: The appointment has been scheduled for 5 p.m.

    Example: The bus will depart at ⑤ o'clock. *(sp)*

Use figures *without* adding *d*, *st*, or *th* after a month to express the day and the year. (Set the year off by commas when it follows the month and day.)

    Example: The Declaration of Independence was signed on July 4, 1776.

    Example: She will retire on August ~~Ninth~~ 9, 200-.

Express the day in ordinal figures (*1st*, *2d*, *3rd*, *4th*, etc.) when the day precedes the month or when the month is omitted. (The preferred abbreviation of *second* and *third* is *2d* and *3rd*, respectively.)

    Example: The state conference will start on the 21st of November.

    Example: The ~~fifth~~ 5th of this month will be a school holiday.

Express in figures dimensions, measurements, and weights.

    Example: The rug measures 10 by 12 feet.

    Example: The fish weighed ~~five~~ 5 pounds.

Rule 10 Express in figures street numbers over ten and all address numbers except *One*. Street numbers above ten may be expressed as either cardinal numbers (*22*) or ordinal numbers (*22d*). However, be consistent and use one style.

> *Example:* Please send the order to 607 South 38th Street.

> *Example:* The art gallery will be located at One Park Drive. *sp*

> *Example:* The parade will begin at the corner of Main and ⑼th Street.

Rule 11 Express as figures numbers following nouns such as *page*, *chapter*, *room*, *rule*, and *policy*.

> *Example:* Our final statement begins at the bottom of page 41 in Chapter 4.

> *Example:* According to Rule ~~six~~ ⁶, the motion is not needed.

Rule 12 Express in figures amounts of money, decimal amounts, percentages, and interest periods that include the year, month, and day.

> *Example:* The cost per person will be $9.97.

> *Example:* Money that is deposited into the account will earn ~~five~~ ⁵ percent interest.

Spell out the word *cents* for amounts under a dollar (*15 cents*, not *$.15*).

> *Example:* The small souvenirs can be sold for 47 cents each.

> *Example:* Be sure to add ~~six~~ ⁶ cents to the total for the tax.

Express even amounts of money without zeros or decimal points (*$10*).

> *Example:* The special ticket price will be $8 per person through Friday.

> *Example:* The necklace will cost ~~nine dollars~~ *$9* when it is on sale.

In legal documents, express amounts of money in both words and figures.

> *Example:* In consideration of One Hundred Sixty Dollars ($160), the contract will be binding on both parties.

> *Example:* Upon payment of Four Hundred Thirty-two Dollars and Twenty-one Cents, the loan will be considered paid in full. *($432.21)*

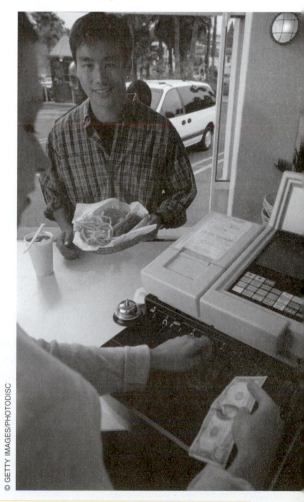

The cost of his lunch was $4.29.

© GETTY IMAGES/PHOTODISC

Exercise 6-2 PROOFREAD AND MARK

Use the appropriate proofreaders' marks to correct the errors in number expression. If the sentence is correct, write **C** to the left of the number.

1. The candidates' meeting will be held at 876 East 5th Street.

2. She purchased 4 $100,000 policies for her business.

3. The council approved the start of construction of an office building at 976 South Sixteenth Street.

4. On the questionnaire, she stated her son's age as 6 years, 6 months, and 27 days.

5. He purchased thirty-six 9-inch dividers for the file cabinets.

ZIP CODES

To assist the post office, addresses on all letters and envelopes should include the correct two-letter state abbreviation and ZIP Code. Whenever possible, the ZIP Code should contain nine digits.

The proofreader should be sure the ZIP Code on the envelope is the same as the ZIP Code in the letter address. Accuracy in ZIP Codes is important because errors cause delays in delivery of correspondence. The Appendix contains a list of the two-letter abbreviations for states and U.S. territories. When in doubt about a ZIP Code, check the official ZIP Code directory available from the U.S. Postal Service. You may also find ZIP Code information on the Internet.

Note: The U.S. Postal Service requests that envelope addresses be single-spaced and keyed in all capital letters with no punctuation.

> *Example:* MS DEBBIE GONZALEZ
> 547 INDIANA AVENUE
> CENTER POINT WV 26339-0487

Exercise 6-3 PROOFREAD AND MARK

Proofread the envelope addresses by comparing them to the correct letter addresses on the left. Correct the envelope addresses using the appropriate proofreaders' marks. If the envelope address is correct, write **C** to the left of the number.

Letter Address	Envelope Address
1. Ms. Hilda Morales 431 Maiden Way Denver, CO 80233-0499	MS HILDA MORALES 431 MAIDEN WAY DENVER CO 80233-0499

2. Mr. Chuck Hansen

Crest Insurance Company

P.O. Box 1923

Garland, TX 75046-1623

MR. CHUCK HANSEN

CREST INSURANCE COMPANY

P.O. BOX 1923

GARLAND TX 70546-1623

3. Feather Duster, Inc.

Attention: Credit Department

807 Second Street South

Kalamazoo, MI 49009-1208

FEATHER DUSTER INC.

ATTENTION CREDIT DEPARTMENT

870 SECOND SOUTH STREET

KALAMAZOO MI. 49009-1208

4. Professor Anita Sandoval

Marysville State College

546 South Cleveland Road

Memphis, TN 38104-3232

PROF ANITA SANDOVAL

MARYSVILLE STATE COLLEGE

564 SOUTH CLEVELAND ROAD

MEMPHIS TENN 38104-3223

5. Mr. Lynwood Johnreit

Vice President of Sales

West Fisheries Company

901 Jefferson Boulevard

Vancouver, WA 98660-3692

MR LYNWOOD JOHNRIET

VICE PRESIDENT OF SALES

WET FISHERIES COMPANY

901 JEFFERSON BOULEVARD

VANCOUVER Wa 98660-3692

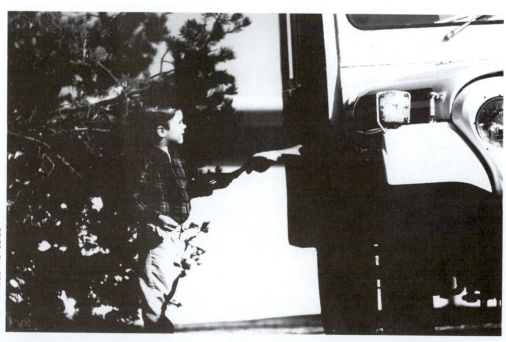

Accuracy in ZIP Codes is important because errors cause delays in delivery of correspondence.

CONFUSED AND MISUSED WORDS

can	*v.* to be able to do something
may	*v.* to be possible; to give permission

Can you type 50 words per minute?

Mrs. Colby, **may** I help you grade today's quiz?

cent	*n.* 1/100; penny
scent	*n.* a distinctive odor; perfume; a sense of smell
sent	*v.* past tense and past participle of *send*

Bank tellers must balance to the **cent** each day.

Your perfume has an unusual **scent.**

Miguel **sent** his resume to 15 companies.

complement	*n.* something that adds to or completes a whole; v. to complete or make perfect
compliment	*n.* an expression of praise; v. to praise

A black portfolio will **complement** most interview ensembles.

Mr. Tuttle did **compliment** me on my perfect attendance.

- Check the accuracy of all extensions, calculations, and totals of numbers.

- Verify the accuracy of numbers against their source document.

- Check the alignment of decimals that appear within a column.

- Although the style of expressing numbers as words or figures may vary depending on the formality of the document, follow one style consistently within a document.

PROOFREADING APPLICATIONS

Proofread the following paragraphs to locate errors in number expression. Use the appropriate proofreaders' marks to show the corrections.

CLASS RUNION TIME

You are cordially invited to attend the reunions for the Classes of 1980–1985. They will be held on Friday, January 15th, in Room fourteen of the Central Conference Center, 469 Grand Avenue East in Birmingham. Registration and the social hour will begin at 5:30 o'clock p.m. The dinner will begin at 6:30 p.m. and the program at 7:30 p.m.

We anticipate that the program will be over by 9:30. The rest of the evening will be available for remembering and listening to the music of THE ORANGE APPLES, an old-time music pep band from the high school.

2 copies of a questionnaire are enclosed for you to share with us your "personal history" since the big day in the early eighties. Please complete the questionnaire, and return it in the enclosed envelope to the high school secretary's office as soon as possible. We'll include a summary of the responses in the Early Eighties booklet you will get when you register. This booklet will be a wonderful compliment to your library.

Your friends and mine have done many things since they left the alma mater. Here's the chance to catch up in a hurry in 1 evening! See you there!

Enclosure

Exercise 6-5 SPELLING AND WORD USAGE CHECK

Compare the words in Column A with the corresponding words in Column B. Use the appropriate proofreaders' marks to correct the misspelled or misused words. If both columns are correct, write **C** to the left of the number.

Column A	Column B
1. secrateries	secretaries
2. complience	compliance
3. emergency	emergency
4. questionaire	questionnaire
5. pryor	prior
6. categories	catagories
7. government	goverment
8. business	buisness
9. correspondance	correspondence
10. excellent	excellent
11. consensus	consensis
12. vendur	vendor
13. Can I leave now?	I may attend the conference.
14. He sent the letter yesterday.	The cent made me ill.
15. What a nice complement!	She paid the chef a nice compliment.

Exercise 6-6 INTERNATIONAL VOCABULARY

Compare the Spanish words in Column A with the corresponding words in Column B. If the word in Column B is different from the word in Column A, use the appropriate proofreaders' marks to correct Column B. If the words in both columns are the same, write **C** to the left of the number.

Column A	Column B
1. ejercicio	ejerciccio
2. empresa	empressa
3. esperar	espearar
4. frijoles	friholes
5. gustar	gustar

Exercise 6-7 MEMORANDUM

Proofread the printed memo that follows by comparing it with the correct handwritten memo on page 86. Mark all errors using the appropriate proofreaders' marks.

TO: Laurine Rantzeed
             Budget Office

FROM: Trent Washington, Manger
             Communication Center

DATE: October 10, 200-

SUBJECT: BUDGET REQUEST FOR NEXT YEAR

Enclosed with this note is our completed budget request for next year. Please note several items:

29 reams of orange offset paper have been requested because next year we will be publishing and distributing the environmental promotion flyer each month.

The postage amount has been increased to $950.00 because of an expected rise in postal rates.

The BHD Company has informed us that the next version of its word proccesing software program will be available on the 6 of August; therefore, we will need at least $825.00 of the equipment budget to receive the appropriate software upgrade.

In addition, the literature for the newest model of BHD's computer should be scent on or shortly after August 31st. Finally, the miscellaneous amount has been increased by seven percent for use in an emergency situation.

Enclosure

TO: Laurine Rantzeed
Budget Office

FROM: Trent Washington, Manager
Communication Center

DATE: October 10, 200-

SUBJECT: BUDGET REQUEST FOR NEXT YEAR

Enclosed with this note is our completed budget request for next year. Please note several items:

Twenty-nine reams of orange offset paper have been requested because next year we will be publishing and distributing the environmental promotion flyer each month.

The postage amount has been increased to $950 because of an expected rise in postal rates.

The BHD Company has informed us that the next version of its word processing software program will be available on the 6th of August; therefore, we will need at least $825 of the equipment budget to receive the appropriate software upgrade.

In addition, the literature for the newest model of BHD's computer should be sent on or shortly after August 31. Finally, the miscellaneous amount has been increased by 7 percent for use in an emergency situation.

Enclosure

Exercise 6-8 LETTER

Proofread the printed letter that follows by comparing it with the correct handwritten letter on page 88. Mark all errors using the appropriate proofreaders' marks.

NATIONAL ACTIVITIES ASSOCIATION
632 Grandy Building
278 Balsam Avenue, Boise, ID 83701-1609
(208) 555-0162 • Fax (208) 555-0163

December 19, 200-

Ms. Alyssa Gater, President
Emerald City Enterprises, Inc.
363 North Raintree Avenue
Portland, OR 97222-0384

Dear Ms. Gater:

Thank you for your kind hospitality during my recent visit with you and the planning committee. I have reviewed the notes that Mr. Giles prepared, and I hasten to ask that whether the following corrections might be made:

1. The business meeting should be scheduled for Room Seven rather than 17.

2. The 4 seminars on Friday morning should be planned to accommodate at least 40 people per session.

3. The banquet on Friday night will start at 7 p.m. rather than 8:00 p.m.

4. The shuttle buses will need to leave the main hotel every fifteen minutes.

5. The special V.I.P. reception on Saturday should be planned for thirty-one people.

If you have any questions, be sure to let me know.

Sincerely,

Agnes Woo

tis

December 19, 200-

Ms. Alyssa Gater, President
Emerald City Enterprises, Inc.
363 North Raintree Avenue
Portland, OR 97222-0348

Dear Ms. Gater:

Thank you for your kind hospitality during my recent visit with you and the planning committee. I have reviewed the notes that Mr. Giles prepared, and I hasten to ask whether the following corrections might be made:

1. The business meeting should be scheduled for Room 7 rather than 17.
2. The four seminars on Friday morning should be planned to accommodate at least 40 people per session.
3. The banquet on Friday night will start at 7 p.m. rather than 8 p.m.
4. The shuttle buses will need to leave the main hotel every 15 minutes.
5. The special VIP reception on Saturday should be planned for 31 people.

If you have any questions, be sure to let me know.

Sincerely,

Agnes Woo

tis

PROOFREADING AT THE COMPUTER

Exercise 6-9 MEMORANDUM

1. Open 06-9 from the Chapter 06 folder on the Student CD. (This is a computer copy of Application 6-7.)

2. Proofread the memo on the screen. Correct all errors on the screen copy that you indicated with proofreaders' marks in Application 6-7.

3. Format the memo using default left and right margins and a 2″ top margin.

4. Save the memo as 06-9R, and print it.

5. Proofread the printed document. If you find any additional mistakes, correct the errors on both the hard copy and the screen.

6. Save and print the revised document.

Exercise 6-10 NOTICE

1. Mark the necessary changes for the rough draft notice that follows on page 90.

2. Open 06-10 from the Chapter 06 folder on the Student CD.

3. Proofread the copy on the screen by comparing it with the rough draft notice.

4. Correct all mistakes.

5. Format the notice using default left and right margins and a 2″ top margin.

6. Save the notice as 06-10R, and print it.

7. Proofread the printed document. If you find any additional mistakes, correct the errors on both the hard copy and the screen.

8. Save and print the revised document.

Exercise 6-11 E-MAIL MESSAGE

1. Open 06-11 from the Chapter 06 folder on the Student CD.

2. Proofread the e-mail message, and make all necessary corrections.

3. Save the document as 06-11R, and print it.

4. Proofread the printed document. If you find any additional mistakes, correct the errors on both the hard copy and the screen.

5. Save and print the revised document.

PROMOTION CEREMONIES

Students, your deadline to participate in the midyear promotion ceremonies for the short-term business programs is quickly approaching. Applications must be filed by Friday, November 11th, for your paperwork to be processed and your name to appear on the printed program. You may obtain an application form from your counselor or in the business division office. Please submit completed applications to Cherise in the business division office. Hours are Monday through Friday from 7:30 to 4:30 p.m.

You are encouraged to invite your family members and friends to attend; however, there is a maximum of 8 guests per student. The ceremonies will take place on Saturday, December 10th, in the Warnor Theater, 1400 Fulton Road, Fresno. Doors will open at 12:30 p.m.; the program will begin at 1 o'clock p.m. We anticipate that the program will be over by 3:00. Soft drinks, coffee, and cookies will be served in the lobby after the ceremony.

We look forward to seeing you and celebrating your achievement. Congratulations on a job well done!

CUMULATIVE APPLICATION

Exercise 6-12 ANNOUNCEMENT

Work with a partner to proofread this printed document. One of you should read from the correct handwritten document on page 92 while the other checks the announcement below, paying special attention to numbers. Mark all errors using the appropriate proofreaders' marks.

Teamwork

ANNOUNCEMENT

Congratulations on your eligibility to attend the Outstanding Business Students Conference this year! Our goal is to provide information that will compliment the education of your emerging business leaders. We are looking forward to hosting students from the top 10 business schools in the country and are working dilagently to provide an attractive program.

Please indicate below the number of students you anticipate will be attending the various breakout sessions, and submit the information by September 21. My Associate, Kevin Crenshaw, will return your confirmation schedules by the 5 of October.

1 additional highlight will be the dinner banquet on Saturday from 5:30–9:30 p.m. This will include three enticing buffet lines and displays from 15 local employers. Let us know if we may assist you farther.

Breakout sessions:

Entreperneurship	BE-218	8:30–11:50	_____
Managerial Leadership	BE-129	8:00–9:50	_____
Free Enterprise	BE-219	10:00–11:50	_____
Globalization	BE-123	1:00–2:50	_____
Conflict Management	BE-215	1:00–4:30	_____
Resume/Interview	BE-217	3:00–4:30	_____

ANNOUNCEMENT

Congratulations on your eligibility to attend the Outstanding Business Students Conference this year! Our goal is to provide information that will compliment the education of your emerging business leaders. We are looking forward to hosting students from the top ten business schools in the country and are working dilagently to provide an attractive program.

Please indicate below the number of students you anticipate will be attending the various breakout sessions, and submit the information by September 21. My Associate, Kevin Crenshaw, will return your confirmation schedules by the 5 of October.

One additional highlight will be the dinner banquet on Saturday from 5:30–9:30 p.m. This will include three enticing buffet lines and displays from 15 local employers. Let us know if we may assist you farther.

Breakout sessions:

Entreperneurship	BE-218	8:30–11:50	_____
Managerial Leadership	BE-129	8:00–9:50	_____
Free Enterprise	BE-219	10:00–11:50	_____
Globalization	BE-123	1:00–2:50	_____
Conflict Management	BE-215	1:00–4:30	_____
Resume/Interview	BE-217	3:00–4:30	_____

© DIGITAL VISION

Sentence Construction Errors, Part 1

Spotlight on **ACCURACY**

In business communication, your writing style is important. Your mastery of a clear, concise writing style is essential to success because how you say something may be as important as what you say. A poor writing style can result in confusion, to both your company and your customers. Think of the confusion that may have resulted from the following sentences written by people completing an accident report:

- The accident happened when the right back door of a car came around the corner without signaling.

- The other car hit my truck without giving warning of its intentions.

- He had been driving 45 years before falling asleep and having an accident.

- No one was to blame for the accident, but it would never have happened if the other person had been alert.

Objectives

- Recognize incomplete sentences (fragments).

- Find and mark errors in subject-verb agreement.

- Find and mark errors in singular/plural nouns.

- Identify intervening modifiers and indefinite pronouns.

- Find and mark errors in compound and collective nouns.

- Spell correctly 12 frequently misspelled words.

- Use correctly three sets of commonly confused and misused words.

Your instructor writes on your term paper "You done a well job!" What is your reaction? Are you pleased? Yes, you are happy about the complimentary remark and the high grade you earned. But are you impressed with your instructor's use of English grammar? Not likely. In fact, you may react negatively and lose confidence in your instructor's ability to communicate correctly and effectively.

Businesspeople react the same way. A person is judged on his or her ability to communicate clearly and correctly—when speaking or writing. Your ability to communicate effectively in the business world is extremely important.

Proofreading for correct grammar requires patience and attention to detail. You must be alert and look for errors in grammar usage and sentence construction.

Chapters 7, 8, and 9 will discuss the most important principles of correct grammar. In this chapter you will review and apply the rules of basic sentence structure. You will learn to recognize complete sentences and sentence fragments. You will learn to identify and use singular, plural, compound, and collective nouns. You will also learn how intervening modifiers and indefinite pronouns affect subject-verb agreement.

If you locate a grammar error when proofreading, draw a line through the error and write the correction above the error. If you are unsure of the correct grammatical structure or the writer's intended message, write a question mark in the right or left margin of the page. The question mark indicates to the writer that the meaning is not clear and that the sentence should be revised or rewritten.

		MARKED COPY	CORRECTED COPY
Change copy as indicated.	——	Ten resumes ~~was~~ *were* received.	Ten resumes were received.
Question the writer.	⸮ /	If I have a ⸮ question. /	If I have a question, I will ask her.

SENTENCE STRUCTURE

A **complete sentence** is a group of words that has a subject and a verb and expresses a complete thought. The **subject** is the person, place, or thing the sentence is about. It may be a noun or a personal pronoun (*I, you, he, she, it, we,* or *they*) that takes the place of the noun. The **verb** tells what the subject is or does. Verbs express either action or a state of being.

Action verbs often include **helping verbs** that indicate the **tense** (timing) of the verb. The main helping verbs are *is, are, be, am, was, were, has, have,* and *had.* Other helping verbs include *may, might, must, ought, can, could, would, should, shall, will, do, does,* and *did.* Helping verbs are easy to recognize; they help the main verb tell what the subject is doing.

ACTION VERBS	STATE-OF-BEING VERBS
Dexter *drives* a green Jaguar.	Juana *is* an actuary.
I *jog* five miles every day.	The food *looks* delicious.
The manager *uses* the computer.	I *am* the chairperson.

A **verb phrase** consists of the main verb plus any helping verbs. (A **phrase** is a group of words that does not contain both a subject and a verb.) In the following examples, the subjects are underscored once and the verb phrases are underscored twice.

Example: Lunch will be served in the Sunset Room.

Example: Cruise ships are designed for passenger comfort.

Example: How many cruises have you taken?

Linking verbs are state-of-being verbs. The most common linking verbs are forms of the verb *be* (*is, am, are, was, were, being, has been, have been,* and *had been*). Other linking verbs include *appear, become, feel, look, seem, taste,* and *sound.* Linking verbs answer the question *What?* and are followed by nouns, pronouns, or adjectives (called *complements*). **Complements** are words used after linking verbs to describe or rename the subject of the sentence.

The difference between a helping verb and a linking verb is that the helping verb is part of the verb phrase containing an action verb and helps to ask questions, give commands, or make statements. The linking verb "links" the subject of the sentence to the word (noun, pronoun, or adjective) that immediately follows the linking verb and completes the meaning of the subject by describing or renaming it.

In each of the following examples, the subject is underscored once and the linking verbs (or verb phrases) are underscored twice. Can you find the complements in the sentences?

Example: Gunther looks worried. (Gunther looks what?)

Example: Sarah is the cruise director. (Sarah is what?)

Example: Tuesday's activities were fun. (Activities were what?)

Example: Cruises are becoming favorite vacation choices. (Cruises are becoming what?)

Example: Liv celebrated by taking a yacht cruise. (Liv celebrated by what?)

Exercise 7-1 PROOFREAD AND MARK

In each sentence underline the subject once and the verb or verb phrase twice.

1. The president of the travel agency is Ron Tellez.

2. The cruise ship was refurbished two years ago.

3. Santa Barbara seems like a popular port of call.

4. The barge cruise on the River Nile sounds exciting.

5. Luxury cruises have become very competitive.

SENTENCE FRAGMENTS

A group of words that contains a subject and a verb is a complete sentence. If either the subject or the verb is missing, it is an incomplete sentence— more commonly known as a **sentence fragment**. When you locate a sentence fragment, write a question mark in the left or right margin of the page. This will alert the writer to explain the meaning of the sentence or to revise it. If the correction appears obvious, simply correct the fragment by changing it into a complete sentence.

SENTENCE FRAGMENT	COMPLETE SENTENCE
When you talk to travel agents. ?⟋	When you talk to travel agents, they will explain all the options.

Exercise 7-2 PROOFREAD AND MARK

Write a question mark in the margin if the group of words is a fragment. Correct the copy if the error is obvious. If the group of words is a complete sentence, write **C** to the left of the number.

1. The king of vacations.

2. Choosing which cruise to take. One of life's most delectable dilemmas.

3. A wide variety of itineraries from which to choose.

4. The new addition to The Diamond Dining Room. Built by Panthos Contracting in 2003.

5. Accommodations range from inside cabins to penthouse suites.

SINGULAR AND PLURAL NOUNS

The subject and verb must agree in number (singular or plural) and in person (first person: *I, we, our/ours*; second person: *you, your/yours*; third person: *he, she, it, they, theirs*). A singular subject requires a singular verb. A plural subject requires a plural verb. Most singular present-tense verbs in the third person end with an *s*. Therefore, an *s* ending on most verbs indicates that the verb is singular. In the examples the subjects are underscored once and the verbs are underscored twice.

Example: Cruising offers value that other kinds of travel do not offer.

Example: Rachel and Celia ~~is~~ *are* fortunate to be able to travel in Europe.

Example: The cruise director's position require*s* enthusiasm and stamina.

Note: When *there* or *here* introduces a sentence, the subject follows the verb. *There* and *here* are never used as subjects of sentences. In the following examples, the subjects are underscored once and the verbs are underscored twice.

Example: There are culinary artists preparing food fit for royalty.

Example: Here ~~are~~ *is* the list of five-star cruise ships.

Example: There are cruise lines that offers special-interest programs.

> ### Exercise 7-3 PROOFREAD AND MARK

In these sentences correct the verb rather than the subject. Use the appropriate proofreaders' marks to correct the errors in subject-verb agreement. If the sentence is correct, write **C** to the left of the number.

1. Fantasy Cruise Line offer special group rates.

2. There was many shipboard activities to keep us busy.

3. Some passengers fears becoming seasick on a cruise ship.

4. Here are the list of ports on the Mexican Riviera cruise.

5. We highly recommend cancellation insurance.

INTERVENING MODIFIERS

The subject and verb must always agree in number, even if modifiers of a different number separate them. A **modifier** is a word or a word group that describes and is usually related to the subject of the sentence. Modifiers that occur between subjects and verbs are called **intervening modifiers**. When proofreading for errors in subject-verb agreement, disregard intervening modifiers. The intervening modifiers are italicized in the following examples. The subjects and verbs are also identified. (Remember, the verbs must agree with the subjects, not the modifiers.)

> *Example:* Proper <u>attire</u>, *as well as courtesy and civil behavior*, <u>is expected</u>
> on any cruise ship.

> *Example:* Travel <u>agents</u> *with training and experience* <u>are</u> very helpful.

> *Example:* The <u>ports</u> *of call* <s>is</s> *are* usually considered in selecting a cruise
> vacation.

> *Example:* Travel <u>counselors</u> *who assist people in selecting the right tour*
> <u>agrees</u> that satisfaction is based on attitude and flexibility.

Exercise 7-4 PROOFREAD AND MARK

Use the appropriate proofreaders' marks to correct the errors in subject-verb agreement. If the sentence is correct, write **C** to the left of the number.

1. *Stardream*, like its partner ship *Stardust*, have a similar deck plan.

2. Active programs, as well as total relaxation, adds to your enjoyment.

3. The attendant who cleans and furnishes your cabin daily are responsible for your ultimate comfort during the cruise.

4. Everyone, from the captain to the assistant waiter, is devoted to treating you like a VIP.

5. Travel videotapes about every type of cruise imaginable is available for your viewing pleasure.

COMPOUND SUBJECTS

Sentences that contain two or more subjects are said to have **compound subjects**. Compound subjects, usually joined by the word *and*, require plural verbs. In the following examples, the compound subjects are underscored once and the verbs are underscored twice.

> *Example:* Quality <u>food</u> and excellent <u>service</u> <u>are featured</u> on every cruise.

When a compound subject refers to one person or thing, use a singular verb.

> *Example:* My <u>friend</u> and <u>colleague</u> <u>is</u> an experienced world traveler.

When the compound subject is preceded by *each*, *every*, *many a*, or *many an*, use a singular verb.

Example: Many a client and travel agent has wished he or she could communicate more effectively.

Example: Every man and woman who signed up has been entered in the mystery passenger contest.

When a compound subject is joined by *or* or *nor*, the verb may be either singular or plural. Use a singular verb when two or more singular subjects are joined by *or* or *nor*. Use a plural verb when both subjects are plural. If one of the subjects is singular and the other is plural, the verb should agree with the subject closest to the verb. In these examples the subjects are underscored once and the verbs are underscored twice.

Example: The chief purser or the assistant is always ready to help.

Example: Neither the main showroom nor the lounges are large enough.

Example: The dining room captains or the restaurant manager accept special requests.

Exercise 7-5 PROOFREAD AND MARK

Use the appropriate proofreaders' marks to correct the errors in subject-verb agreement. If the sentence is correct, write **C** to the left of the number.

1. Reading and sunning are two popular deck activities.

2. Destination and ports of call has always been considered important factors in selecting a cruise.

3. My associate and bridge partner, Natalia Suvarov, have decided to join me on the Rhine River cruise.

4. Evening dining or dancing do not always require formal dress.

5. The cruise director and entertainers has excellent voices.

COLLECTIVE NOUNS

A noun that denotes a collection of persons or things regarded as one unit is called a **collective noun**. Examples of collective nouns are *team*, *choir*, *chorus*, *flock*, *herd*, *audience*, *staff*, *crowd*, *faculty*, *orchestra*, *committee*, *company*, *group*, and *people*.

When a collective noun refers to the collection as a whole, use a singular verb. When a collective noun refers to members of the collection as separate persons or things, use a plural verb. In the following examples, the collective nouns are underscored once and the verbs are underscored twice.

Example: The cruise <u>staff</u> <u>was</u> on duty day and night. (The staff is acting as a single unit.)

Example: The cruise <u>staff</u> <u>were introduced</u> at the welcome party. (Each member of the staff was introduced individually.)

Example: The <u>audience</u> <u>~~were~~ *was* pleased</u> with the ship's entertainment.

Note: Do not treat a collective noun as both singular and plural in the same sentence.

Example: The <u>audience</u> <u>was</u> positive with ~~their~~ *its* praise.

Exercise 7-6 PROOFREAD AND MARK

Use the appropriate proofreaders' marks to correct the errors in subject-verb agreement. If the sentence is correct, write **C** to the left of the number.

1. The ship's entertainers rehearse at 3:15 p.m. daily.

2. The committee were undecided about which tour to give.

3. The deck staff has been assigned to different duties.

4. The game team consist of six people.

5. A flock of seagulls follow the ship everywhere.

INDEFINITE PRONOUNS

An **indefinite pronoun** does not refer to or specify a particular noun. Some indefinite pronouns are always singular, others are always plural, and still others may be either singular or plural depending on their relationship to other words in the sentence. Study the following indefinite pronouns to become familiar with their number.

ALWAYS SINGULAR			ALWAYS PLURAL	SINGULAR OR PLURAL
anybody	everybody	neither	both	all
anyone	everyone	nobody	few	any
anything	everything	somebody	many	more
each	many a	someone	none	most
either	many an	something	several	
every			some	

Indefinite pronouns used as the subject of the sentence must agree in number with the verb. When a pronoun may be either singular or plural, check the noun to which the pronoun refers. The noun often occurs in a phrase beginning with *of*, as the following examples show. In the examples the subjects (in some cases, indefinite pronouns) are underscored once and the verbs are underscored twice.

Note: Be careful when using the indefinite pronouns *most*, *some*, and *both*. Nouns immediately following these words are used as adjectives—not pronouns. When the phrase *of the* precedes a noun, *most*, *some*, and *both* are used as pronouns.

Example: Either of the two cabins is adequate for two people. (*Either* is singular and the subject of the sentence.)

Example: Both cabins are adequate for two people. (*Both* is used as an adjective.)

Example: Both are adequate for two people. (*Both* is plural and the subject of the sentence.)

Example: Most of the passengers are happy with the cruise. (*Most* refers to *passengers*, which is plural and the subject of the sentence.)

Example: Most passengers are happy with the cruise. (*Most* is used as an adjective.)

Example: Most of the events is designed for group participation. *(are)*

Example: Everyone seem to be enjoying the cruise. *(s)*

Example: Everybody are in a festive mood tonight. *(is)*

Exercise 7-7 PROOFREAD AND MARK

Use the appropriate proofreaders' marks to correct the errors in subject-verb agreement. If the sentence is correct, write **C** to the left of the number.

1. Most of the cruise staff also works as entertainers.

2. Many passengers considers entertainment and food more important than accommodations.

3. Nobody in our group have gained weight on this cruise.

4. Some of the duty-free items in the boutique is being offered at a 40 percent price reduction.

5. Everyone who performs in the passenger talent show receives a souvenir medal.

CONFUSED AND MISUSED WORDS

assure	*v.* to give confidence to; to feel sure; to convince
ensure	*v.* to make sure, certain
insure	*v.* to cover with insurance; to guarantee; to secure from harm

I want to **assure** you that you did the right thing.

Please **ensure** that the door is locked before you leave.

You will want to **insure** this building for $250,000.

capital	*n.* official seat of government; money to invest
capitol	*n.* a building in which a legislature meets

The **capital** of Iowa is Des Moines.

The U.S. Senate meets in Washington in the **Capitol**.

cite	*v.* to quote; to acknowledge
sight	*v.* a vision; *v.* to see or observe
site	*n.* a location

She was able to **cite** the Gettysburg Address.

You are a **sight** to behold!

Lawrence purchased a new **site** for our business.

- When proofreading for errors in subject-verb agreement, be alert for nouns whose singular and plural forms are spelled differently.

Singular	**Plural**
analysis	analyses
basis	bases
criterion	criteria (or criterions)
medium	media

- Use the team method of proofreading to improve accuracy, especially for longer documents.

PROOFREADING APPLICATIONS

Exercise 7-8 SENTENCES

Proofread the following sentences, and mark all sentence construction errors using the appropriate proofreaders' marks. If the sentence is correct, write **C** to the left of the number.

1. Scammon Bay in Alaska appears to be a beautiful city to visit.

2. All of your travel arrangements is to be completed by May 1.

3. Sherri and Jamel was instrumental in designing the brochure.

4. Rated among the state's top ten attractions. Is the mighty Mendenhall Glacier.

5. Holiday Travel Inc. are offering a trip to Germany.

6. There was more than a dozen daily activities in which we could participate.

7. Everyone, from the pilot to the flight attendant, were helpful.

8. Each man and woman have been participating in the contest.

9. The ship's bursar or the captain accept valuables for safekeeping.

10. The cruise director and the singers received our applause.

11. The group have signed up for another tour to Australia.

12. Either of the two associates are eligible for the honor.

13. Most of the passengers were thrilled with their arrangements.

14. The captain assured us that we was about to see something extraordinary.

15. Is you as excited to visit this site as I am?

Exercise 7-9 SPELLING AND WORD USAGE CHECK

Compare the words in Column A with the corresponding words in Column B. Use the appropriate proofreaders' marks to correct the misspelled or misused words. If both columns are correct, write **C** to the left of the number.

Column A	Column B
1. descriptive	discriptive
2. orientation	oriention
3. planing	planning
4. pursue	pursue
5. brochure	broshure
6. consistant	consistent
7. efficient	efficeint
8. impliment	implement
9. successfull	successfull
10. responsibilities	responsabilities
11. arrangements	arrangments
12. internationl	international
13. I want to ensure this diamond ring.	I assure you nothing will go wrong.
14. You will need to raise some capitol.	Let's meet at the capital building.
15. Please meet me at the new work sight.	Were you able to cite your references?

Exercise 7-10 INTERNATIONAL VOCABULARY

Compare the Spanish words in Column A with the corresponding words in Column B. If the word in Column B is different from the word in Column A, use the appropriate proofreaders' marks to correct Column B. If the words in both columns are the same, write **C** to the left of the number.

Column A	Column B
1. oscilatorio	oscilitorio
2. encomiar	encomair
3. aventajar	aventajir
4. recurrir	recurir
5. pasatiempo	pasatiempo

Exercise 7-11 TRAVEL BROCHURE

Proofread the following brochure, and correct all errors using the appropriate proofreaders' marks.

DISCOVER ALASKA'S INSIDE PASSAGE!

The pristine waters of the Inside Passage leads you to some of the friendliest little towns in the world. Each one of the towns are unique and rich in history and heritage. Totems depict the Indian spirits of the bald eagle, the whale, and the raven. Russian onion-domed churches gleams with gold icons. The many wonders of Alaska awaits your discovery. Let's visit two of Alaska's most popular sites.

Ketchikan. The Tongass Tribe of Tlingit call this historic "First City of Alaska" its home. Fishing along the Ketchikan Creek established this town as the "Salmon Capital of the World." Equally impressive are the large collection of totem poles. Fly over or cruise to Misty Fjords National Monument. Waterfalls cascades down sheer granite walls. Abundant wildlife is.

Wrangell. The Russians and the British flew their flags here before. The United States purchased Alaska in 1867. The bust of three gold rushes surely made this a flourishing timber industry town. Everything in this small but spirited town are within walking distance—shops, restaurants, galleries, and museums.

Exercise 7-12 BUSINESS LETTER

Proofread the following letter, and correct all errors using the appropriate proofreaders' marks.

January 16, 200-

Diamond Cruise Line
432 North Shore Avenue
San Francisco, CA 94114-1642
Phone: 415-555-0147
Fax: 415-555-0149

Mr. and Mrs. Hector Romero
9067 Vista Avenue
Albuquerque, NM 87108-4631

Dear Mr. and Mrs. Romero

Thank you for the generous comments about your successful Caribbean cruise aboard the *Blue Diamond*. Our captain and I is delighted that you had a pleasant experience.

All of us at Diamond Cruise Line is looking forward to an exciting year! We have enclose information on our voyages for 200-. Please note the highlighted announcements of two new cruise routes—the North Cape and the Mediterranean/Black Sea cruises. Both cruises offers overnight visits to such cities as Honnisvag, Norway, in the Arctic, and Odessa, Ukraine, the "Pearl of the Black Sea."

You, as a member of our Diamond Society, knows that we take our responsibility for our clients seriously. Our goal is to provide consistent, high-quality products and efficient, friendly service. As a former cruise passenger, you are entitled to a special members-only savings of $500 on staterooms and $1,000 on penthouse suites for our 13- and 14-day sailings from July through September. All cruises includes the fly-free bonus from any of our gateway cities. And a $100 on-board credit per person.

Don't wait! Either of our two 5-star jewels, the *Blue Diamond* or the *White Diamond*, still have space available. Make travel arrangements today for your next cruise!

See you on board!

Sincerely

Eugene K. Patterson
Manager

rjs

Enclosure

PROOFREADING AT THE COMPUTER

Exercise 7-13 BUSINESS LETTER

1. Open 07-13 from the Chapter 07 folder on the Student CD. (This is a computer copy of Application 7-12.)

2. Proofread the letter on the screen. Correct all errors on the screen copy that you indicated with proofreaders' marks in Application 7-12. Use the spelling checker.

3. Format the letter using default left and right margins and a 2″ top margin.

4. Save the letter as 07-13R, and print it.

5. Proofread the hard copy, and mark all additional errors.

6. Correct the errors on the screen copy.

7. Save and print the revised document.

Exercise 7-14 MAGAZINE ARTICLE

1. Open 07-14 from the Chapter 07 folder on the Student CD.

2. Proofread the article on the screen, and make all necessary corrections.

3. Format the article using default left and right margins.

4. Save the article as 07-14R, and print it.

5. Proofread the printed document. If you find any additional mistakes, correct the errors on both the hard copy and the screen.

6. Save and print the revised document.

Exercise 7-15 E-MAIL MESSAGE

1. Open 07-15 from the Chapter 07 folder on the Student CD.

2. Proofread the e-mail message on the screen, and make all necessary corrections.

3. Save the document as 07-15R, and print it.

4. Proofread the printed document. If you find any additional mistakes, correct the errors on both the hard copy and the screen.

5. Save and print the revised document.

CUMULATIVE APPLICATION

Exercise 7-16 ANNOUNCEMENT

Proofread the following announcement, and correct all errors using the appropriate proofreaders' marks.

CRUISE REVIEW

Thank you for sailing with Diamond Cruise Line. We appreciate your business, and serving you have been our pleasure.

Our goal is to provide a cruise vacation that you will want to experience again and again. You can greatly assist us in achieving this objective by completing the enclosed cruise review questionaire.

You comments are very important to us, and every cruise review are read. Your responses are completely confidential, so please give us your honest opinion. About every aspect of this cruise.

Thank you for taking a few moment of your time to complete this Cruise Review. Those who return the completed questionnaire within 3 weeks will be invited to a complimentary reception on their next cruise. We look forward to welcoming you aboard again soon, and we ensure you we will do our best to make your cruise comfortable.

Danielle F. Schilla, President
Diamond Cruise Line

Enclosure

Sentence Construction Errors, Part 2

Spotlight on **ACCURACY**

Your writing style provides information about you as a writer. Did you mean what you wrote? Will other people interpret your message in the same way you meant it to be understood? How might a doctor interpret the following items found in patients' medical charts?

- Patient has chest pain when he lies on his right side for over a year.

- On the third day the knee was better, and on the fourth day it had completely disappeared.

- By the time she was admitted in the emergency room, her rapid heart had stopped and she was feeling great.

- Appears mentally alert but forgetful.

Objectives

- Locate and correct errors in pronoun-antecedent agreement.

- Identify and correct errors in pronoun case.

- Spell correctly 12 frequently misspelled words.

- Use correctly three sets of commonly confused and misused words.

Like proofreading for other types of grammar errors, identifying errors in the proper use of pronouns requires reading the copy carefully and having a good understanding of the nature of pronouns. Because a pronoun acts as a substitute for a particular noun, the pronoun must give clear and correct reference to the noun. In addition, pronouns have various forms depending on their relationship to other words in the sentence. In this chapter you will learn to identify and correct misused pronouns.

PRONOUN AND ANTECEDENT AGREEMENT

A **pronoun** is a word used in place of a noun. The noun that the pronoun replaces is called the **antecedent**. In the sentence "Roslyn was complimented for her professional attitude," the pronoun *her* refers to the antecedent *Roslyn*. To be correct, pronouns must agree with their antecedents in three ways:

- **Person:** A *first-person* pronoun (*I, we*) refers to the person speaking, a *second-person* pronoun (*you*) refers to the person spoken to, and a *third-person* pronoun (*he, she, it, they*) refers to the person spoken about.

- **Number:** A singular pronoun (*I, you, me, he, she, it*) refers to a singular noun. A plural pronoun (*we, you, ours, they, theirs*) refers to a plural noun.

- **Gender:** A feminine pronoun (*she, her*) refers to a feminine noun (*Christina, woman, girl, lady*). A masculine pronoun (*he, him*) refers to a masculine noun (*Robert, man, boy, gentleman*). The neutral pronoun *it* may be used when no gender is designated.

	1ST PERSON	2ND PERSON	3RD PERSON
Singular	I, me, my, mine	you, your, yours	he, him, his, she, her, hers, it, its
Plural	we, us, our, ours	you, your, yours	they, them, their, theirs

In the following examples, the pronouns and antecedents are italicized.

Example: *Donald* paid *his* dues for the ski club. (The masculine, singular pronoun *his* agrees with the masculine, singular noun *Donald*.)

Example: Ten club *members* qualified for the tour, and *they* were all experienced players. (The plural pronoun *they* agrees with the plural noun *members*.)

Example: The *university* will send ~~their~~ *its* sports director to the
tournament. (The singular pronoun *its* agrees with the singular
noun *university*.)

Example: Lori was thrilled with ~~their~~ *her* sports trophy. (The feminine,
singular pronoun *her* agrees with the feminine, singular noun
Lori.)

> ### Exercise 8-1 PROOFREAD AND MARK

Proofread the sentences, and correct the pronouns. If the sentence is correct,
write **C** to the left of the number.

1. The motorized cart carrying the softball team's equipment
was on their way to the field.

2. After making his speech, the coach was pleased to hear that
the audience enjoyed their talk.

3. The rookies are habitually leaving their extra bats in the
dugout.

4. The fans enjoyed the photo opportunity with its softball
team, and she had a good time.

5. Sun Beach, the Heat's winter training camp, is ideal
because of their location and weather.

Collective Nouns as Antecedents

When proofreading for agreement of pronouns and antecedents, watch for
collective nouns used as antecedents. Words such as *committee*, *team*, *audience*, and *jury* are called collective nouns because they refer to a collection
of objects, people, or animals. (Refer to Chapter 7, page 99, for other examples of collective nouns.) If the members of the collective noun act as a singular unit, use a singular pronoun. If the members of the collective noun act
individually, use a plural pronoun. In the following examples, the pronouns
and antecedents are italicized.

Example: The *team* made *its* decision after careful analysis of the alternatives. (The collective noun *team* is acting as one unit and
agrees with the singular pronoun *its*.)

Example: The *audience* left ~~its~~ *their* seats immediately after the rally. (The
plural pronoun *their* agrees with the collective noun *audience*.
In this instance, the pronoun refers to individuals in the
audience acting independently.)

Compound Antecedents

Just as the verb must agree in number with the compound subject, the pronoun must also agree in number with compound antecedents. A **compound antecedent** consists of two or more nouns. Apply the following rules for compound antecedents. The pronouns and antecedents are italicized in the examples.

Rule 1 Two or more nouns joined by *and* require a plural pronoun.

> *Example:* *Claire, Paolo,* and *Tim* received *their* applications a week ago.

> *Example:* The team *captain* and the *players* were honored for *their* success.

Rule 2 Two or more nouns joined by *or/nor* require a singular pronoun when both antecedents are singular.

> *Example:* Neither the *board* of directors nor the *commission* is willing to change *its* position regarding the trading policy.

Rule 3 Two or more nouns joined by *or/nor* require a plural pronoun when both antecedents are plural.

> *Example:* Neither the *coaches* nor the *players* have sent *their* lists of goals.

Rule 4 If one antecedent is singular and the other is plural, the pronoun must agree with the nearer antecedent.

> *Example:* Neither the *captain* nor the *players* were ready for *their* speech.

Indefinite Pronoun Agreement

In Chapter 7 you learned that some indefinite pronouns are always singular, others are always plural, and still others may be either singular or plural. When the first pronoun is indefinite and is used as an antecedent, the second pronoun that follows the antecedent must agree in number with the first.

> *Example:* *Each* of the men took *his* turn in demonstrating the techniques. (*His* agrees with the singular antecedent *each*.)

> *Example:* *Both* of the players were sorry for *their* actions. (*Their* agrees with the plural antecedent *both*.)

> **Exercise 8-2** PROOFREAD AND MARK

Proofread the sentences, and correct the pronouns. If the sentence is correct, write **C** to the left of the number.

1. The field hockey team's tournament committee made their flight arrangements for the trip.

2. Neither Bette nor Tammy has consulted their director regarding the itinerary.

3. Both Coach Palmer and Coach Isobe have made his final selections for the starting players for tonight's game.

4. One of the women left her golf clubs in the locker room.

5. The boxing team voted to double their effort for the duration of this season.

THE CASE OF THE PRONOUN

Incorrect usage of personal pronouns often occurs because pronouns have different forms known as **cases**. A personal pronoun case changes its form according to its relationship to other words in the sentence. Notice the two masculine pronouns in the sentence "When John called, he said not to wait for his reply." Even though *he* and *his* both refer to John, the cases are different because the two pronouns have separate functions in the sentence.

The three cases of pronouns are **nominative**, **objective**, and **possessive**. Study the three different pronoun cases, and learn to use them correctly. In the examples that follow, all of the pronouns are italicized.

Nominative Case

Nominative case pronouns include the singular pronouns *I*, *you*, *he*, *she*, and *it* and the plural pronouns *we*, *you*, and *they*. The nominative case is used in two ways.

Rule 1 **Subject pronoun.** Use the nominative case when the pronoun acts as the subject of the sentence (subject of the verb). The verb may be the main verb of the sentence or the verb within a clause. (Clauses will be discussed in Chapter 9.)

> *Example:* *He* canceled the game because *we* had to work that week. (Both pronouns are the subjects of verbs—*canceled* and *had*, respectively.)

> *Example:* Two players were hurt during the first quarter, but *they* were not injured seriously. (The pronoun is the subject of the verb phrase *were injured*.)

> *Example:* Peter and Teresa will officiate while *you* and ~~*her*~~ *she* are away.

> *Example:* Sumio and ~~me~~ *I* play well together.

Rule 2 **Predicate pronoun.** Use the nominative case when the pronoun immediately follows a form of the linking verb *be* (*am*, *is*, *are*, *was*, *were*, *be*, *has been*, *have been*, *had been*). When a pronoun follows a linking verb, it is called a **predicate pronoun**. A predicate pronoun is used after a verb and refers to the same person or thing as the subject of the verb. A predicate pronoun is always in the nominative case.

> *Example:* It was *I* who called about the schedule. (*I*, a predicate pronoun, follows *was*, a form of the linking verb *be*.)

> *Example:* The star player for today's game is *she*. (*She*, a predicate pronoun, follows *is*, a form of the linking verb *be*.)

> *Example:* The only students who complained were *you* and ~~*him*~~. *he*

> *Example:* The winner of the Satellite News 20-K run was ~~*her*~~. *she*

Exercise 8-3 PROOFREAD AND MARK

Proofread the sentences, and correct the pronoun case errors. If the sentence is correct, write **C** to the left of the number.

1. If the junior players were treated like the varsity players, would they do as well?

2. It was not me who requested that the seats be changed; it was Lee and her.

3. The senior track coach and him can meet with the press today.

4. The person in the photograph is her when she played on the championship team in 1998.

5. The athletics office had a good year because they have an experienced staff.

Objective Case

Objective case pronouns include the singular pronouns *me, you, him, her,* and *it* and the plural pronouns *us, you,* and *them*. Because objective case pronouns always function as objects, they are used with action verbs. Objective case pronouns are never used with linking verbs, such as *is, are, was, were, seem,* or *become*. The objective case pronoun is used in three ways.

Rule 1 Direct object of the verb. Use the objective case when the pronoun answers the question *what* or *whom* and the pronoun receives the action of the verb (called the object of the verb).

> *Example:* When you call your brother, tell *him* to meet us at Gate 15. (You tell *whom*?)

> *Example:* They selected *him* to be the team captain. (They selected *whom*?)

Rule 2 **Indirect object.** Use the objective case when the pronoun tells *to whom* or *for whom* something is done.

> *Example:* Mother gave *me* the play-off tickets for my birthday. (tells that Mother gave to me the tickets—the preposition *to* is omitted)

> *Example:* My niece bought *me* a sweater. (tells that my niece bought for me a sweater—the preposition *for* is omitted)

Rule 3 **Object of the preposition.** Use the objective case when the pronoun is used as the object of the preposition. **Prepositions** are words that relate a noun or pronoun to other words in the sentence. Some common prepositions are *about, after, at, before, between, by, for, from, in, of, on, over, since, to, until,* and *with*. A preposition and its object form a **prepositional phrase**. In the following examples, the prepositional phrases with the objective case pronouns are italicized.

> *Example:* Caitlin discussed the gymnastics trials *with her*.

> *Example:* Just *between you and me*, I won't be going to the game today.

> *Example:* Are you saving this seat *for he̶ and I̶*? ~~he~~ *him* ~~I~~ *me*

> *Example:* You are assigned to work *with Lucio, Jeff, and she̶*. ~~she~~ *her*

Note: When *to* is followed by a verb, the phrase is called an **infinitive phrase**. No other preposition can be used as an infinitive. Do not confuse the preposition *to* with the infinitive *to*.

> *Example:* Auri mailed *to him* an Olympic souvenir program. (shown as a prepositional phrase)

> *Example:* I plan *to take* the bus to Friday's championship game. (shown as an infinitive phrase)

> ### Exercise 8-4 PROOFREAD AND MARK

Proofread the sentences, and correct the pronouns. If the sentence is correct, write **C** to the left of the number.

1. The lacrosse coach sent Glenn and he copies of next week's practice schedule.

2. The sports public relations office will arrange interviews for you and I.

3. I decided to go to the game with Judy and her.

4. The tournament director called the team managers and I to confirm the lineups for the game.

5. After the team won, the owner gave a bonus to he.

Who and Whom

The use of the pronouns *who* and *whom* is troublesome, even for experienced writers and speakers. Remember, the rules that apply when using nominative and objective pronouns also apply when using *who* and *whom*.

Who is a nominative case pronoun that may be used as the subject of the sentence or clause. *Who* must also follow a form of the linking verb *be* (predicate pronoun).

Whom is an objective case pronoun that is used as the direct object of the verb, indirect object, or object of the preposition.

To help you decide which pronoun is correct, mentally rearrange the sentence and substitute the pronoun *he*, *she*, or *they* in place of "who" and *him*, *her*, or *them* in place of "whom."

> *Example:* *Who* signed up for the tour? (*She* signed up for the tour.)
>
> *Example:* *Whom* did the agent call? (The agent called *him*.)
>
> *Example:* To *who*^m did you sell the car? (You sold the car to *her*.)
>
> *Example:* The boy in the photo is *whom*? (*He* is the boy in the photo.)

If *who* or *whom* appears within a clause, determine the pronoun's use within the clause, ignoring the rest of the sentence. Then substitute another pronoun in place of *who* or *whom*. In the following examples, the dependent clauses are italicized.

> *Example:* Jeanette is the person *who will represent us*. (*Who* is the subject of the dependent clause. *She* will represent us.)
>
> *Example:* The member *whom we elected* is most qualified for the position. (*Whom* is the direct object of the verb elected. We elected *him*.)
>
> *Example:* Clyde, *whom* we know is ill, cannot attend the qualifying match. (*Who* is ill?)
>
> *Example:* Sorphea is the person *who*^m the league selected as the sportsmanship award winner. (The league selected *whom*?)

Exercise 8-5 PROOFREAD AND MARK

Proofread the sentences, and correct the pronouns. If the sentence is correct, write **C** to the left of the number.

1. Kelli, who you know well, is a very intense player.

2. Whom is making our travel arrangements?

3. Whom did you ask to take the basketball team's photographs?

4. Is she the person who you wish to interview?

5. Who do you want for a roommate this year?

Possessive Case

The possessive case includes the singular pronouns *my*, *mine*, *your*, *yours*, *his*, *her*, *hers*, and *its* and the plural pronouns *our*, *ours*, *your*, *yours*, *their*, and *theirs*. Possessive pronouns show ownership, and they are always written without the apostrophe.

Note: Don't confuse the contractions *it's* (it is), *they're* (they are), *who's* (who is), and *you're* (you are) with the possessive pronouns *its*, *their*, *whose*, and *your*.

> *Example:* All of the league teams mail *their* subscription season tickets.

> *Example:* *Whose* racket case has the blue and red piping?

> *Example:* The painting was restored because of *it's* deterioration.

> *Example:* *Your's* were the best score predictions.

Possessive pronouns are also used immediately before a **verbal noun** or **gerund** (a verb ending in *ing* that is used as a noun). In the following examples, the gerunds are italicized.

> *Example:* Travis takes his *jogging* very seriously.

> *Example:* Their *complaining* has ruined the game for everyone.

> *Example:* I appreciate your *working* late this week.

Using Pronouns with *Than* or *As*

When using pronouns in comparing two persons or things, the pronoun that follows *than* or *as* can be nominative or objective, depending on the use of the pronoun. Because the clause has been deliberately omitted after the pronoun, mentally restate the clause to determine the correct use of the pronoun. Study these examples carefully.

> *Example:* Mick is taller than *I*. (Mick is taller than I am tall.)

> *Example:* Corrine knows him as well as *I*. (Corrine knows him as well as I know him.)

> *Example:* Corrine knows him as well as *me*. (Corrine knows him as well as Corrine knows me).

> *Example:* My sister keys faster than *I*. (My sister keys faster than I key.)

> *Example:* You helped them more than *I*. (You helped them more than I helped them.)

> *Example:* You helped them more than *me*. (You helped them more than you helped me.)

She practices her *riding* every day.

© GETTY IMAGES/PHOTODISC

Exercise 8-6 PROOFREAD AND MARK

Proofread the sentences, and correct the pronouns. If the sentence is correct, write **C** to the left of the number.

1. The team's local ticket office offers the best prices for their home games.

2. The NFL announced their football schedule for the season.

3. You insisting on an aisle seat for the game was a good idea.

4. She was allowed more time for practice than I.

5. Ask Joy and Lenny if her time will allow for another match.

CONFUSED AND MISUSED WORDS

correspondence   *n.* a communication by exchange of letters
correspondents   *n.* those who write letters

They kept in touch through **correspondence**.
All volunteer **correspondents** write five letters a day.

currant   *n.* small, seedless raisin
current   *adj.* up-to-date; *n.* electricity

I have an easy recipe for **currant** jelly.
Marcy enjoys writing about **current** events.

device   *n.* a machine or gadget
devise   *v.* to invent or to plan

Arturo has a **device** that will automatically turn the lights on and off.
Can you **devise** a way to surprise them?

- **Double-check the document. Read the copy the first time for content. Read the copy a second time for consistency and correct grammar.**

- **Use available references if you have questions about correct grammar.**

PROOFREADING APPLICATIONS

Exercise 8-7 SENTENCES

Proofread the following sentences; and mark all pronoun, spelling, and word usage errors using the appropriate proofreaders' marks. If the sentence is correct, write **C** to the left of the number.

1. Team owner Fay Sollenberger is one of the persons who's winning record was acknowledged at the sports awards banquet.

2. To whom did you write about the receipt?

3. It was very noticeable that you played better than me during today's match.

4. The news staff said its two correspondence will not be attending the banquet.

5. The star player for the team is her.

6. The Rhine Curling Club announced that anyone can attend their meetings.

7. The meeting of the Whitland Athletic Club was disrupted by his arriving late.

8. Mail you're reply in the enclosed envelope before the May 30 deadline.

9. When the members of the International Olympic Committee meets, it is required to show their identification cards at the gate.

10. It is she whom we recommend for membership in the Garfield Spirit Club.

11. Between you and I, the new Milwaukee Sports Arena is the most outstanding facility of its kind in the country.

12. To who should you address an inquiry about parallel parking at the stadium?

13. Members of the golf team has its own ideas of how quality training helps.

14. My sister-in-law is a noticeably better pianist than me.

15. The U.S. skating team will perform its exhibition program tonight.

Exercise 8-8 SPELLING AND WORD USAGE CHECK

Compare the words in Column A with the corresponding words in Column B. Use the appropriate proofreaders' marks to correct the misspelled or misused words. If both columns are correct, write **C** to the left of the number.

Column A	Column B
1. acknowledge	acknowlege
2. noticeable	noticable
3. convenience	convience
4. facilities	facilities
5. monitoring	monitering
6. occasionally	occassionally
7. reciept	receipt
8. particpation	participation
9. paralel	parallel
10. processing	proccessing
11. quality	guality
12. perseverance	perseverance
13. The correspondents are here.	The correspondence may use e-mail.
14. What is the currant year?	The current administration is busy.
15. The devise is interesting.	The new device works well.

Exercise 8-9 INTERNATIONAL VOCABULARY

Compare the Spanish words in Column A with the corresponding words in Column B. If the word in Column B is different from the word in Column A, use the appropriate proofreaders' marks to correct Column B. If the words in both columns are the same, write **C** to the left of the number.

Column A	Column B
1. helado	hellado
2. horario	horrario
3. informe	infrome
4. juegos	juegos
5. lavar	lavaar

Exercise 8-10 BUSINESS LETTER

Proofread the following letter, and correct all errors using the appropriate proofreaders' marks.

SAN JOSE PANTHERS
Southern City Stadium
48322 Buckingham Avenue • San Jose, CA 95136-2382
(408) 555-0128 • Fax (408) 555-0129

February 28, 200-

Ms. Jeanne R. Hudson
400 Lake Street
Seattle, WA 98125-4130

Dear Ms. Hudson:

You are among a select group of baseball fan who we believe will be interested in a once-in-a-lifetime opportunity to meet and socialize with it's favorite team. At the same time, you will enjoy a regimen of healthful diet, exercise, and sleep.

The baseball team are the San Jose Panthers. For the past two years, the team have provided a limited group of its fans the unprecedented opportunity to join them during spring training for two weeks. You will become a part of the team themselves, participating in planning sessions, all strategy meetings, practice sessions, etc. You will also have available the full services of our training staff to help you avoid that occasional cramp and to treat them if it does occur.

The enclosed brochure will provide information for the two sessions scheduled. The price for both sessions include all expenses: lodging, food, transportation, and gratuities. We are also providing a currant brochure describing the hotel accommodations and tours available in the area.

As we anticipate a considerable response to this offer, we would appreciate your returning your correspondents promptly in the enclosed self-addressed envelope.

Yours truly,

Darrell T. Underwood
President

rks

Enclosures   Brochures
              Self-Addressed Envelope

Exercise 8-11 MEMORANDUM

Proofread the following memo, and correct all errors using the appropriate proofreaders' marks.

TO: All Supervisors

FROM: Darrell T. Underwood, President

DATE: March 30, 200-

SUBJECT: TRAINING SESSION FOR SAN JOSE PANTHERS' FANS

We am attaching a copy of my letter of February 28, 200-, and the brochure entitled *Guidelines for Training Session*. These were sent to a select group of baseball fans who has indicated an interest in joining the San Jose Panthers for a limited time during spring training at the Marina facilities.

You will be contacted individually by Vice President Dawn Burnside in connection with logistics and related handling. However, I would like to take this opportunity to encourage you to extend yourself in making the participants in this program feel as though he is joining our family.

Remember, these people are more than guests; these people are sincere and dedicated fans of the Panthers whom have cheered the players when they were up and encouraged them when they were down. Its easy to acknowledge the applause and wave the pennants when "Lady Luck" is smiling. But it takes a special, dedicated fan to remain devoted to us team.

Please make use of the many convenient and exclusive touches we deviced to be used in this excellent program, such as the extensive menu that can be tailored to accommodate individual preferences as well as needs. Food is a most important part of this program, and we want to make sure that even those guests who have restricted diets enjoy his meals.

So I am asking for your assistance in monitoring this program to ensure that our guests enjoy their stay with us. When they return home, their happy memories will encourage them to join us again next year.

Thank you for you're continued support in making this an outstanding program.

Attachments

PROOFREADING AT THE COMPUTER

Exercise 8-12   MEMORANDUM

1. Open 08-12 from the Chapter 08 folder on the Student CD. (This is a computer copy of Application 8-11.)

2. Proofread the letter on the screen. Correct all errors on the screen copy that you indicated with proofreaders' marks in Application 8-11.

3. Format the memo using default left and right margins and a 2″ top margin.

4. Save the memo as 08-12R, and print it.

5. Proofread the printed document. If you find any additional mistakes, correct the errors on both the hard copy and the screen.

6. Save and print the revised document.

Exercise 8-13   ENUMERATED LIST

1. Open 08-13 from the Chapter 08 folder on the Student CD.

2. Proofread the list, and make all necessary corrections.

3. Format the list using default left and right margins and a 2″ top margin.

4. Save the list as 08-13R, and print it.

5. Proofread the printed document. If you find any additional mistakes, correct the errors on both the hard copy and the screen.

6. Save and print the revised document.

Exercise 8-14   E-MAIL MESSAGE

1. Open 08-14 from the Chapter 08 folder on the Student CD.

2. Proofread the e-mail message, and make all necessary corrections.

3. Save the document as 08-14R, and print it.

4. Proofread the printed document. If you find any additional mistakes, correct the errors on both the hard copy and the screen.

5. Save and print the revised document.

CUMULATIVE APPLICATION

Exercise 8-15 LETTER

Proofread and correct all errors using the appropriate proofreaders' marks.

December 27, 200-

Mrs. Gloria Ayala
Health department
4300 North DeWolf Ave.
Clovis, CA 93611-0956

Dear Mrs. Ayala

We aplaud the recent move of your district to prohibit sales of soft drinks to junior high students. To help educate students about better nutritional choices, we are asking for you're assistants in distributing this information.

Since the effect of a healthy diet helps increase students' concentration and overall learning expereince, we believe this is a worthwhile effort. Perhaps among our two organizations we can help students devise a plan for making healthier choices. We will hold a public forum in the cafeteria on January 6th for anyone who wish to obtain more information.

Drink (8 oz.)	Carbs (g)	Calories	Sodium (mg)	Sugars (g)	Calcium
1% Milk	—	120	160	15	35%
Aple Juice	28	110	35	28	--
Soda	33	130	35	33	--
Orange Juice	27	110	25	24	2%
Frappuccino®	38	190	180	32	15%

Nutritionally yours

Marcus Taylor, R.N.

rrh

Sentence Construction Errors, Part 3

Spotlight on ACCURACY

Your writing style includes the six Cs of communication: courtesy, clarity, conciseness, correctness, completeness, and coherence. When you edit your documents, check that the message will be clear to your audience. How seriously do you think the principal took the following excuses when she received them?

- Please accuse Sam for being absent on February 29, 30, and 31.

- Sandy is under our doctor's care and should not take physical education. Please execute her.

- Rosangela has been absent because she had two teeth taken out of her face.

Objectives

- Understand the significance of phrases and clauses.

- Find and mark errors in parallel structure.

- Identify and correct dangling and misplaced modifiers.

- Use bias-free language.

- Spell correctly 12 frequently misspelled words.

- Use correctly three sets of commonly confused and misused words.

In Chapter 7 you learned that a sentence contains a subject and a verb and expresses a complete thought. Generally, sentences contain other elements that help to convey the writer's message. The alert proofreader must check that these elements are positioned correctly to ensure consistency and clarity. The proofreader must also check the language for any bias.

SENTENCE ELEMENTS

In addition to the words that act as subjects and verbs, most sentences also contain phrases and clauses. A **phrase** is a group of two or more related words without a subject and a verb. The entire phrase in a sentence may act as a noun, a verb, an adjective, or an adverb. Phrases may also modify nouns and verbs. Phrases that function as adjectives or adverbs are usually positioned near the words they modify. The phrases are italicized in the following examples.

Example: *The certified public accountant* audited their accounting records. (noun phrase acting as the subject)

Example: David *should work together* with Augustina on the assignment. (verb phrase)

Example: The book *lying on the table* belongs to Beatriz. (adjective phrase that modifies the noun *book*)

Example: My first class started *on time*. (adverb phrase that modifies the verb *started*)

Example: *Running late*, I forgot my 3 p.m. appointment. (participial phrase that modifies the subject *I*)

Example: Amelia will return *in the morning*. (prepositional phrase that is used as an adverb and modifies the verb *will return*)

Example: The sweatshirt *with the gold stripes* is mine. (prepositional phrase that is used as an adjective and modifies the noun *sweatshirt*)

Example: Ellis wants *to retire*. (infinitive phrase that is used as a noun and is the direct object of the verb *wants*)

Clauses are groups of words that contain a subject and a verb. If the clause expresses a complete thought, it is a sentence and is called an **independent clause**. If the clause does not express a complete thought, it is called a **dependent clause**. In the following examples, the independent clauses appear in bold and the dependent clauses in italics. The subject and verb of both clauses are identified.

Example: **The representative returned my call.**

Example: *If you leave your number,* **I will call you tomorrow.**

Example: *When the package arrives,* **Helio will sign for it.**

Exercise 9-1 PROOFREAD AND MARK

In each of the sentences, identify the underlined group of words. To the left of the number, write **P** for phrase, **IC** for independent clause, or **DC** for dependent clause.

1. <u>If we are to arrive on time</u>, we must follow their directions.

2. <u>You shouldn't leave the interview</u> without asking when they will contact you with a decision.

3. <u>When you volunteer for the position</u>, consider the work hours and your ability to complete the necessary tasks.

4. <u>The grievance committee has total commitment</u> to further the work.

5. <u>For most people</u>, satisfaction is an important consideration.

PARALLEL STRUCTURE IN SENTENCES

Words, phrases, or clauses within a sentence that are related in meaning should be written in the same grammatical form. Using the same form makes the ideas **parallel**. When adjectives are parallel to adjectives, phrases are parallel to phrases, and clauses are parallel to clauses, the meaning of the sentence is clear and logical. When you find a sentence that sounds awkward, revise it so that related ideas are expressed in the same way.

Example: Michelle's career interests are *advertising* and *modeling*. (parallel noun forms, or gerunds)

Example: We are looking for someone who is *courteous*, *dependable*, and *considerate*. (parallel adjectives)

Example: Roland couldn't decide whether *to buy* a laptop computer or *to spend* the money on a trip to visit his brother. (infinitive phrases used as the objects of the verb *decide*)

Example: We will ski and ~~we will be~~ climbing mountains during our vacation. (unparallel verbs)

Example: Sharon is tall, ~~with~~ *has* brown eyes, and has a *cheerful* disposition ~~that is cheerful~~. (unparallel adjectives) *Also correct:* Sharon is tall, brown-eyed, and cheerful.

Example: I have limited experience using desktop publishing, but *I use* word processing ~~is being used~~ extensively in my present job. (unparallel clauses)

She went *rock climbing* and *camping* in the mountains last week.

Errors in parallelism occur frequently within enumerations. All related elements must be stated in the same grammatical structure. Additionally, the same grammatical structure must follow conjunctions that appear in pairs, such as *both ... and, either ... or, neither ... nor,* and *not only ... but also.* These pairs are called **correlative conjunctions**. The parallel elements are italicized in the examples. Note that all of the elements end in *ing*.

Example: Past job experience includes the following tasks:

1. *Keying* original copy and *proofreading* first drafts

2. *Saving* documents

3. *Printing* and *proofreading* hard copy

4. *Retrieving* and *revising* documents

Example: Daniel stated *that you had changed your mind* or *that you had canceled your reservation.*

Example: The topics to be covered include the following:

1. Identifying the purpose and audience

2. To plan~ning~ the message

3. Write~ing~ the message

4. Editing the message

5. *Writing* Direct and indirect messages

Example: Suzette not only serves on the Personnel Committee but ~she is~ also on the Constitution Committee.

Exercise 9-2 PROOFREAD AND MARK

Correct errors in parallelism using the appropriate proofreaders' marks. If the sentence is correct, write **C** to the left of the number.

1. We will hire only employees who are hardworking, ambitious, and who are trustworthy.

2. The guidelines were written for upgrading all employees, improving the morale, and to augment income.

3. A supervisor was hired to manage the new plant and that he would recommend changes in hiring practices.

4. The equipment now being installed can number the sections, rearrange the margins, and listing the corrections.

5. The editor called me about the manuscript draft and wanted more information about tomorrow's meeting.

DANGLING AND MISPLACED MODIFIERS

A **modifier** is a word, a phrase, or a clause that describes another word in the sentence. To clarify the relationship between the modifier and the word it describes, the modifier must be placed in the correct position. If the modifier does not logically describe any word in the sentence, it is called a **dangling modifier**. If it is not close enough to the word it describes, it is called a **misplaced modifier**. You should place the modifier as close as possible to the word it modifies. Study the placement of the modifiers below.

DANGLING MODIFIER	CORRECTED
Keying very rapidly, the report had three errors.	Keying very rapidly, the operator made three errors in the report.

MISPLACED MODIFIER	CORRECTED
Mara bought a canary for her friend that sings beautifully.	Mara bought her friend a canary that sings beautifully.

Errors frequently occur when introductory phrases and clauses do not modify the subject of the sentence. To correct a dangling or misplaced modifier, revise the sentence so that the subject completes the action described in the introductory phrase. If you are unsure about the subject of the sentence, ask the question *who* or *what* after the introductory phrase. The answer is the sentence's subject, which should immediately follow the introductory phrase. Compare the following sentences.

DANGLING MODIFIER	CORRECTED
Before deciding which van to buy, three agencies were visited by Christopher.	Before deciding which van to buy, Christopher visited three agencies. (Who visited three agencies?—Christopher)

MISPLACED MODIFIER	CORRECTED
While jogging on the sidewalk, a cyclist hit Donita.	While jogging on the sidewalk, Donita was hit by a cyclist. (Who was jogging?—Donita)

Exercise 9-3 PROOFREAD AND MARK

Revise the sentences that contain dangling or misplaced modifiers. If the sentence is correct, write **C** to the left of the number.

1. Adept at using software applications, the department decided to hire Tom.

2. The document was accidentally picked up by Myra lying on the desk.

3. Though all of the applicants are qualified for the positions, they need improvement in some skills.

4. Ciarra showed the supervisor how she used the equipment appearing somewhat doubtful.

5. When leaving for lunch today, a phone message for the supervisor was left by the receptionist.

BIAS-FREE LANGUAGE

A writer or speaker should never send a message that could alienate employees or potential customers. Instead, messages should be unbiased, ethical, and fair to all. **Bias-free language** avoids insensitive language regarding gender, race, ethnic group, age, religion, or disability.

Avoid Gender Bias

Traditionally, writers have used *he* or *man* to represent both genders. The practice of gender bias is outdated and no longer acceptable. It is inappropriate to use *he* or *his* to refer to both men and women. Likewise, it is incorrect to assume that certain jobs are "men's work" or "women's work." Today men and women are employed in all occupations; and the *Dictionary of Occupational Titles* was rewritten to reflect job titles, not gender. To classify secretaries, elementary school teachers, or nurses as women and pilots, farmers, or police officers as men would be to stereotype occupations.

To treat men and women fairly, follow these general rules:

Rule 1 Use the plural pronouns *they, their, theirs,* or *them* or nouns such as *people* or *persons* when referring to a group that consists of both men and women.

> *Example:* Salespersons must have their weekly reports completed by Monday.

Rule 2 Rewrite the sentence to avoid using pronouns if it is possible to do so without affecting the meaning.

Example: Sales reports are due on Monday.

Rule 3 Shift the sentence to second person.

Example: As an employee, you are responsible for reporting expenses correctly.

Rule 4 If you must use a singular pronoun, use both *he/she* and *his/her*. Do not overuse these expressions, for they can become annoying and sound repetitious.

Example: Each salesperson must have his or her report completed by Monday. (both genders used)

Rule 5 Use parallel phrasing if you must refer to people by gender. Use "women and men," "females and males," "boys and girls," or "ladies and gentlemen" for parallel structure. You would not say "men and girls" or "women and males."

Example: The boys and girls toured our offices.

Rule 6 Use business terms that do not imply the gender of a person.

OUTDATED (AVOID)	CURRENT (USE)
airline steward or stewardess	flight attendant
businessman	businessperson, executive, entrepreneur, professional
businessmen	businesspeople, people in business
chairman	chair, chairperson, group leader, moderator, president, presiding officer
coed	student
congressmen	members of Congress, congressional representatives, representatives of Congress
foreman	supervisor, manager, executive
housewife	homemaker
mankind	persons, people, humanity, everyone, humankind
man-made	handmade, custom-made, custom-built
manpower	human resources, human power, human energy, workforce, personnel

repairman	repairer, repairperson, service technician
salesman	salesperson, sales agent, sales representative
spokesman	speaker, spokesperson, advocate, proponent
statesman	politician, public official, political leader, public servant, government leader
waiter/waitress	server
workmen	workers, employees, personnel

Avoid placing the words *man*, *male*, *lady*, *female*, or *woman* before or after an occupational title. Compare the differences in these examples:

AVOID	USE
lady or female doctor	doctor
male nurse	nurse
policewoman, policeman	police officer
fireman, female firefighter	firefighter
male elementary school teacher	elementary school teacher

The children pay close attention to their elementary school teacher.

© GETTY IMAGES/PHOTODISC

Exercise 9-4 PROOFREAD AND MARK

Revise the sentences that contain inappropriate language. If the sentence is correct, write **C** to the left of the number.

1. An elementary school teacher must demonstrate that she can teach art in her classes.

2. Evangelina Torres was just named chairman of the Hospitality Committee.

3. More manpower will be required to complete the installation quickly.

4. Humankind must be aware of the importance of the environment.

5. The January sales meeting brought together more than 500 salesmen.

Avoid Race and Ethnic Group, Age, Religion, and Disability Bias

The principle for writing messages that are sensitive to race and ethnic group, age, religion, or disability is as follows: *Avoid emphasizing race and ethnic group, age, religion, or disability when those categories have no relevance to your message.* The emphasis in business writing should be on competence and relevance, not on categories such as race, age, or religion.

◆ Race and Ethnic Group Bias

Mention race or ethnic group only when the race or ethnic group is relevant. Likewise, avoid language that suggests that all members of a certain racial or ethnic group have the same characteristics.

UNACCEPTABLE	ACCEPTABLE
Yens Weimer is an unusually fast German runner.	Yens Weimer is an unusually fast runner. (Being German is not relevant.)
Celine Casiano, the Spanish clerk, was selected for promotion.	Celine Casiano was selected for promotion. (Being Spanish is not relevant to her promotion.)

◆ Age Bias

Mention the age of a person only when age is relevant.

UNACCEPTABLE	ACCEPTABLE
Lu Chou, 29, was hired last month.	Lu Chou was hired last month. (His age, 29, was not relevant in being hired.)
Kay Aspen, the 51-year-old president of our company, has resigned.	Kay Aspen, president of our company, has resigned. (Her age, 51, was not relevant in her resignation.)

◆ Religion Bias

Religion usually has no relevance in a business setting and should not be mentioned.

UNACCEPTABLE	ACCEPTABLE
Mavis Mann, the Jewish account executive, gave a presentation on using laptop computers.	Mavis Mann gave a presentation on using laptop computers. (Being Jewish is not relevant.)

◆ Disability Bias

There is no polite way to label people with a physical, cognitive, or emotional disability. Eliminate mention of the disability if possible. If you must refer to people in terms of their disabilities, refer to the person first and the disability second. In addition, avoid using terms such as *handicapped, crippled, afflicted, retarded,* or *victim.*

UNACCEPTABLE	ACCEPTABLE
A diabetic, Everett is always the first person to arrive.	Everett is always the first person to arrive. (Being a *diabetic* has no bearing on when he arrives.)
The crippled worker, Kip, faces barriers on the job.	Kip, who is disabled, faces many barriers on the job. (Avoid using terms such as *crippled*, and refer to Kip by name prior to listing his disability.)

Exercise 9-5 PROOFREAD AND MARK

Revise the sentences that contain inappropriate language. If the sentence is correct, write **C** to the left of the number.

1. Marco Galeone, former Italian-American mayor of our city, plans to run for U.S. senator.

2. Cedric's temper flared when he was questioned about his frequent tardiness.

3. Joachim, a member of the ELCA church, took the bus to Albuquerque.

4. Arianna, 22, will be joining our Accounting Department upon her graduation.

5. As a cancer victim, Janelle MacDonald is being treated for her disease.

© GETTY IMAGES/PHOTODISC

CONFUSED AND MISUSED WORDS

cooperation   *n.* working together
corporation   *n.* a legal entity

Your **cooperation** is greatly appreciated.
This **corporation** is traded on the New York Stock Exchange.

council   *n.* an assembly of people
counsel   *v.* to give advice or guidance; *n.* a lawyer or group of lawyers; *n.* advice received

The **council** recommended that we approve the request for funding.
Your **counsel** was well received.

dairy   *n.* a commercial firm that processes and/or sells milk and milk products
diary   *n.* a daily personal record of events, experiences, and observations

She works at the **dairy** in Burnsville.
Have you read his **diary** for December 1?

- Select words carefully to eliminate insensitivity regarding gender, race, ethnic group, religion, age, or physical condition. Emphasis in business writing should be concerned with competence and relevance, not on categories such as gender, religion, or age.

- Read one word at a time—the opposite of speed-reading—especially for copy that contains specialized or highly technical vocabulary. Read unfamiliar words syllable by syllable or letter by letter.

- Check a dictionary to determine whether a compound word is written as one word, as two words, or as a hyphenated word.

PROOFREADING APPLICATIONS

Exercise 9-6 SENTENCES

Proofread the following sentences, and mark all sentence construction errors using the appropriate proofreaders' marks. If the sentence is correct, write **C** to the left of the number.

1. Maurice was excited to take courses in marketing, entrepreneurship, and also a course in accounting.

2. Dana and I plan to visit San Francisco and stopping in San Jose.

3. The best qualified candidates have three or more years' work experience, a degree in management, and have a strong work ethic.

4. This software package allows me to correct words, insert comments, and the merging of documents.

5. Before hiring a new account rep, four candidates were interviewed by Cylea.

6. Tawni purchased a new laptop computer for her son that weighs less than four pounds.

7. The new textbook was found by Lynn on the floor.

8. Stewardesses are able to fly almost anywhere in the world.

9. The men and women who passed the Certified Public Accountant exam were hired by Garver Inc. to work in the Accounting Department.

10. One of the firemen will be promoted to captain.

11. The conference was attended by at least 1,500 salesmen.

12. Milo, whose parents are Italian, was appointed to the Personnel Committee.

13. In 2005 Jessie Bulatov, 35, received her doctorate in Computer Information Systems from The Ohio State University.

14. As a victim of lupus, Collette has an appointment with her doctor every six months.

15. Conrad Lieber eats sauerkraut at least once a week because of its anticancer compounds.

Exercise 9-7 SPELLING AND WORD USAGE CHECK

Compare the words in Column A with the corresponding words in Column B. Use the appropriate proofreaders' marks to correct the misspelled or misused words. If both columns are correct, write **C** to the left of the number.

Column A	Column B
1. acaddemic	academic
2. applicants	applicants
3. cleint	client
4. decision	decisoin
5. develope	develop
6. eligible	eligable
7. featured	faetured
8. installation	instalation
9. libary	library
10. percent	per cent
11. possibility	possability
12. recommendation	recomendation
13. Their cooperation was tremendous.	The cooperation declared bankruptcy.
14. The counsel meets on Wednesday.	I will accept your council.
15. I frequently visit the dairy.	The information in your dairy is fascinating!

Exercise 9-8 INTERNATIONAL VOCABULARY

Compare the Spanish words in Column A with the corresponding words in Column B. If the word in Column B is different from the word in Column A, use the appropriate proofreaders' marks to correct Column B. If the words in both columns are the same, write **C** to the left of the number.

Column A	Column B
1. fulgurar	fulgurar
2. emborronar	enborronar
3. contrarrestar	contrarrestir
4. sainete	saintee
5. afabilidad	afabillidad

Exercise 9-9 BUSINESS LETTER

Proofread the following letter; and correct all errors in placement of phrases, parallel structure, misplaced or dangling modifiers, and gender stereotyping. Use the appropriate proofreaders' marks to make the corrections.

July 24, 200-

Mr. Alton K. Ladene
4090 Strawberry Circle
Denver, CO 80123-4102

THE GOURMET SOCIETY
143 Grant Plaza • 1621 West Market Avenue
San Francisco, CA 94105-1362
(415) 555-0173 Fax (415) 555-0177

Dear Alton

I am excited about your decision to be spokesman at the fall meeting of The Gourmet Society.

This dinner meeting will be held in the Ruby Room of the Hotel Goldstrike, 9006 Mission Street, San Francisco, CA 94105-3428, at 7 p.m., Tuesday, September 6, 200-. Following the dinner meeting, we will have refreshments and also have dancing in the Diamond Room.

I enjoyed your recent article titled "The Many Faces of Pasta" in the June edition of *Cooking Western Style*. Most of our members would be pleased to have you speak on this subject. Topics you may want to develop in your presentation include the following:

1.   Selecting the right pasta for the right dish
2.   Pasta calories count
3.   How to find the stores that offer the largest selection of pasta

You asked if I know any one-liners on the subject of food or dining that you can use in your presentation. I don't keep a library of jokes, but I'm enclosing some jokes that I've laughed at in the past. I am sure you will find these jokes to be tasteful, funny, and I think relevant for this dinner meeting.

All meeting arrangements will be handled by this office. You can be sure we will do everything possible to ensure a successful evening and that would be delightful.

Again, thank you for agreeing to be our spokesman. As your client, we look forward to your presentation. Just between us, I think the meeting is going to be a smash!

Sincerely

THE GOURMET SOCIETY

Gretel Von Rotteck, Director

yha

Enclosure

Exercise 9-10 NEWSPAPER ARTICLE

Proofread the following article, and correct all errors using the appropriate proofreaders' marks.

THE SMART FOOD SHOPPER

Smart food shopping equals saving money—and there is no better place to save money than at the supermarket. You don't have to go to different markets just to save 20 cents on a can of vegetables, fruit, or maybe a can of meat. A little planning can make a dent in your food budget and putting money back in your pocket.

First, before you leave home develop the habit of making a list of the food items you need. Write down items before you run out of them, thus eliminating a last-minute dash to the corner convenience store where you'll likely pay much higher prices.

Planning a food list is elementary—just like when you balance your checkbook. Whether you need a certain item now or later, if it is on sale, buy it—in quantity. A good deal is a good deal, right? But watch out! The larger size isn't always less expensive. If a sale item is out of stock, ask your stock boy for a rain check so you can buy the item at the reduced price when it is restocked.

Do you clip, save, and have you used coupons? I do, but only for a limited number of national brands. Today store brands are often as good as nationally advertised brands and sell for less.

Be on the lookout for ripe but still quite usable fruits and vegetables. Bananas are to be eaten when they begin to darken; but ripe bananas are perfect for making breads, cookies, and are good for cakes. Specially marked vegetables are ideal for make soups, stews, and casseroles.

With a list of items and a handful of coupons, the amount you save may surprise you. And remember, make it a habit to glance at the cash register to be sure the checkout lady rings up the right price. Happy shopping!

PROOFREADING AT THE COMPUTER

Note to the Student:

- Beginning with this chapter, directions for saving, printing, and proofreading the hard copy and reprinting the document will not be repeated. These functions are standard procedures that you should follow for the applications listed in Proofreading at the Computer.

- Also, formatting instructions will not be provided for the documents. If necessary, refer to your text-workbook for assistance.

Exercise 9-11 NEWSPAPER ARTICLE

1. Open 09-11 from the Chapter 09 folder on the Student CD. (This is a computer copy of Application 9-10.)

2. Proofread the newspaper article on the screen. Correct all errors on the screen copy that you indicated with proofreaders' marks in Application 9-10. Use the spelling checker.

3. Produce the newspaper article in correct format following the standard procedures described in previous chapters.

Exercise 9-12 NOTICE

1. Open 09-12 from the Chapter 09 folder on the Student CD.

2. Proofread the notice on the screen. Correct all errors.

3. Produce the notice following the standard procedures.

Exercise 9-13 E-MAIL MESSAGE

1. Open 09-13 from the Chapter 09 folder on the Student CD.

2. Proofread the e-mail message on the screen. Correct all errors.

3. Produce the e-mail message following the standard procedures.

CUMULATIVE APPLICATION

Exercise 9-14 NOTICE

Proofread and correct all errors using the appropriate proofreaders' marks.

Crescent City Fire Department—Station 47

NOTICE

TO: ALL FIREMEN ASSIGNED TO STATION 47

EFFECTIVE AUG. 5, 200-

A time-honored tradition in the fire department is that all firefighters assigned to a given station participate, on a rotation basis, in meal preparation. This plan has work well for us.

In an effort to be more aware of different dietary requirements, I reccommend we use these herbs to prepare our meals.

1. <u>Basil</u>. Having a sweet flavor with an aromatic odor, basil is used whole or ground. It is good with lamb, ground beef, vegetables, dressing, and when you make omelets.

2. <u>Chives</u>. With a sweet mild flavor of onion, this herb are excellent in salads, fish, soups, and potatoes.

3. <u>Dill</u>. Both seeds and leaves of dill is flavorful. Leaves may be used to garnish or cook with fish, soup, and beans.

4. <u>Sage</u>. Sage may be used fresh or dried in tomatoe juice, fish, omelets, beef, poultry, and stuffing.

Use these herbs in small amounts, and taste before adding more. Our firemen are guaranteed to enjoy these refreshing tastes!

Jake Magnuson, Captain

Comma Errors

Spotlight on ACCURACY

Punctuation causes problems for many people. It appears that some people punctuate whenever they pause; others rarely punctuate. But when is punctuation necessary? The purpose of any punctuation mark should be to help the reader correctly interpret a written message. How does punctuation change your interpretation of the following sentences?

- We are going to eat Monte before we take another step.
  We are going to eat, Monte, before we take another step.

- The meeting ended, happily.
  The meeting ended happily.

- The Democrats, say the Republicans, are sure to lose.
  The Democrats say the Republicans are sure to lose.

Objectives

- Identify and correct errors in the use of commas as they apply to compound sentences, introductory elements, and series.

- Identify and correct errors in comma usage as they apply to nonessential elements, consecutive adjectives, direct quotations, dates, addresses, and titles.

- Spell correctly 12 frequently misspelled words.

- Use correctly three sets of commonly confused and misused words.

THE IMPORTANCE OF PUNCTUATION MARKS

Why are punctuation marks so important in written communication? Why do you need to proofread for punctuation errors? If punctuation marks are used incorrectly or omitted, the meaning of the text may be unclear to the reader.

Punctuation marks are like traffic signals—they tell the reader when to stop, slow down, or proceed. *Terminal* (ending) punctuation marks appear at the end of a sentence and tell the reader to stop. *Internal* (within or inside) punctuation marks tell the reader when to pause and help the reader to interpret the sentence as the writer intended.

Terminal punctuation marks will be discussed in Chapter 11. In Chapter 10 you will review the rules pertaining to the use of the comma. Because the comma is the most frequently used punctuation mark, this entire chapter will be devoted to comma usage. Use the following proofreaders' marks to show comma corrections:

		MARKED COPY	CORRECTED COPY
Insert a comma.	⋏	The class had already started but I walked in anyway.	The class had already started, but I walked in anyway.
Delete a comma.	⌿	Rob, and Bianca will graduate in May.	Rob and Bianca will graduate in May.

THE COMMA

The comma is an important internal punctuation mark. When used correctly, commas make the relationship between elements (words, phrases, and clauses) in the sentence clear. You learned in Chapter 9 that a clause is a group of related words that contains a subject and a verb. A clause may be either a dependent clause, which does not express a complete thought, or an independent clause, which does.

Independent Clauses

A sentence may contain a combination of independent and dependent clauses separated by commas. A sentence that consists of two or more *independent* clauses is called a **compound sentence**. When the independent clauses are joined by the conjunction *and, but, or, nor, for,* or *yet,* separate the clauses with a comma. The word *independent* means "able to stand alone"; thus, independent clauses in a compound sentence may also be written as two separate sentences. The two clauses are joined with a conjunction simply because they are closely related in meaning. If the two independent clauses are very short, the comma can be omitted.

> *Example:*   I called and she answered.

In all of the examples that follow, the subject and the verb of each independent clause are identified. The conjunctions are italicized.

> *Example:*   Alicia's strength is her work ethic, *but* her weakness is her
>   lack of time management skills.

> *Example:*   Secretaries are called administrative assistants, *and* they are
>   knowledgeable in office management and computer technology.

> *Example:*   Garrett may work in the garden *or* he may attend the concert.

Note: When "you" is understood to be the subject in both clauses, a comma is still required.

> *Example:*   (You) Attend the annual meeting in person *or* (you) vote by
>   proxy.

Note: The following sentence contains a compound verb (three verbs). It is still a simple sentence—not a compound sentence. Therefore, a comma is not required.

> *Example:*   He will hire a taxi or rent a car and drive to the meeting site.

Exercise 10-1   PROOFREAD AND MARK

Use the appropriate proofreaders' marks to correct the errors in comma usage. If the sentence is correct, write **C** to the left of the number.

1. Silas attended the meeting but no new business was introduced.

2. Daphne sent the edited minutes to Jackie and Arlene sent the treasurer's report to Julio.

3. San-li wrote a poem entitled "I Can Do It!" and sent it to the local newspaper for publication in Friday's edition.

4. Edith is responsible for editing the monthly newsletter and she takes minutes at weekly meetings.

5. *Robert's Rules of Order Newly Revised* shows the correct format for minutes and it also includes a list of motions.

Introductory Elements

Insert a comma after most introductory words, phrases, or clauses that come before the independent clause.

> *Example:*   *Therefore*, I have decided to enroll in the computer class.
>   (introductory word)

Example: *In other words*, the course is designed to develop basic skills on three application programs. (introductory phrase)

Example: *When you are ready to study*, I'll meet you at the library. (introductory clause)

Example: No‸you were not late for the first session.

Example: As a rule‸the chairperson's duty is to keep the meeting moving.

Example: When the package arrives‸check its contents to make sure nothing is broken.

Commas are generally not required after introductory words or restrictive, short phrases that answer the questions *when, how often, where,* or *why*.

Example: Tomorrow I will begin my diet. (I will begin my diet *when*?)

Example: In the margin you will find a short definition of new terms. (*Where* will you find a short definition of new terms?)

Commas do not set off noun phrases or noun clauses that function as the subjects of sentences (not introductory). The italicized phrases or clauses in the following examples function as subjects of the sentences and, therefore, are not set off by commas. Note that all of the italicized phrases in the following examples answer the question *what*.

Example: *Learning a new video game* can be both fun and frustrating.

Example: *To win this game* will require real team effort.

Example: *Whether we win or lose* will make no difference in our standing.

Jogging long distances is one of her favorite weekend activities.

© GETTY IMAGES/PHOTODISC

Exercise 10-2 PROOFREAD AND MARK

Use the appropriate proofreaders' marks to correct the errors in comma usage. If the sentence is correct, write **C** to the left of the number.

1. When the delegates arrive they must register at the desk and receive name tags.

2. Using recycled paper to publish our company newsletter, has significantly decreased our supplies and printing costs.

3. Incidentally who has the agenda for the May meeting?

4. Completing my assignments on time is at the top of my list of goals.

5. Regardless of what the outcome might be Felicita is determined to bring the matter, before the Academic Board.

Series

Insert a comma after each item in a series (words, phrases, or clauses) except the last item.

Example: I invited Concepcion, Hunter, Wakako, and Reggie to the beach party. (series of words)

Example: Zach did not tell us where he would meet us, whom he would be with, or when his flight would arrive. (series of clauses)

Example: I scored 76, 94 and 85 on the last three science quizzes.

Example: Please read the chapter, complete the review and study for the test.

Example: Felix and Myrna will be the game organizers, Teresita and Darwin will be the race timers, Noriko and Bernardo will be the scorekeepers and I will be the official starter.

Note: Do not use commas when each item in the series is connected by *and*, *but*, *or*, or *nor*.

Example: We need Vince and Jorge and Sarit to watch the monitors.

Example: Neither Deon nor Sue nor Owen were available.

Exercise 10-3 PROOFREAD AND MARK

Use the appropriate proofreaders' marks to correct the errors in comma usage. If the sentence is correct, write **C** to the left of the number.

1. Worth County's top five cities are Grafton, Manly, Kensett, Bolan and Lake Mills.

2. This home unit CD player features full programmability, direct access, shuffle-repeat play functions and remote control.

3. You must have an education degree to teach courses in computers, math, science, and languages.

4. If you buy, sell, develop, manufacture or use RightWord software, you can't afford to miss the RightWord training session this weekend.

5. Her new checking account provides free checks, a Brava credit card, free credit consolidation and a $5,000 credit line.

Nonessential Elements

Nonessential elements consist of information that is not necessary to the meaning of the sentence. They include appositives, interrupting expressions, and nonrestrictive phrases or clauses. Set off nonessential elements with commas.

Appositives are words or phrases that rename a preceding noun or pronoun. Commas are used to set off appositives because they are not essential to the meaning of the sentence but provide further identification of the noun or pronoun. The appositives are in italics in the following examples.

Example: Suzanne Russo, *the president*, will preside at the annual meeting next month.

Example: San Francisco, *the City by the Bay*, is a popular vacation and convention site.

Example: Byron Canton, *a local real estate broker*, will respond to your question.

Example: Their first song, *written while they were teenagers*, was a tremendous success.

Interrupting (also called *parenthetical*) **expressions** include such nonessential words or phrases as *furthermore, however, in addition*, and *of course*. Such expressions often indicate the writer's feelings.

Example: Ruth will, *of course*, accept your dinner invitation.

Example: Bennett, *however*, is an exceptionally talented pianist.

Example: Saturday's ballgame, *on the other hand*, may attract a large crowd of college students.

Example: We are determined, *nevertheless*, to finish today.

Nonrestrictive elements include phrases or clauses that further explain or describe the noun or pronoun they modify. However, the information is considered to be nonessential because it is not necessary in understanding the meaning of the sentence. Nonrestrictive clauses often begin with *which, who,* or *whom*. Analyze the following two examples. The nonrestrictive elements are italicized.

Example: Mr. Kline, *who works in the president's office*, will address the March meeting. (The nonrestrictive element does not affect the principal message in this sentence, which is that Mr. Kline will address the meeting in March.)

Example: We have been unable to complete the Jorgensen contract, *which you had negotiated so successfully*. (The nonrestrictive element has no bearing on the completion of the Jorgensen contract.)

Do not set off **restrictive phrases** or **clauses**, those that are essential to the meaning of the sentence. The restrictive clauses appear in italics in these examples:

Example: Those people *who are registered to vote* may cast their ballots in the school board election. (The restrictive clause identifies the people who may cast their ballots and is essential to the meaning of the sentence.)

Example: We have been unable to complete the contract *that you just negotiated.* (The restrictive clause identifies which contract is not yet completed.)

Example: The Lundgren bid arrived *after we had made our decision.* (The restrictive clause tells when the bid arrived.)

Example: The shops *that are located in Westwood Mall* are open on the Fourth of July. (The restrictive clause tells which shops are open.)

© GETTY IMAGES/PHOTODISC

Mr. Petersen, who is a prosecuting attorney, is always working.

Exercise 10-4 PROOFREAD AND MARK

Use the appropriate proofreaders' marks to correct the errors in comma usage. If the sentence is correct, write **C** to the left of the number.

1. Corporal Lance Mitchell left the army, as a computer programmer, and started his own software company.

2. Everyone, listed on the attached sheet, will receive a copy of the workshop report.

3. Lake Superior, on the other hand, is the largest of the lakes.

4. Ricardo Santiago, general manager of the Corvallis store has been with the company for 14 years.

5. A photograph and a position statement which each candidate running for office is required to submit will be published with the election ballot.

OTHER COMMA USES

In addition to their very important role of setting off sentence elements, commas perform a variety of other roles.

Consecutive Adjectives

Use commas to separate consecutive adjectives that are parallel and not joined by a conjunction. Parallel adjectives describe the same noun to the same degree. To determine whether adjectives should be separated by commas, reverse the order of the adjectives and insert the word *and* between them.

Example: Joyce is a sincere, delightful person. (Joyce is a delightful *and* sincere person.)

Example: The student is faced with a difficult, frustrating decision. (The student is faced with a frustrating *and* difficult decision.)

Example: The tall handsome fellow in the photograph is my husband.

Example: They are looking for an intelligent enterprising young person.

Exercise 10-5 PROOFREAD AND MARK

Use the appropriate proofreaders' marks to correct the errors in comma usage. If the sentence is correct, write **C** to the left of the number.

1. They enjoyed the sleek simple design.

2. Gentleness, and sincerity, are two personal traits that I look for in people I meet.

3. Fritz read the informative, entertaining articles.

4. Listening to soft soothing classical music is my favorite pastime.

5. She wants to purchase tough dependable tools to use around the house.

Direct Quotations

Use commas to set off the exact words of a speaker. Do not set off an indirect quotation. An indirect quotation is a rewording of the person's exact words and is usually introduced by *that* or *whether*.

> *Example:* The director said, "You should return your music after the concert." (Direct quotation—a comma and quotation marks are required.)

> *Example:* Jane asked the director whether we should return our music after the concert. (Indirect quotation—no comma or quotation marks are needed.)

When a direct quotation is broken up into two parts, such as in the next example, place a comma *after* the first part of the quotation (inside the quotation mark) and another comma *before* the second part.

> *Example:* "The class colors," said Chuong, "are pink and green."

> *Example:* Andrei stated, "I believe you made the right decision."

> *Example:* I said that "the mail will be picked up at 3:10 p.m."

> *Example:* "On the other hand," Savita remarked, "I may surprise you."

Note: Commas and periods at the end of a quotation are *always* placed inside the quotation marks. Other punctuation marks used with quotation marks will be discussed in Chapter 11.

▸ Exercise 10-6 PROOFREAD AND MARK

Use the appropriate proofreaders' marks to correct the errors in comma usage. If the sentence is correct, write **C** to the left of the number.

1. "Furthermore" Keith said "you must finish painting before you quit for the day."

2. I thought you said that "you would cancel your appointment with your accountant."

3. Le Van Loc asked me yesterday whether you plan to go skiing this weekend.

4. "I never think about age" Marvin said "because age is only an attitude."

5. "Entertaining, uplifting, and funny" wrote the movie critic "and fiendishly clever too".

Dates and Addresses

Use commas to set off the year when it follows the month and the day or to separate the weekday from the calendar date. Commas are not required when only the month and the year are given or when military style is used in expressing dates.

Example: August 31, 200-, is the deadline for filing applications for classes next semester.

Example: Our high school received its first laptop computers in May 200-.

Example: The letter from General Kraft dated 11 May 200- was misplaced when the office was remodeled.

Example: The perishable supplies were shipped by air freight on Thursday, June 30, 200-.

Example: Clarissa graduated in June 200-.

Use commas to separate address parts when the address appears in text format. Do not use a comma to separate two-letter state abbreviations and ZIP Codes.

Example: The address is Majestic Records, 3090 Brookline Boulevard, Suite 254, Newark, NJ 07110-3201.

Melanie started her new job in April 2005.

Direct Address and Titles

Use commas to set off a person's name or title when addressing the person directly.

Example: Please reserve a conference room, Noel, for October 14.

Example: Thanks for helping me with my homework⌃Dad.

Use commas after names of people when academic and professional titles are used. Do not separate personal titles, such as *Jr.*, *Sr.*, *II*, or *III*, unless you know that the individual prefers to do so.

Example: Professor Navara, Ph.D., is also a certified professional planner.

Example: Melissa Eby, CPA, will lead the panel discussion.

Example: Duane Simpson⌀Jr. will arrive tomorrow morning.

Example: Bridget Brostrom⌃Ed.D.⌃ is the coordinator of the seminars.

Setting Off *Inc.* and *Ltd.*

Use commas to set off the abbreviations or words for *Inc.* and *Ltd.* when they follow the name of the company, unless you know the official company name does not use a comma.

Example: We will notify United Movers, Inc., of the change of address.

Example: Braniff⌃Limited⌃has been awarded the contract for next year.

Exercise 10-7 PROOFREAD AND MARK

Use the appropriate proofreaders' marks to correct the errors in comma usage. If the sentence is correct, write **C** to the left of the number.

1. My driver's license expires on Friday, December 28.

2. The return address on the envelope shows 218 South Front Avenue Liberty PA 12981-4825.

3. Can you help me Micha, in solving this difficult problem?

4. Aurelia be sure to call the airline to cancel the flight.

5. Afton Companies Inc. is located at 9770 Grandview Street Omaha NE 67115-0893.

CONFUSED AND MISUSED WORDS

farther	*adv.* more distant
further	*adj.* to a greater degree; additional

Ashley can run **farther** than Samantha.
Tremaine is **further** along in math than Chad.

its	*adj.* possessive form of *it*
it's	contraction of *it is* or *it has*

The bank will post **its** interest rates today.
It's my turn to drive.

lay	*v.* to place or set down an object
lie	*v.* to rest; to recline

Lay the pen on the desk, Francesco.
Tina, **lie** down and rest.

PEP Tip

- Punctuation marks are designed to add clarity. Check for errors in punctuation that may cause confusion or misunderstanding.

- When debating the placement of a comma, identify the rule or rules that apply.

- Keep a reference manual handy when proofreading; use it as needed.

- Proofread in a quiet place; noise can be distracting.

- Pay attention to important information, such as dates, names, addresses, and amounts. Do not assume they are correct.

PROOFREADING APPLICATIONS

Exercise 10-8   SENTENCES

Proofread the following sentences, and correct all comma errors using the appropriate proofreaders' marks. If the sentence is correct, write **C** to the left of the number.

1. In the future, you may wish to make your hotel reservations online.

2. Jenae's strength is her desire to excel but her weakness is her lack of direction.

3. Ismael may work on the car or he may go for a bike ride.

4. Ms. Bell you have been promoted to vice president of purchasing.

5. Our president, Mr. Richards will be in Japan all next week.

6. Rose wrote a poem entitled "You Can Succeed!," and sent it to the local newspaper for publication in Saturday's edition.

7. I scored 89, 90 and 100 on my last three Spanish quizzes.

8. The book you ordered, Bonnie, will be shipped immediately.

9. "On the other hand," Stedman remarked "I may go golfing."

10. Professor Corbett, Ph.D., is also a certified linguist.

11. Kaley is an upbeat charming individual.

12. On Friday September 8, the surprise party will take place.

13. When you are ready to print select the desired printer.

14. Can you help me Terrell, with my golf swing?

15. Guardian, Limited has been awarded the new contract.

Exercise 10-9 SPELLING AND WORD USAGE CHECK

Compare the words in Column A with the corresponding words in Column B. Use the appropriate proofreaders' marks to correct the misspelled or misused words. If both columns are correct, write **C** to the left of the number.

Column A	Column B
1. article	artical
2. assessment	assesment
3. custermer	customer
4. environment	enviroment
5. equipment	equipement
6. interrupt	interrupt
7. maneger	manager
8. orientation	orientation
9. perposal	proposal
10. recognise	recognize
11. representative	representitive
12. session	session
13. Please respond further.	I ran further than Nel.
14. It's time to leave.	They say its going to rain.
15. May I lay on your couch?	Please lay the shirt on the bed.

Exercise 10-10 INTERNATIONAL VOCABULARY

Compare the Spanish words in Column A with the corresponding words in Column B. If the word in Column B is different from the word in Column A, use the appropriate proofreaders' marks to correct Column B. If the words in both columns are the same, write **C** to the left of the number.

Column A	Column B
1. leche	lache
2. llegada	lledaga
3. lunar	lunar
4. mundial	mundail
5. negocios	negocois

Exercise 10-11 EDITORIAL LETTER

Proofread the following editorial letter, and correct all errors using the
appropriate proofreaders' marks.

LETTER TO THE EDITOR, June 6, 200-

The Examiner, Loma Linda, California

Dear Editor:

I would like to offer an assessment of the latest trend in TV programming: reality-based
television. On Friday May 13, 200-, I arrived home early and interrupted my six-year-old
son, who was watching television. I said, "Brandon, what are you watching?" He replied,
"Justice Agents." I asked what it was about and he said that "this program depicted the dis-
pensing of justice by agents of a city swat-team-type organization." Yes, six-year-olds do
talk like that today. I recognize that young children live in a fantasy world when they watch
TV, but they often imitate what they see and hear. Sitting with Brandon for a few minutes,
I was startled to see that the last part of the show was an uninterrupted, violent gun battle
between the good guys and the bad guys.

My assessment is that it is not all right for a child to see this kind of realism on television.
As a responsible parent and a customer of commercial television, I asked myself, "Is this a
reality-based show and if so whose reality is it?" More importantly I wonder if this is a
proper environment for a child.

I later asked myself whether such programs should be available at a time when young
children can view them and the answer is that they shouldn't. We must recognize that
a show of this kind has the potential for disaster. I don't believe it is necessary to show
such an extreme negative environment in such detail. To a six-year-old, the actor is not just
practicing a craft. The child, even an adult, is watching someone being brutalized or killed.

I have a proposal to make. Perhaps the corporation network would air an orientation
session demonstrating the art of artifice and makeup so that the young, inexperienced and
naive viewer can see the difference between make-believe and reality.

If any reader of this newspaper shares my views voice your opinion by writing to the
network, Station KVRT, 408 South Bascom Avenue, Loma Linda, CA 90097-4213.

Curtis Bolt Jr.

Exercise 10-12 BUSINESS LETTER

Proofread the following business letter, and correct all errors using the appropriate proofreaders' marks.

June 10, 200-

Mr. Curtis Bolt, Jr.
14009 Van Ness Avenue
Loma Linda, CA, 90405-0332

Dear Mr. Bolt:

I appreciated your letter to the editor of *The Examiner* dated June 6, 200- concerning reality-based television.

Having a son who is seven, I agree that this program is not suitable for viewing by primary school-age children. Since we are concerned, with children viewing inappropriate programs, scheduling is closely audited by Station KVRT. We did not anticipate that young children would be in the viewing audience at that time.

Reality-based television leaves much to be desired, and should not be used as a means of categorizing programs. We live in an age when people strongly believe in personal rights and they want to decide what programs to watch.

I like your idea, for a program that educates the young to be aware that what they see on television is playacting—that it has no application to real-life situations. So we invite your son and his classmates to tour Station KVRT. The tour will include sessions with various departments, such as costume, makeup and editing, and end with lunch at our cafeteria. Please limit the number of people in your group to no more than 30.

You may call Mrs. Loretta Huerta, a representative of our Public Relations Department to discuss final arrangements.

Sincerely,

Alfred P. McRay, President

c Mrs. Loretta Huerta Manager
  Public Relations Department

PROOFREADING AT THE COMPUTER

Exercise 10-13 BUSINESS LETTER

1. Open 10-13 from the Chapter 10 folder on the Student CD. (This is a computer copy of Application 10-12.)

2. Proofread the letter on the screen. Correct all errors on the screen copy that you indicated with proofreaders' marks in Application 10-12.

3. Produce the letter in correct format following the standard procedures described in the previous chapters.

Exercise 10-14 MAGAZINE ARTICLE

1. Open 10-14 from the Chapter 10 folder on the Student CD.

2. Proofread the letter on the screen. Correct all errors.

3. Produce the article following the standard procedures.

Exercise 10-15 E-MAIL MESSAGE

1. Open 10-15 from the Chapter 10 folder on the Student CD.

2. Proofread the e-mail message on the screen. Correct all errors.

3. Produce the e-mail message following the standard procedures.

CUMULATIVE APPLICATION

Exercise 10-16 MEMO

Proofread and correct all errors using the appropriate proofreaders' marks.

TO: All Department Heads

FROM: Patrick E. O'Malley, Vice president, Marketing

DATE: July 14, 200-

SUBJECT: LETTER TO THE EDITOR

On June 6, *The Examiner* published a letter to the editor from Mr. Curtis Bolt, Jr. about reality-based television. Mr. Bolt stated the need for caution in scheduling programs because of the negative affects programs may have on young children. As a result our president, Mr. Alfred P. McRay, invited the classmates of Mr. Bolt's son to visit our studio. This is how Mr. Bolt described the tour.

Like Dorothy in *The Wizard of Oz*, we had a feeling that we were no longer in Kansas when we past through the magic portals of Station KVRT. The maze of camera equipment, sets miniature cities, and sky-scrapers appeared to be twenty stories tall. Everyone's favorite department was makeup.

Lunch was especially enjoyable to the young enthusiastic visitors because many teenage stars was eating at the same time and didn't mind being asked for autographs.

Our tour also had a serious side. The children learned never to try the jumps, falls, or other stunts that they see on television because these actions are performed by professionals.

We thank Station KVRT for a fun, educational session.

rkt

Other Punctuation Errors

Spotlight on **ACCURACY**

An incorrectly placed comma in a sales contract once cost an American company $70 million. In Europe commas are used instead of periods to mark decimal points. This American company misplaced a comma by one decimal point in an international contract. According to a company spokesperson, the customer held the American company to the price quoted, resulting in a loss of $70 million!

Objectives

- Identify and correct errors in end-of-sentence punctuation.

- Identify and correct errors in the use of semicolons and colons.

- Identify and correct errors in the use of apostrophes, underscores, and quotation marks.

- Identify and correct errors when using quotation marks with other punctuation marks.

- Spell correctly 12 frequently misspelled words.

- Use correctly three sets of commonly confused and misused words.

n addition to the comma, other punctuation marks appear in written material. In this chapter you will review the use of end-of-sentence punctuation marks—the period, the question mark, and the exclamation mark. You will also learn to correctly use semicolons, colons, apostrophes, underscores, and quotation marks. Finally, you will learn to recognize errors when other punctuation marks are used with quotation marks.

When correcting errors for these punctuation marks, use the following proofreaders' marks:

		MARKED COPY	CORRECTED COPY
Insert a period.	⊙	Please send me your check⊙	Please send me your check.
Insert a question mark.	⌄? ?⌃	How did you do on the test⌄	How did you do on the test?
Insert an exclamation mark.	⌄/ /⌃	Don't touch it⌄	Don't touch it!
Insert a semicolon.	⌄; ;⌃	Please come to the fund-raiser⌄ we could use your help.	Please come to the fund-raiser; we could use your help.
Insert a colon.	⌄: :⌃	Follow these steps⌃ 1. Revise copy. 2. Save copy.	Follow these steps: 1. Revise copy. 2. Save copy.
Insert an apostrophe.	⌄'	the bikers helmet	the biker's helmet
Underscore or italicize.	—— or *ital.*	<u>Do not</u> be late to the meeting. <u>Do not</u> be late to the meeting. *ital.*	<u>Do not</u> be late to the meeting. *Do not* be late to the meeting.
Insert quotation marks.	⌄" "⌃	King's new book is a ⌄must⌃ read.	King's new book is a "must" read.

THE PERIOD, THE QUESTION MARK, AND THE EXCLAMATION MARK

There are three **terminal punctuation marks**: the period, the question mark, and the exclamation mark. They are used at the ends of sentences and tell the reader when to stop.

Rule 1 Use a period after (1) a statement of fact, (2) an indirect question, or (3) a courteous request. A **statement of fact** is something declared or stated. An **indirect question** is a reworded question or another person's statement. A **courteous request** is not a question, but it is sometimes incorrectly punctuated as a question because it sounds like one. When deciding whether to use a period or a question mark, remember: If the person is expected to answer in words, use a question mark. If the person is expected to respond with action, use a period.

STATEMENT	INDIRECT QUESTION	COURTEOUS REQUEST
They delivered the new furniture on Wednesday.	Bea asked if you were available to help.	Would you please send this order today.

Rule 2 Use a question mark after a **direct question**—it requires an answer. When a sentence contains a series of short questions related to one idea, place a question mark at the end of each question in the series. (See example.) Within the series, only the first part is a full question; the rest are not. Therefore, capitalize only the first word of the first part; **do not** capitalize the first word of each remaining part.

QUESTION	INDIRECT QUESTION	SERIES OF QUESTIONS
Did you receive the report?	He asked if you received the report.	Do you wish to look better? feel healthy? lose weight? trim inches?

Example: Do you remember when the report was sent?

Example: I asked what the features on Model 72K15J were.

Example: After graduation, are you planning to do anything? to travel? to enter college? to work? Have you considered joining the military?

Rule 3 Use an exclamation mark after a sentence that expresses strong emotion, excitement, surprise, or urgency.

Example: Wow! What a game! But we lost!

Example: Congratulations! You got the job!

Example: Fantastic, Gary!

> **Exercise 11-1** PROOFREAD AND MARK

Use the appropriate proofreaders' marks to correct the errors in the use of the period, question mark, and exclamation mark. If the sentence is correct, write **C** to the left of the number.

1. She asked when she could expect the delivery?

2. Did you remember to send a card for his birthday.

3. Ouch. That really hurt.

4. Will you please send us a copy of the book when it is reprinted.

5. How will we continue the trip? by car. by ferry. by air?

THE SEMICOLON

Within a sentence the semicolon provides a stronger break than a comma, but a weaker break than a period.

Rule 4 Use a semicolon—not a comma—between two independent clauses of a compound sentence when the clauses are not joined by a coordinating conjunction (*and, but, or, nor, for, yet*).

Example: Wisdom is in knowing what to do next; virtue is in doing it.

Example: The package arrived; it was slightly damaged.

Example: The truths of life are not inborn, each generation must learn them through experience. ⌄;

Example: I will accept the job if it is offered, I would enjoy working for the firm. ⌄;

Rule 5 Use a semicolon between two independent clauses when they are joined by transitional expressions such as *however, moreover, consequently, namely, nevertheless, therefore, in addition, likewise, on the other hand, besides,* and *accordingly*. A comma is used after a transitional expression of more than one syllable or when a strong pause is needed after one-syllable words such as *hence, yet, thus,* and *then*. Remember, a semicolon comes *before* and a comma usually *follows* such expressions.

Example: The workshop will be held July 12–15; in addition, a second workshop is scheduled for August 9–12.

Example: I studied five months for this certification exam; consequently, I was confident that I would pass.

Gina got a puppy for her birthday; it was what she had always wanted.

© GETTY IMAGES/PHOTODISC

Example: We will meet five hours on Monday; then we are free to work on other projects.

Example: The presentation was scheduled for 9:30 a.m., unfortunately, the speaker missed her flight.

Example: The computer parts arrived this morning, therefore, we can proceed with the repairs.

Rule 6 Use a semicolon—not a comma—between two or more independent clauses of a compound sentence when the clauses are joined by a coordinating conjunction *and* when either or both of the independent clauses already contain commas.

Example: Hiking, boating, and camping are within easy driving distance from the city; but all of these activities require special permits.

Example: Claudine was interested in shopping, eating, and dancing, but Ethan was more interested in swimming, camping, and hunting.

Rule 7 Use a semicolon—not a comma—in a series when one or more of the items in the series already contain commas.

Example: The firm has branch offices located in Fort Lauderdale, Florida; Pueblo, Colorado; and Montgomery, Alabama.

Example: Interviews are scheduled for Friday, May 14, Monday, May 31, and Wednesday, June 16.

Exercise 11-2 PROOFREAD AND MARK

Use the appropriate proofreaders' marks to correct the errors in the use of the semicolon. If the sentence is correct, write **C** to the left of the number.

1. Knowing the rules of the game is one thing; applying them

   is another.

2. The rules of business etiquette are not well known, it takes

   time to learn to apply the rules properly.

3. The jury, after six weeks of testimony, deliberated for nine

   days, but it did not reach a verdict until Friday.

4. The last order of the season was sent this morning, there-

   fore, we will close an hour earlier today.

5. Next year we will vacation in Aspen, Colorado, Hilo, Hawaii,

   or Hartford, Connecticut.

THE COLON

A colon shows anticipation. It alerts the reader that what follows the colon will explain what came before it.

Rule 8 Use a colon before items such as a list, a series, or an explanation of what came before the colon.

Note: If the items appearing in a vertical list are not complete sentences, do not capitalize the first word in each item. Omit periods after the items unless one or more of the items is a complete sentence, a long phrase, or a dependent clause.

Example: Determine the following points for each career:
nature of the work
satisfaction from the job
advancement opportunities

Example: The job requirements are these: experience working in a medical office, ability to work independently, competence in using spreadsheets, and superior communication skills.

Example: Evaluate potential employers in terms of the following factors:
1. Are there opportunities for advancement?
2. Are the salary and fringe benefits attractive?
3. Does top management support the position?

In the following example, a colon is used after the first clause because the second and third independent clauses explain the first one.

Example: The representative says that the resort has it all: It has an excellent location, and it has outstanding food and entertainment.

Do not use a colon to introduce a list following a preposition or verb. Do not capitalize lists that are not in vertical form unless each item is a complete sentence.

Example: The secretary has the responsibilities of (1) keying the report, (2) sending a cover memo with the final results to the manager, and (3) filing the hard copy.

Example: The group includes Jessica, Pedro, Lani, and Herman.

Rule 9 Use a colon in the following situations: after the salutation of a letter that uses mixed punctuation, within ratios, and between hours and minutes. When time is expressed exactly on the hour, do not include the colon and the zeros.

Example: Dear Mr. Ybarra:

Example: The portions are 3:1 olive oil and water.

Example: The flight leaves at 1:49 p.m.

Example: Report to the principal's office at 3 p.m. sharp.

Example: Every dollar contributed will be matched 1/1.

Example: Set your alarm for 5:00 a.m.

Exercise 11-3 PROOFREAD AND MARK

Use the appropriate proofreaders' marks to correct the errors in the use of the colon. If the sentence is correct, write **C** to the left of the number.

1. Study the following requirements of each project.

    1. short-term benefits.

    2. five-year requirements.

    3. long-term potential.

2. We require the following information to complete the order. the catalog number; the date of delivery; and the method of payment.

3. Do you have revenue estimates for: the quarter ending March 31, the quarter ending June 30, and the quarter ending December 31?

4. The list of duties includes opening incoming mail, distributing priority mail, and resetting timers.

5. The Executive Committee will meet at 9:00 a.m. and reconvene after lunch at 130 p.m.

THE APOSTROPHE

The apostrophe is used to form contractions, the possessive case of nouns, and the plural forms of some words and letters. Watch for errors in the use of the apostrophe.

Rule 10 Add an apostrophe and *s* (*'s*) to form the possessive case of singular nouns not ending in an *s* sound.

    Example: the committee's decision   (the decision of the committee)

    Example: the manager's office   (the office of the manager)

    Example: year's end   (the end of the year)

    Example: Marcia's children   (the children of Marcia)

    Example: The book's cover is torn.

    Example: The company's warehouse is located in Milpitas.

Rule 11 Add an apostrophe and *s* (*'s*) when a new syllable is formed in the pronunciation of the possessive.

>   *Example:*   Congress's vote (the vote of Congress)
>
>   *Example:*   Tess's car (the car owned by Tess)
>
>   *Example:*   Mr. Harris' report
>
>   *Example:*   Mrs. Lopez' plans

Add only an apostrophe if an extra syllable would make a word ending in an *s* sound hard to pronounce.

>   *Example:*   Mr. Osters' suit (the suit belonging to Mr. Osters)
>
>   *Example:*   Ms. Hastings' proposal (the proposal submitted by Ms. Hastings)
>
>   *Example:*   Mr. Marcos' doctor
>
>   *Example:*   Miss Burroughs' investments

Rule 12 Add only an apostrophe to form the possessive case of plural nouns that end in an *s* sound.

>   *Example:*   the girls' pep club (the pep club of the girls)
>
>   *Example:*   the students' behavior (the behavior of the students)
>
>   *Example:*   The candidates' names must be on file.
>
>   *Example:*   Mr. Donohue announced the winners' names at yesterday's assembly.

Rule 13 Add an apostrophe and *s* (*'s*) to form the possessive of plural nouns that do not end in an *s* sound.

>   *Example:*   women's organizations (organizations of women)
>
>   *Example:*   the alumni's reunion (the reunion of the alumni)
>
>   *Example:*   The sheep's wool was sheared.
>
>   *Example:*   The children's favorite fruits are apples and bananas.

Rule 14 Add an apostrophe and *s* (*'s*) to only the final name when an item is jointly owned by more than one person.

>   *Example:*   Dan and Carolyn's wedding (the wedding of Dan and Carolyn)
>
>   *Example:*   Yoko and Magdalena's boutique (the boutique of Yoko and Magdalena)
>
>   *Example:*   Hank's and Toby's ice cream is the best.
>
>   *Example:*   For superior service, take your vehicle to Dom's, Rick's, and Mary's Auto Shop.

Thomas's coin collection includes many rare pieces.

When two names indicate separate ownership, each name is possessive.

> *Example:* Beau's and Donna's companies (two companies, separate ownership)
>
> *Example:* Andrew's and Martha's signatures (each signature is separate)

Rule 15 Use the apostrophe to form the contraction of two words. Place the apostrophe at the point of the missing letter(s).

> *Example:* don't (do not) haven't (have not)
>
> *Example:* it's (it is) you're (you are)
>
> *Example:* who's (who is) I'll (I will)
>
> *Example:* They're not here yet. But we're going to start because it's getting late.

Rule 16 Use an apostrophe to form the following: (1) the plurals of lower-case letters and the plurals of some abbreviations with two or more interior periods (to avoid misreading an expression for a word) and (2) acronyms. An **acronym** is a word formed from the initial letters of a series of words. Acronyms are usually written in all capital letters and without periods.

> *Example:* dot your i's (*not* "is") all A's (*not* "As")
>
> *Example:* x's and y's (*not* "xs" and "ys") M.A.'s and Ph.D.'s
>
> *Example:* SADD's monthly meeting will be held May 3, 200-.

Rule 17 Use the apostrophe as a symbol for feet in measurements. (The quotation mark is the symbol for inches.)

> *Example:* 4' x 8' (4 feet by 8 feet)
>
> *Example:* 6'2" tall (6 feet 2 inches tall)

Exercise 11-4 PROOFREAD AND MARK

Use the appropriate proofreaders' marks to correct the errors in the use of the apostrophe. If the sentence is correct, write **C** to the left of the number.

1. Mr. Arness's computer equipment will be delivered in Ryans' van by years end.

2. Your evaluation of Professor Cummings lecture was positive.

3. Tad's and Ivan's acceptance of Talia and Solange's recommendation was predictable.

4. Dont' forget that students receiving their M.A.s have graduation practice next Friday.

5. The company's fiscal year ended October 31, 200-.

UNDERSCORING AND ITALICS

Both underscoring (underlining) and *italics* are marks of emphasis. Italic type is the preferred means of giving special emphasis to words and phrases and to literary titles and artistic works. The following examples show the use of italics and the underscore. With underscores any space between consecutive words should be underscored. However, a punctuation mark immediately following a word or phrase is not underscored (except periods within abbreviations).

Rule 18 Use italics or the underscore to set off titles of complete literary works, such as books, magazines, newspapers, movies, or plays.

> *Example:* I subscribe to *TIME* and *The Wall Street Journal.*

> *Example:* We have purchased the DVD of The Sound of Music.

> *Example:* My subscription to Quick Cooking *ital* expires in November.

> *Example:* I saw The Lion King on Broadway last summer.

Rule 19 Use italics or the underscore to emphasize or identify special words or phrases.

> *Example:* Choose a computer that offers ease of use *and* compatibility.

> *Example:* The word site means "a location."

> *Example:* I said I was not going! *ital*

> *Example:* Where were you going at that time of night?

QUOTATION MARKS

Quotation marks are used primarily to enclose direct quotations.

He buys the *Enquirer* to read the "Smart Investor" column.

Rule 20 Use quotation marks to enclose all parts of direct quotations and words used in an unusual way.

> *Example:* "The solution," announced the speaker, "is quite obvious."

> *Example:* I heard Cindy tell Richie, "Get lost." So he did.

> *Example:* "Bookworm" and "nerd" are not necessarily nice nicknames.

> *Example:* "Come after school," Ronice said, "and we'll study for the exam."

Rule 21 Use quotation marks to set off parts of complete works, such as chapters within a book, titles of articles and feature columns, titles of essays, short poems, sermons, unpublished works, and songs.

> *Example:* The most popular column in the *Recorder* is "Ask the Editor."

> *Example:* Answer the questions from Chapter 1, "Office Ethics."

Rule 22 Use quotation marks with other punctuation marks in the following manner:

- Periods are placed *inside* quotation marks.

    Example: The editor said, "Please send all chapter drafts by Priority Mail."

- Commas are placed *inside* quotation marks.

    Example: "When I fly," I said, "I plan to fly first class."

- Exclamation marks and question marks are placed *inside* the quotation marks when the punctuation mark applies *only* to the quoted material.

    Example: Miles exclaimed, "Watch out!"

    Example: Marquetta replied, "What did you say?"

- Exclamation marks and question marks are placed *outside* the ending quotation mark when the exclamation or question applies to the entire sentence.

    Example: Why did you ignore Lauralee after she said, "Get out of here now!"?

- Semicolons and colons are placed *outside* the ending quotation mark.

    Example: I marked the package "fragile"; despite this fact, Morris handled the package carelessly.

    Example: Please send me the following items from the folder marked "Confidential": the proposal salary schedule, Bryce's evaluation, and the new employee contract.

Exercise 11-5 PROOFREAD AND MARK

Use the appropriate proofreaders' marks to correct the underscore and quotation mark errors. If the sentence is correct, write **C** to the left of the number.

1. Please send me copies of your most recent issue of the

   Avid Gardener and the Garden Gate.

2. The allocation covers daily expenses and lodging.

3. "We have an answer, the host said, to your first question."

4. He told me I'm over the hill, it's not true!

5. I found the article titled Internet Anxiety to be very informative.

CONFUSED AND MISUSED WORDS

envelop	*v.* to cover with a wrapping
envelope	*n.* a paper container for correspondence

We will **envelop** the air conditioner with plastic before winter begins.
I will place your contract in this **envelope**.

foreword	*n.* an introduction; a preface
forward	*adj.* at or near the front; *v.* to send mail

Anne wrote the **foreword** for my new book.
Constantine **forwarded** the check to my new address.

later	*adv.* after
latter	*adj.* the second of two

They arrived **later** than Stephen and Brook arrived.
August and September are both excellent times to visit, but I prefer the **latter**.

- **Train your eye to check the terminal punctuation of each sentence.**

- **Check that the punctuation mark conveys the proper meaning. If in doubt, ask the originator.**

- **Check that the closing quotation marks have not been omitted.**

PROOFREADING APPLICATIONS

Exercise 11-6 SENTENCES

Proofread the following sentences, and mark all punctuation errors using the appropriate proofreaders' marks. If the sentence is correct, write **C** to the left of the number.

1. Your assignment is due on Tuesday, November 6

2. Would you please let me know when you are ready?

3. Autumn is one of my favorite seasons, I enjoy watching the trees change colors.

4. The team plays its first game on November 12, however, this is a road game.

5. We plan to attend conferences in Des Moines, Iowa; Lansing, Michigan; and Anaheim, California.

6. Employers are looking for these soft skills; team building, active listening, and time management.

7. The group includes: Manuel, Chet, Maureen, and Joni.

8. We were excited to be invited to Doris graduation party.

9. The teams behavior was unacceptable.

10. Our first stop was at Sue's and Will's Resort.

11. Its the best offer I have had since I began interviewing.

12. Fabian subscribes to both BusinessWeek and Money.

13. Dinah was prepared for questions from Chapter 8, "Protecting Your Credit."

14. Bailey asked, Must the candidates names be on file?

15. My subscription to the "Journal of Education for Business" must be paid before the end of the month

Exercise 11-7 SPELLING AND WORD USAGE CHECK

Compare the words in Column A with the corresponding words in Column B. Use the appropriate proofreaders' marks to correct the misspelled or misused words. If both columns are correct, write **C** to the left of the number.

Column A	Column B
1. cooperate	cooperite
2. criterea	criteria
3. curriculum	curriclum
4. development	developement
5. emphasis	emphasis
6. evaluate	evauluate
7. libility	liability
8. minamum	minimum
9. plaque	plaqeu
10. procedure	proceedure
11. reguard	regard
12. volumne	volume
13. The house was enveloped in snow.	He placed a first-class stamp on the envelop.
14. Your forward was well written!	Irene asked that nothing be forwarded to her.
15. Jamir arrived latter than I.	The later item is more popular than the first item.

Exercise 11-8 INTERNATIONAL VOCABULARY

Compare the Spanish words in Column A with the corresponding words in Column B. If the word in Column B is different from the word in Column A, use the appropriate proofreaders' marks to correct Column B. If the words in both columns are the same, write **C** to the left of the number.

Column A	Column B
1. vestidura	vistidura
2. templanza	templanza
3. quintaesencia	quinteasencia
4. minucioso	minuceoso
5. gestionar	gestiomar

Exercise 11-9 BUSINESS LETTER

Proofread the following letter, and correct all punctuation errors using the appropriate proofreaders' marks.

May 15, 200-

THE NEW CAPITOL THEATER
35 Central Avenue
West San Jose, CA 95128-1469
(408) 555-0109 • Fax: (408) 555-0111

Mr. and Mrs. Frank Doolittle
3429 Oak Meadow Road
San Jose, CA 95134-3428

Dear Mr. and Mrs. Doolittle:

Do you remember those lean days in the twenties and thirties. Do you remember enjoying Saturday matinees at the local Bijou? the Orpheum or the Strand. Do you recall the anticipation as you walked to the theater and thought about the enticing smell of popcorn?

Well, this grand environment is not "gone with the wind". It's alive and well, and you can see it all at the New Capitol Theater, a once-popular landmark in San Jose.

Yes, the New Capitol has been rebuilt. The development of this replica of the original Capitol Theater, which opened in April 1926, took three years to complete, and due regard was given to restoring the luxurious ambiance that was so exciting in the heyday of the flapper era.

We also restored two pleasant amenities that were so much a part of attending a movie back then; (1) the usher who guided you to your seat with a pinpoint flashlight and (2) the washroom attendant who was always ready with a needle and thread to mend any clothing.

The enclosed flyer announces our opening double feature, "Footlight Parade" and "Gold Diggers of 1933," and includes a brief review of each movie.

If you know the way to San Jose, come join us for the joy of reminiscence. May we also suggest that you dress in appropriate costume of the twenties and thirties? You will find that the—good old days—were more than fodder for trivia games.

Rah. Rah. The—good old days—are here again.

Sincerely,

Desiree Van Wyke, Owner-Manager

wit

Enclosure

Exercise 11-10 ANNOUNCEMENT

Proofread the following announcement, and correct all punctuation errors using the appropriate proofreaders' marks.

HOLY FAMILY PARISH
555 Newhall Street
San Jose, CA 93334-3248

THE CONTEST OF THE CENTURY

Sponsored by San Joses New Capitol Theater

Guess the gross revenue of the top movie money-makers of the last 50 years, and you will win a fabulous cash prize while helping your parish underwrite the development of the summer curriculum of programs for the whole family. When you cooperate, we all win

Listed here are the names of motion pictures that have grossed enormous sums on their first runs. All you have to do is guess the total revenue of each movie on its first run, right down to the last dollar.

Remember, you need to evaluate the first run only. Obviously, the first run of Gone with the Wind, which came out at the tail end of the depression, will be substantially lower and seem like peanuts when compared with the blockbuster "Batman."

The procedure to enter is simple, anyone can enter, but only one entry per family. List the movie titles and dollar amounts on a 3 x 5 card, and then mail it in an envelope to Holy Family Parish. The address is as follows 555 Newhall Street, San Jose, CA 93334-3248. Thats all you have to do!

Good luck!

THE PICTURES:	Gone with the Wind	Star Wars
	Batman	The Sound of Music
	Ben-Hur	The Wizard of Oz
	The Godfather	Singing in the Rain
	The Bridge on the River Kwai	Dick Tracy
THE PRIZES	First:	$5,000
	Second:	$2,500
	Third:	$1,000

Fr. Martin O'Brien, Pastor

PROOFREADING AT THE COMPUTER

Exercise 11-11 ANNOUNCEMENT

1. Open 11-11 from the Chapter 11 folder on the Student CD. (This is a computer copy of Application 11-10.)

2. Proofread the announcement on the screen. Correct all errors on the screen copy that you indicated with proofreaders' marks in Application 11-10. Use the spelling checker.

3. Produce the announcement in correct format following the standard procedures described in the previous chapters.

Exercise 11-12 MANUSCRIPT PARAGRAPHS

1. Open 11-12 from the Chapter 11 folder on the Student CD.

2. Proofread the manuscript page on the screen. Correct all errors.

3. Produce the manuscript page following the standard procedures.

Exercise 11-13 E-MAIL MESSAGE

1. Open 11-13 from the Chapter 11 folder on the Student CD.

2. Proofread the e-mail message on the screen. Correct all errors.

3. Produce the e-mail message following the standard procedures.

Teamwork

CUMULATIVE APPLICATION

> ### Exercise 11-14 NEWS RELEASE

Proofread the following news release, and correct all errors using the appropriate proofreaders' marks. After you have proofread the news release, team up with one of your classmates to proofread a second time. Your partner will open 11-14 from the Chapter 11 folder on the Student CD and read from the correct list of favorite movies. You should pay particular attention to the names of movies, the years, and the directors' names.

Imagine the excitement provided by early films in the 1920s and 1930s! Here was a chance for people to enjoy a different kind of entertainment. Many of these early films was dramas, epics, romances, or comedies, but regardless of the films classification, people could get away from the events of the day for a few hours.

Following is a list of my favorite movies from the 1920s

- *The Jazz Singer*, 1927, Alan Crosland, Director
- *The Gold Rush*, 1925, King Vidor, Director
- *The General*, 1927, Buster Keaton, Director
- *Sunrise*, 1929, F. W. Murnau, Director
- *The Covered Wagon*, 1923, James Cruze, Directer
- *Ben-Hur: A Tale of the Christ*, 1925, George Niblo, Director

My favorite movies from the 1930s include these:

- *King Kong*, 1933, Merian C. Cooper, Director
- *Way Out*, 1937, James W. Horne, Director
- *Gone with the Wind*, 1939, Sam Wood, Director
- *Red Dust*, 1932, Victor Fleming, Director
- *Bride of Frankenstein*, 1935, Michael Curtiz, Director
- *Les Miserables*, 1935, Richard Boleslawski, Director

What other major films are your favorites from the 1920s and 1930s Let us know at the New capitol Theater and we will try to show your favorite movie in our new facilities.

© FSTOP

Format Errors:
Letters and Memos

Objectives

- Identify errors in block and modified block format.

- Identify format errors in interoffice memorandums.

- Use the appropriate proof-readers' marks to mark format error corrections.

- Spell correctly 12 frequently misspelled words.

- Use correctly three sets of commonly confused and mis-used words.

Spotlight on **ACCURACY**

It is estimated that approximately 20 percent of the adults in the United States are functionally illiterate; they cannot read, write, or calculate above the eighth-grade level. People who are illiterate are unable to read the daily newspaper; read a story to their children; or read the correspondence, memos, e-mail messages, or business reports that businesses need to operate.

Business calls illiteracy one of its most serious problems. An illiterate employee may cost a company thousands of dollars because he or she is unable to read a simple letter or manual. One such employee caused $250,000 worth of damage to an engine because he did not understand the repair manual that came with the machine. The problem of illiteracy costs business and industry billions of dollars every year!

FORMAT

The layout of copy on a page is referred to as **format**. Some formatting considerations include margin settings, spacing between paragraphs, and the organization of document parts. It may also include underlining, capitalizing, and boldfacing letters or words.

Is format important? Yes, it is. The format of a document should enhance the message—not detract from it. The document presentation should reflect the competency of the sender. If a document has a "sloppy" appearance or if the format makes a document difficult to read, the document reflects negatively on the sender. On the other hand, a document that is formatted attractively and printed on high-quality stationery indicates quality and a professional attitude. It is an indication that the sender is a person you can work with and trust.

In this chapter you will learn to recognize incorrectly formatted business letters and interoffice memorandums. Use the following proofreaders' marks to correct errors in format.

	MARKED COPY	CORRECTED COPY
Begin new paragraph. ¶	Attendance was good. ¶ Next year's play will be a comedy.	Attendance was good. Next year's play will be a comedy.
Do not begin new paragraph. *No* ¶	Single-space them. *No* ¶ Memos should always be single-spaced.	Single-space them. Memos should always be single-spaced.
Center.] [	]BASIC OBJECTIVES[	BASIC OBJECTIVES
Align copy. ‖	Bring your pictures. We will design holiday scrapbook pages.	Bring your pictures. We will design holiday scrapbook pages.
Make bold. ~~~	Use the <u>new</u> fax.	Use the **new** fax.

	MARKED COPY	CORRECTED COPY
Move to the left.	We can help you.	We can help you.
Move to the right.	The crew will need it.	The crew will need it.
Move up.	They like to go. would	They would like to go.
Move down.	for My trip provides stops.	My trip provides for stops.

▶ Exercise 12-1   PROOFREAD AND MARK

Use the appropriate proofreaders' marks to revise the copy in the second column according to the instructions in the first column.

1. Center heading.   SUMMARY

                to be present.

2. Move down.   We plan

3. Move left.   Several people will volunteer.

4. Do not begin   I would like to attend.

   new paragraph.   The presentation of the award

                     will be held on Friday, June 12.

5. Move up.   Mr. Marcel Chapelin

                 334 West Draxten Boulevard

© GETTY IMAGES/PHOTODISC

LETTERS

Letters are documents used to communicate with people, such as customers or clients, outside the organization. Therefore, proper format is especially important. Proofreading a letter for correct format includes checking three things: (1) the overall balanced appearance; (2) the correct placement, spacing, and sequence of letter parts; and (3) the consistency in the format of the letter style.

Balanced Appearance

A good proofreader judges whether the overall appearance of a letter creates a favorable or unfavorable impression. Overall balance is achieved when the left and right margins are approximately even and the top and bottom margins are balanced.

Proper balance may be attained by following these general guidelines: Letters are formatted with default (1.25 inches) or 1-inch left and right margins, a 2-inch top margin, and a 1-inch bottom margin. Instead of a 2-inch top margin, letters may be centered vertically using the Center Page feature. To place a letter in reading position, insert two hard returns below the last keyed line.

▶ **Exercise 12-2** **PROOFREAD AND MARK**

Proofread the following letters for their overall balanced appearance. Use brackets to show whether the copy should be moved right, left, up, or down.

1.   **2.**

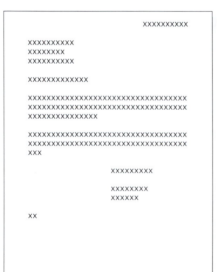

3.

```
                              xxxxxxxxxx

xxxxxxxxxx
xxxxxxx
xxxxxxxxxx

xxxxxxxxxxxxx

xxxxxxxxxxxxxxxxxxxxxxxxxxxxxxxxxxxx
xxxxxxxxxxxxxxxxxxxxxxxxxxxxxxxxxxxx
xxxxxxxxxxxxxxx

xxxxxxxxxxxxxxxxxxxxxxxxxxxxxxxxxxxx
xxxxxxxxxxxxxxxxxxxxxxxxxxxxxxxxxxxx
xxx

              xxxxxxxxx

              xxxxxxxx
              xxxxxx

xx
```

4.

```
                              xxxxxxxxxx

xxxxxxxxxx
xxxxxxx
xxxxxxxxxx

xxxxxxxxxxxxx

xxxxxxxxxxxxxxxxxxxxxxxxxxxxxxxxxxxx
xxxxxxxxxxxxxxxxxxxxxxxxxxxxxxxxxxxx
xxxxxxxxxxxxxxx

xxxxxxxxxxxxxxxxxxxxxxxxxxxxxxxxxxxx
xxxxxxxxxxxxxxxxxxxxxxxxxxxxxxxxxxxx
xxx

              xxxxxxxxx

              xxxxxxxx
              xxxxxx

xx
```

Letter Parts

Most letters are prepared using the same basic letter parts arranged in the same sequence. If any letter part is omitted, the sequence of the other parts should not be affected. When proofreading letters, check to make sure that all of the required letter parts are present and that they are in the correct sequence. Also check that the proper spacing has been used above and below each letter part. The eight basic letter parts include the following items:

1. Heading

2. Date

3. Letter address

4. Salutation

5. Body

6. Complimentary close

7. Writer's name and title

8. Reference initials

Other letter parts, such as the attention line, the subject line, and notations, may be added as needed.

Heading

In business letters the heading is usually preprinted on letterhead stationery. The printed heading includes the name and address of the company. Additional information may include telephone number, fax number, e-mail address, and company logo. This heading is placed only on the first page of a multiple-page letter.

J & E Company, Inc.
279 Highland Park Court
Charlotte, NC 28208-4233

(704) 555-0131 • Fax: (704) 555-0134
JECompany@email.com

If a letter is to be printed on plain paper, the sender's return address should be included on the lines immediately above the date.

```
279 Highland Park Court
Charlotte, NC 28208-4233
December 19, 200-
```

Date

The date includes the month, day, and year. It is positioned 2 inches from the top of the page or a double space below a letterhead that is more than 2 inches deep.

Letter Address

The letter address includes the personal title, name, and complete mailing address of the receiver. If the letter is addressed to an individual, the individual's personal title (*Mr.*, *Mrs.*, *Ms.*) or professional title (*Dr.*, *Professor*) is included as a sign of courtesy. Use *Ms.* when a woman prefers that title or when her preferred title is unknown. The letter address is positioned at the left margin four lines below the date.

The letter address is used as the mailing address on the envelope. Should the letter be sent in a window envelope, the letter address may be keyed in all capital letters without punctuation. The alert proofreader should check that the city, state, and ZIP Code are correct. (The Appendix contains a list of two-letter state abbreviations.) Use one space between the two-letter state abbreviation and the ZIP Code.

Ms. Lidia Ruiz	MS LIDIA RUIZ
Del Sol, Inc.	DEL SOL INC
379 North River Road	379 NORTH RIVER ROAD
Dallas, TX 75212-3682	DALLAS TX 75212-3682

Attention Line

An attention line is included in the letter address when the writer does not know the name of the receiver of the letter or is writing to an organization. The attention line is keyed as the first line of the letter address.

Attention Personnel Director
Del Sol, Inc.
379 North River Road
Dallas, TX 75212-3682

When an attention line is used, the salutation should read *Ladies and Gentlemen*.

> **Exercise 12-3** PROOFREAD AND MARK

Proofread the following list of cities and states by comparing the states in Column A with their two-letter state abbreviations in Column B. If the state abbreviation in Column B is not correct, use the appropriate proofreaders' mark to show what correction should be made. If the abbreviation is correct, write **C** to the left of the number.

Column A	Column B
1. Cedar Falls, Iowa 50613-1822	Cedar Falls, IA. 50613-1822
2. Cincinnati, Ohio 45213-0733	Cincinnati, Oh 45213-0733
3. Bloomer, Wisconsin 54724-9125	Bloomer, WS 54724-9125
4. Minot, North Dakota 58701-8829	Minot, ND 58701-8829
5. Towanda, Illinois 61776-4931	Towanda, LI 61776-4931

Salutation

The salutation is the friendly "hello" of the letter. Depending on the relationship between the sender and the receiver, the salutation may be formal or informal. The salutation should agree with the first line of the letter address in number and gender. When the letter is addressed to a company, you should use the salutation "Ladies and Gentlemen." When the letter is addressed to an individual or position/title, the salutation should be that person's name or position/title.

Letter Address	Salutation
ABC Corporation 555 State Avenue Jamestown, MI 49427	Ladies and Gentlemen
Mr. Leonard Dreese 90 West Boulevard St. Ansgar, IA 50472	Dear Mr. Dreese
Personnel Director ABC Corporation 555 State Street Jamestown, MI 49427	Dear Personnel Director

The salutation is placed at the left margin a double space below the last line of the letter address. A colon follows the salutation when *mixed punctuation* is used; the colon is omitted when *open punctuation* is used. The examples on the next page illustrate various situations.

To an individual (open punctuation):	Dear Mr. Pham
To an organization (mixed punctuation):	Ladies and Gentlemen:
To an individual whose gender is unknown (mixed punctuation):	Dear Dale Komar:

Only when you know the receiver on a personal basis should you use the receiver's first name in the salutation.

Subject Line

The subject line, an optional letter part, states the main topic of the letter. It is positioned at the left margin a double space below the salutation. It is keyed in all capital letters.

| Dear Ms. Cohen: | Dear Mr. Dortch |
| APRIL MADNESS SALE | AWARD WINNERS |

Body

The body contains the message of the letter. It begins a double space below the salutation (or subject line if one is included). The body is single-spaced with a double space between paragraphs.

In general, the body should include at least three paragraphs, which makes the letter look attractive. If the message is long, the body may extend to more than one page. In a multipage letter, maintain a 1-inch bottom margin on the first page. Use plain paper that is the same quality as the letterhead, and begin each succeeding page with a heading. Single-space the heading and include the receiver's name, the page number, and the date. Double-space below the date before continuing the letter.

Mr. Genaro Ordonez
Page 2
November 12, 200-

Complimentary Close

The complimentary close is the social "good-bye" of the letter. It is placed a double space below the last line of the body. Only the first word is capitalized. The style of punctuation used in the complimentary close **must** agree with the style of punctuation used in the salutation. A comma follows the complimentary close when *mixed punctuation* is used (meaning a colon was used after the salutation); the comma is omitted after the complimentary close when *open punctuation* is used (meaning no colon was used after the salutation).

| **Mixed punctuation:** | Dear Dr. Reed: | **Open punctuation:** | Dear Dr. Reed |
| | Sincerely, | | Sincerely |

While several forms of the complimentary close are used—Sincerely yours, Cordially, Truly yours, Very truly yours—the trend is to use only the word *Sincerely*.

Writer's Name and Official Title

The writer's keyed name and job title are positioned on the fourth line below the complimentary close. The job title may be positioned on the same line with the keyed name or immediately below, whichever gives the best balance.

Sincerely,   Sincerely

Georgina Nascimento   Emi Mori, Treasurer
Conference Coordinator

Reference Initials

The initials of the keyboard operator are keyed in lowercase letters, no periods or spaces, at the left margin a double space below the writer's name, title, or department.

Georgina Nascimento
Conference Coordinator

tah

When the writer of a letter keyboards his or her own letter, reference initials are not needed.

Notations

When a document is included with a letter, an enclosure notation is keyed a double space below the reference initials. If a copy of the letter is to be sent to another person, a copy notation is included. The letter c is used, followed by the name(s) of the person(s) who will receive a copy. A postscript would be the last notation in a letter. As shown below, all of these letter parts are positioned at the left margin a double space below the preceding part.

. . . are anxious to work with you.

Sincerely,

Theodore Klements, Manager

mri

Enclosure: Price List

c Andres Miranda

The deadline for the discount is . . .

> ### Exercise 12-4 PROOFREAD AND MARK

Proofread the following letter parts, and correct all format errors using the appropriate proofreaders' marks. If there are no format errors, write **C** to the left of the number.

1. . . . to discuss your proposal.

Sincerely,

Lorna Reinertson

c Jarod Sampson

tis

2. Ms. Gail Jaeckin
763 Jackson Street South
Anchorage, AK 99501-0942

Dear Ms. Jaeckin

HOLIDAY SHOPPING PLANS

Yes, it is time to make your . . .

3. Pavement Prices Co.
9473 Chestnut Boulevard
New Orleans, LO 70118-3811

Dear Sir or Madam

4. MS. MIWAKU YOSHINO
SWEET SUGAR REFINERY
4715 OAHU AVENUE
HILO, HI 96720-4186

Ladies and Gentlemen

5. Mr. Larry Stelter, President
Comfort Homes, Inc.
257 Hampton Avenue
Wilmington, DE 19899-3169

Dear Mr. Stelter

6. . . . and is enclosed for your use.

Sincerely,

Damon Wenisch
Sales Department
tbe

7. . . . and return the enclosed card by June 30.

Sincerely,

Nanette Jungers
National President

Enclosures

AK

8. August 11, 200-

Dr. Barbara Ericson
Hairs and Ribbons
7593 Bradley Circle
Nashua, NH 03063-0269

AWARD WINNERS

Letter Formats

Letters may be prepared in different formats and styles. Business letters are formatted in two basic styles: block and modified block. **Block format** is quick and easy to use because all letter parts begin at the left margin. This style is very popular because there are no paragraph or line indentations.

In **modified block format**, the date, complimentary close, and writer's name and official title *begin* near the horizontal center of the page. Paragraphs may be blocked at the left margin or indented 0.5 inch.

When proofreading letters, check that the letter format has been applied consistently. Also check that either open or mixed punctuation has been used consistently. Figures 12-1 and 12-2, which follow, illustrate the two letter formats.

Figure 12-1

**Block Format with
Mixed Punctuation**

GRAND WRITING INC.

39179 West Outer Drive • Knoxville, TN 37921-2648

Telephone: 865-555-0152 • FAX: 865-555-0153

writing@email.com

May 19, 200-

Ms. Myrtle Dallman
874 South Ash Avenue
Montgomery, AL 36117-1749

Dear Ms. Dallman:

BLOCK FORMAT, MIXED PUNCTUATION

Block format arranges all of the parts of a business letter at the left
margin. Block format is efficient because no tabs are required.

This letter also illustrates mixed punctuation. The salutation is
followed by a colon, and the complimentary close is followed by a
comma.

Block format appeals to firms that look for efficient ways to handle
business correspondence.

Sincerely,

Joan R. Zunder
Communications Specialist

tbe

Figure 12-2
Modified Block
Format with Open
Punctuation

GRAND WRITING INC.
39179 West Outer Drive • Knoxville, TN 37921-2648
Telephone: 865-555-0152 • FAX: 865-555-0153
writing@email.com

May 19, 200-

Ms. Myrtle Dallman
874 South Ash Avenue
Montgomery, AL 36117-1749

Dear Ms. Dallman

MODIFIED BLOCK FORMAT, OPEN PUNCTUATION

Modified block format is similar to block format except that the date, complimentary close, and closing lines begin near the center. This style has a more balanced appearance.

This letter also illustrates open punctuation. There is no colon after the salutation and no comma after the complimentary close.

Modified block format continues to be a favorite of mine. Do you prefer modified block or block format?

Sincerely

Joan R. Zunder
Communications Specialist

tbe

INTEROFFICE MEMORANDUMS (MEMOS)

Interoffice memorandums (memos) are informal documents used for communication within the same organization. Because of this, writers are generally not as concerned about enhancing the company image as they are with letters. However, employees are judged not only on their ability to compose clear and correct documents, but also on their ability to proofread carefully. Therefore, the proofreader must be sure the format is accurate.

Generally, memos address only one topic and include the following parts: receiver's name, sender's name, date, subject of the memo, body or actual message, and reference initials.

Some companies have replaced interoffice memorandums with e-mail. E-mail will be discussed in Chapter 15.

The memo includes four printed headings: TO, FROM, DATE, and SUBJECT.

Side margins are default settings of 1.25 inches. The first line of the body begins a double space below the subject line. The paragraphs are blocked and single-spaced. The initials of the keyboard operator are included a double space below the last line of the body. Memos may be signed or initialed by the sender. Figure 12-3 illustrates the format of an interoffice memo.

Figure 12-3

Interoffice Memo

GRAND WRITING INC. Interoffice Memorandum

TO: Support Staff

FROM: Kyle Haack   *KH*

DATE: April 12, 200-

SUBJECT: FORMAT FOR MEMOS

This memo is designed for use on printed interoffice memorandum forms. If plain paper is used, the headings TO, FROM, DATE, and SUBJECT must be keyed.

1. Side margins are default (1.25 inches) or 1-inch settings.

2. The message begins a double space below the printed headings.

3. Paragraphs are single-spaced, and a double space (one blank line) is left between them. Enumerations are treated as numbered paragraphs.

4. Reference initials are keyed a double space below the last line of the body.

The memo may be signed or initialed by the originator.

tbe

> **Exercise 12-5** PROOFREAD AND MARK

Proofread the following memo, and correct all format errors using the appropriate proofreaders' marks.

GRAND UNION COLLEGE INTEROFFICE MEMO

TO: JoEllen Eustis, Head Librarian

FROM: Marv Eggersgluess, Management Department *ME*

DATE: October 8, 200-

SUBJECT: RESEARCH REPORTS

Thank you for your interest in our Business

     Communications class project. Each student was asked early in the semester to prepare a research report on a topic of his or her choice.

     The reports that have been submitted are well done; and when we receive permission from the authors, we will place them on reserve in the library.

tos

CONFUSED AND MISUSED WORDS

loose	*adj.* not fastened; free
lose	*v.* unable to find; to fail to win
loss	*n.* a person or thing lost; a defeat

The rope is **loose**.

Please don't **lose** the keys.

Our win is their **loss**.

moral	*adj.* concerned with goodness or badness of human action and character; *n.* lesson contained in a story or an event
morale	*n.* attitude of an individual

He has a good **moral** character.

The **morale** of the staff was low after the recent layoffs.

precede	*v.* to come before in time or rank
proceed	*v.* to go forward

Babette will **precede** you in the graduation lineup.

You may **proceed** with your plans.

- In addition to the body, remember to proofread the special parts of a letter or memo. Also check to be sure that no parts have been omitted.

- When preparing more than one letter, be sure that each letter is inserted into the correctly addressed envelope. Check to be sure that all enclosures are, in fact, enclosed with the letter.

- When proofreading a letter for format, check that one letter style and one punctuation style have been used consistently throughout.

PROOFREADING APPLICATIONS

Exercise 12-6 BUSINESS LETTER LAYOUT

Place the letter parts in Column A in the correct order in Column B.

Column A	Column B
Attention line	1. _____
Body	2. _____
Complimentary close	3. _____
Date	4. _____
Heading	5. _____
Letter address	6. _____
Reference initials	7. _____
Salutation	8. _____
Subject line	9. _____
Writer's name and official title	10. _____

Identify the punctuation style in each of the following:

1. _____   2. _____

Dear Mr. Wong:	Dear Ms. Perea
. . . to thank you for your help.	. . . was most appreciated.
Sincerely,	Yours truly
Roscoe Long	Lavonne Lahammer

> **Exercise 12-7** SPELLING AND WORD USAGE CHECK

Compare the words in Column A with the corresponding words in Column B. Use the appropriate proofreaders' marks to correct the misspelled or misused words. If both columns are correct, write **C** to the left of the number.

Column A   **Column B**

1. beginning   begining
2. priviledge   privilege
3. salary   salery
4. pertinent   pertnent
5. similar   similiar
6. safety   safety
7. technical   technicle
8. especialy   especially
9. transferred   transfered
10. submited   submitted
11. accomodate   accommodate
12. established   establishd
13. We'll loose the game.   Don't lose your homework.
14. You will face moral issues.   The pay increase boosted employee moral.
15. The meeting will proceed.   Payment must proceed shipment.

> **Exercise 12-8** INTERNATIONAL VOCABULARY

Compare the Spanish words in Column A with the corresponding words in Column B. If the word in Column B is different from the word in Column A, use the appropriate proofreaders' marks to correct Column B. If the words in both columns are the same, write **C** to the left of the number.

Column A   **Column B**

1. Nos vemos   Nos vemos
2. orenada   orendada
3. periodismo   peroidismo
4. profesora   professora
5. quisiera   quiseira

Exercise 12-9 LETTER IN MODIFIED BLOCK FORMAT

Proofread the following letter formatted in modified block style with mixed punctuation. Correct all errors using the appropriate proofreaders' marks.

CITY FUNDERS ASSOCIATION OF NEW ENGLAND (CFANE)
3790 Poplar Boulevard • Providence, RI 02915-1388
Telephone: 401-555-0190 • Fax: 401-555-0199

October 23, 200-

Darlene Andross, President
Grand Apple Equipment Corporation
2469 North River Boulevard
Hartford, CT 01609-2331

Organizational Meeting

Ladies and Gentlemen:

The organizational meeting of the new Board of Governors of the City Funders Association of New England has been scheduled for Tuesday, November 20. The meeting will be held in the Baker Room of the Grant Street Hotel beginning at 2 p.m.

On behalf of the Nominating/Elections Committee, I would like to welcome you to the CFAEN board. We look forward to your technical assistance in helping us meet our goal for the annual fund drive and identify those projects and activities that are most in need of financial assistance.

Issues that may be addressed at future meetings include fund safety, salary issues, security devices, and other topics that are pertinent to our board.

Sincerely

Angeline Tigner, President
tis

Proofread the following memo for all format errors. Mark the corrections using the appropriate proofreaders' marks.

GENERAL MANUFACTURING, INC. Interoffice Memorandum

TO: Faustino Colon

FROM: Antoinette Davies

DATE: November 30, 200-

SUBJECT: Recognition of staff

President Yuan has received several letters of commendation on the excellent job you did at the national convention last week. We have submitted copies of your letters to Personnel to be placed in your employee file. Congratulations!

Please complete the enclosed form by Friday so that we can include the information in the next issue of *General Notes.* This newsletter will be published at the end of next week. Don't lose out on this opportunity to highlight the excellent work that you did!

Also, please send us a photograph that we can use with the article.

Tih

PROOFREADING AT THE COMPUTER

Exercise 12-11   LETTER IN BLOCK FORMAT

1. Open 12-11 from the Chapter 12 folder on the Student CD. (This is a computer copy of Application 12-9.)

2. Proofread and correct all errors on the screen copy that you indicated with proofreaders' marks in Application 12-9.

3. Produce the letter in correct format following the standard procedures described in the previous chapters.

Exercise 12-12   MEMORANDUM

1. Open 12-12 from the Chapter 12 folder on the Student CD.

2. Proofread the memo on the screen. Correct all errors.

3. Produce the memo following the standard procedures.

Exercise 12-13   LETTER IN BLOCK FORMAT

1. Open 12-13 from the Chapter 12 folder on the Student CD.

2. Proofread the letter on the screen. Correct all errors.

3. Produce the letter using mixed punctuation and following the standard procedures.

CUMULATIVE APPLICATION

Exercise 12-14   BUSINESS LETTER

Proofread the following letter formatted in block style with open punctuation. Correct all errors using the appropriate proofreaders' marks.

CORNSBURG DISTRIBUTING COMPANY
976 Oak Lane NE
Salt Lake City, UT 84115-3199
(801) 555-0166 • Fax (801) 555-0167

Mr. Girard Heitner

Mountain View Advertising

15 S. Jackson Way

Albuquerque, MN 87108-2713

Dear Mr. Heitner;

Our marketing staff recently decided to contact your company about advertising rates for our campaign in New Mexico. Late this summer we will be introducing our new line of packing boxes at outlets throughout the western UnitedStates.

In each state we will ask an ad agency to be responsible for promotion. You are one agency we are considering for the state of New Mexico. We were especially impressed with the ad campaign your developed for the Geneva Company last year.

Please send us your response within the next fourteen days so we can finalize our advertising plans.

Sincerely

Luisa Diaz, Manager

Marketing Department

be

© BRAND X PICTURES

Format Errors: Reports and Job Search Documents

Spotlight on ACCURACY

Your letter of application in a job search is similar to a sales letter. The purpose of this letter is to match your qualifications with the employer's needs in the best way possible. Because of its importance, your letter must be perfect—no errors. Consider the impression you might make on a potential employer if these errors were found in your letter:

- I have worked in sales since 1098.

- I am enclosing my resume, along with other important parts of me.

- I have taken the following curses in my studies: keyboarding, business law, communications, and entrepreneurship.

Objectives

- Recognize format errors in reports.

- Recognize format errors in job search documents.

- Use the appropriate proof-readers' marks to indicate corrections in format.

- Spell correctly 12 frequently misspelled words.

- Use correctly three sets of commonly confused and misused words.

REPORTS

Reports are used to provide or analyze information and to communicate within a company or with other companies. Business reports can be used for financial, managerial, operational, sales, planning, forecast, and other informational reporting. There is a standard format for most reports, just as there is for letters and resumes. School reports, such as themes, book reports, and term papers, are usually prepared in the standard report format as well.

Reports may be formatted as unbound, leftbound, or topbound documents. The most common format is the unbound report. Although the spacing and arrangement of report parts may vary somewhat from writer to writer, you will review the basic unbound format in this chapter.

Report Parts

When proofreading a report, check closely for consistency and correctness among report parts. For example, check that the spacing above and below similar headings is the same throughout the report. Report parts vary depending on the length and formality of the report. The basic parts, however, include the title page, the body, and the references pages.

◆ Title Page

The title page includes the title of the report, the writer's name and school or organization, and the date. Figure 13-1 illustrates the format and spacing of a title page in an unbound report.

◆ Body

The body, the message of the report, begins with the **main heading**— placed approximately 2 inches from the top and keyed boldface using 14-point type. If there is a **secondary heading**, it is centered a double space below the main heading. The main heading is the title of the report, also found on the title page; the secondary heading provides further information about the message of the report. So the information is easy to read, the body is organized under one or more levels of headings. The first level of headings is called a **side heading**; the next level is called a **paragraph heading**. Figure 13-1 illustrates an acceptable format.

Enumerations are often used to emphasize certain facts or to present information in an easy-to-read format. Enumerations are indented 0.5 inch from the left margin and blocked at that point.

Margins and spacing should be consistent throughout the report. For an unbound report, the side margin is the default of 1.25 inches or 1 inch. The bottom margin is 1 inch. The top margin for the first page is 2 inches; on all other pages, it is 1 inch. Generally, reports are double-spaced and paragraphs are indented 0.5 inch. Pages are numbered beginning with the second page, where the page number is positioned at the top using right alignment.

Title Page:

2 inches
from top ⟶ **FORMAT FOR UNBOUND REPORTS**

5 inches from top ⟶ Karen E. Mikelson

Eastern Cottonwood College

Approximately 9 inches ⟶ April 19, 200-
from top

Sample Page 1:

2 inches ⟶ **FORMAT FOR UNBOUND REPORTS**
Side margins: default

General Guidelines

Double-space ⟶   Indention: 0.5 inch

When proofreading reports, the proofreader's responsibility includes checking for all mechanical errors, including format errors. Although this is a big responsibility, the writer has ultimate responsibility for the correctness of the report.

⟵ Double-space

The writer is responsible for the correct presentation of the entire paper—all the preliminary, illustrative, and reference matter as well as the text. The person preparing the manuscript, if other than the writer, is responsible for accurate transcription of the copy, the layout of the components as illustrated in chapter 14, and the general appearance of the final manuscript, but not for content.[1]

⟵ Double-space

Follow these guidelines to format unbound reports.

⟵ Double-space
⟵ Side Heading

Spacing and Margins

Reports may be either single- or double-spaced. School reports and manuscripts are usually double-spaced. Business reports are often single-spaced.

Regardless of the spacing, the top margin for the first page is 2 inches. The top margin on all other pages is 1 inch. Side and bottom margins are at least 1 inch. Paragraphs are indented 0.5 inch. Quoted material that is four or more lines is single-spaced and indented 0.5 inch from the left margin.

⟵ Double-space
⟵ Double-space

[1]Kate L. Turabian, A Manual for Writers of Term Papers, Theses, and Dissertations. 6th ed. (Chicago: The University of Chicago Press, 1996), 230.

Sample Page 2:

Page number at right margin ⟶ 2

Headings

Main heading. Center a main heading (or title) in all capital letters. If the heading has two or more lines, allow one blank line between them. Leave a double space between the heading and the first line of the body.

Side headings. Side headings begin at the left margin. The first letter of the first word and all other main words are capitalized. Side headings are set boldface.

Paragraph headings. All paragraph headings are indented and set boldface. Only the first letter of the first word is capitalized. The heading at the start of this paragraph is an example of a paragraph heading.

Page Numbers

It is not necessary to number the first page. All other pages are numbered at the top using right alignment.

Guidelines for Dividing Copy

Follow these guidelines when dividing words and paragraphs within the body of the report:

1. Use the wordwrap feature when you key a document. Words are rarely divided at the end of a line.

2. If it is necessary to divide a paragraph between two pages, at least two lines of the paragraph should appear on each page.

References Page:

2 inches from top ⟶   REFERENCES   Side margins: default
Double-space ⟶   Indention: 0.5 inch

Fulton-Calkins, Patsy and Karin Stultz. Procedures and Theory for Administrative Professionals, 5th Edition. Thomson/South-Western, 2004.

Peng, Yeo (December 1997). "Tips for Reading Faster." Executive World [Online]. Available: http://www.informatics.edu.sg/ics-sin/businessletters.htm [January 3, 2000].

Jack P. Hoggatt, Jon A. Shank, and Jerry W. Robinson. Century 21 Computer Applications & Keyboarding. 7th ed. Cincinnati: South-Western/Thomson Learning, 2002.

Turabian, Kate L. A Manual for Writers of Term Papers, Theses, and Dissertations. 6th ed. Chicago: The University of Chicago Press, 1996.

Figure 13-1

Unbound Report Format, Including Title Page, Sample Pages, and References Page

◆ References

If references have been used in writing the report, they are listed at the end. The references may be placed a quadruple space after the last line of the body of the report *or* on a separate page. The references are listed under the heading REFERENCES, WORKS CITED, or BIBLIOGRAPHY. The heading is keyed boldface in all capital letters using 14-point type.

Each entry is single-spaced, with a double space between entries. The first line of each entry begins at the left margin, but all other lines are indented 0.5 inch from the left margin. This is called the **hanging indent style**. Figure 13-1 illustrates a *REFERENCES* page.

Because of the increased use of electronic sources as references, you should also know how to document electronic citations. An electronic citation includes the following reference components: Author. "Title of Work." URL (Date you accessed this site).

Powell, Jim. "The Education of Thomas Edison." http://www.self-gov.org/freeman (27 April 2001).

Documentation

When using another person's ideas or quoting statistics or other specific information, the writer must indicate the sources from which the information was taken. Reference to the originator adds credibility to the report and gives credit to the originator. The most common means of documentation for business writers include textual citations, footnotes, and endnotes. More formal documentation styles include the MLA and APA styles of notation.

◆ Textual Citations

Textual citations have grown in popularity. They usually include the last name of the author(s), the year of publication, and page number(s). Textual citations are placed in parentheses within the body of the report. The complete references are then listed in alphabetical order by author surnames under the heading REFERENCES or BIBLIOGRAPHY at the end of the report. (See the section entitled "References.") If the report in Figure 13-1 had used a textual citation instead of a footnote, the reference would have appeared as follows:

> When proofreading reports, the proofreader's responsibility includes checking for all mechanical errors, including format errors. Although this is a big responsibility, the writer has ultimate responsibility for the correctness of the report.
>
> The writer is responsible for the correct presentation of the entire paper—all the preliminary, illustrative, and reference matter as well as the text. The person preparing the manuscript, if other than the writer, is responsible for accurate transcription of the copy, the layout of the components as illustrated in chapter 14, and the general appearance of the final manuscript, but not for content (Turabian, 1996, p. 230).

The Modern Language Association (MLA) and the American Psychological Association (APA) styles of citation are used in formal reports. The MLA style is used primarily in preparing scholarly manuscripts and lists in parentheses the author's last name and the page number (*Author 53*). The APA style is used primarily by writers in the social and behavioral sciences and lists in parentheses the last name of the author, the year of publication, and the page number (*Author, 200-, p. 53*).

◆ Footnotes

Footnotes are numbered consecutively throughout the report. They appear at the bottom of the page on which the references are cited. Superscripts are used to number footnotes. Figure 13-1 illustrates the correct format for footnotes.

If you are using the Footnote and Endnote feature of your word processing program, the feature will automatically insert a superscript number and position your footnotes correctly at the bottom of the page.

◆ Endnotes

Endnotes are essentially the same as footnotes. But unlike footnotes, endnotes are listed together on a separate page at the end of the report.

If you are using the Footnote and Endnote feature of your word processing program, it will automatically insert a superscript number and place the endnote at the end of your document.

Exercise 13-1 PROOFREAD AND MARK

Proofread the following paragraph from a bound report. Use the appropriate proofreaders' marks to correct the errors. If the line is correct, write **C** to the left of the number.

1. Deere & Company, with Headquarters in Moline Illinois is

2. one of the worlds oldest and respected most companis. Deere

3. & Com. manufactures, distributes and finance a full line of

4. agriculturel equipment, as well as a braod range of

5. construction and forestry equipment.

JOB SEARCH DOCUMENTS

Three documents are crucial to a person's application for employment—a resume (also called a data sheet or vita), an application (cover) letter, and (following an interview) a follow-up letter. Because of the importance of these documents in the employment process, each should show the employer the highest standard of work of which the applicant is capable. Since each document should be submitted without error, careful proofreading is crucial.

Resume

Prospective employers use resumes to screen individuals for an interview. As such, the resume should summarize a person's background in several important sections—personal, education, work experience, and related activities. Other sections might include your career objective, summary of qualifications, computer experience, and references.

The most common resume formats are chronological, functional, and combination. The **chronological format** lists your employment history in reverse chronological order, with your most recent employment first. This resume emphasizes your work stability and experience.

The **functional resume** focuses attention on your qualifications or skills rather than on your past employment history. Applicable skills may include areas such as communication, management, human relations, and computer software. The functional resume is appropriate for applicants who lack related work experience or who have gaps in their employment history.

The **combination resume** takes advantage of the best features of both the chronological and the functional resume. The combination resume emphasizes the applicant's skills or qualifications and includes a job history.

◆ Personal

This section is at the top of the page and includes your name, home address, e-mail address, and telephone number(s). Do not include a telephone number or an e-mail address from your current place of employment.

◆ Education

This section should include the name and address of the schools attended—the most recent one listed first (reverse chronological order). Only the city and state are needed as the address. It is also appropriate to include the dates you attended each school, your GPA, and those courses that have provided special preparation for the desired position.

◆ Work Experience

In this section you should list any previously held jobs, even though they may not directly relate to the desired job. Whether you have worked in agriculture, a service industry, or an office position, a prospective employer is interested in your experience in working with people, your attitude toward work, and your values. Work experience shows the prospective employer that you know how to take initiative and responsibility for your actions.

◆ Related Activities

This section shows your involvement in organizations and athletics during your years in school, as well as any awards, honors, or scholarships you may have received. Include the name of the organization, as well as the time you were a member, and indicate any officer positions you may have held.

◆ Optional Sections

Try to limit the resume to one page. What differentiates you from all other applicants? If the information is not important to an employer, it should not be included on your resume.

Since many jobs today require specific computer experience, consider having a separate section that identifies your background in computers. You might also include this information under "education."

While a separate "references" section was important in the past, most employers today are not interested in a list of references until later in the interview process. For example, an employer might request a list of references from the top candidates. Instead of listing references on your resume, take a separate list with you to the interview. Each entry on this list should include the name and courtesy title of the person; his or her official title (coach, teacher, principal, supervisor); complete mailing address; telephone number(s); and e-mail address. Always ask for permission before listing someone as a reference.

Many companies now request a resume as an electronic submission. The computer looks for key words and phrases during the scanning process and selects only those resumes that included those key words. Information on your resume should be formatted so that the reader can understand it easily. Figure 13-2 illustrates a correctly formatted resume.

Teachers may be used as references if they give you their permission.

© DIGITAL VISION

Application (Cover) Letter

The application (cover) letter should be keyed on plain paper with a return address, as described in Chapter 12. The body of the letter should include three to five paragraphs.

You should begin the first paragraph by identifying the position; telling the reader where you heard of the position (placement office, newspaper ad, counselor, teacher, etc.); explaining what you understand the title of the position to be; and saying that you are a candidate for the job.

In the middle paragraphs of the letter, you should briefly tell the reader about your interest in and background for the job. Discuss your key qualifications, education, and work experience as they relate to this position; do not repeat everything listed on your resume. In this section you should also state that you are enclosing your resume.

Because an interview is a crucial aspect of any employer's decision process, in the last paragraph you should ask for an interview at the reader's convenience. It is appropriate to suggest specific dates. If you end the paragraph by calling attention to your address and telephone number "on the enclosed resume," the reader will most likely look at the resume in more detail. Figure 13-3 shows a sample application letter.

JANEEN K. GENTRY
218 South Andrew
Whitewater, WI 53190-1118
608.555.0168
janeen.gentry@auburn.net

EDUCATION

Northview Public Schools, Whitewater, Wisconsin, 2003–2007
    (Will receive high school diploma, May 2007)
    Graduated with High Honors (3.65 on a 4.00 scale)

Special Preparation:
    Completed courses in English, math, science, and business
    Key 65 words per minute

COMPUTER SOFTWARE EXPERIENCE

Experienced in using the following software applications:
Word, PowerPoint, Microsoft Excel, Microsoft Access, and PageMaker

WORK EXPERIENCE

<u>Administrative Assistant</u>, Dayton Office Supplies, Inc., Fort Atkinson,
    Wisconsin, May 2005–December 2006
    Worked 15 hours each week after school and on weekends

Responsibilities:
- Answered telephones
- Deposited cash
- Stocked and ordered supplies
- Trained employees in using Word and PowerPoint

RELATED ACTIVITIES

National Honor Society, 2007
Student Council Senior Class Representative, 2007
Future Business Leaders of America
    President, 2006, and Publicity Committee Chair, 2005
Volleyball and Soccer, 2006

Figure 13-2 Sample Resume

218 South Andrew
Whitewater, WI 53190-1118
May 23, 200-

Ms. Rita Joseph
Human Resources Department
Hummel Manufacturing
37 Main Street
Whitewater, WI 53190-4498

Dear Ms. Joseph:

Mr. Timothy Tabin, my business teacher at Northview High School, told me about the opening you have at Hummel Manufacturing for a technical assistant. Please consider me an applicant for this position.

As you will see from the enclosed resume, I will graduate next week from Northview High School. In addition to taking advanced courses in English, math, and science, I worked with Mr. Tabin in training students in word processing and desktop publishing. I am comfortable working with most software applications, and I am a quick learner.

I have worked part-time at Dayton Office Supplies, Inc. During my time there, I have been given increased responsibilities. I was also commended by my supervisor for my human relations skills and technical competence in using software applications.

I would appreciate the opportunity to discuss with you my qualifications for this position. I will telephone you next week to request an appointment, or you may call me at your convenience at (608) 555-0168.

Sincerely,

Janeen K. Gentry

Enclosure

Figure 13-3   Sample Application (Cover) Letter

Follow-up Letter

After you have had an interview, you should send a short thank-you note to the interviewer, expressing your appreciation and explaining again your interest in the job. Your thank-you note should be sent within 24 hours after the interview. Figure 13-4 illustrates a sample follow-up letter.

Figure 13-4

Sample Follow-Up Letter

218 South Andrew
Whitewater, WI 53190-1118
June 2, 200-

Ms. Rita Joseph
Human Resources Department
Hummel Manufacturing
37 Main Street
Whitewater, WI 53190-4498

Dear Ms. Joseph:

Thank you for meeting with me yesterday about the technical assistant position at your company. Your description of what the job requires was very helpful in learning what would be expected of me. I particularly liked the opportunity to tour the company and to meet with members of your technical team.

As a result of our meeting and the tour, I am even more interested in being a part of the "Systems Team" and helping Hummel Manufacturing meet its objectives.

If you need additional information, please let me know. I'm excited about the possibility of working for your company.

Sincerely,

Janeen K. Gentry

CONFUSED AND MISUSED WORDS

lean   *adj.* thin; not fat; meager; *v.* to slant away from a vertical position

lien   *n.* the right to sell property of a debtor

Ted is a very **lean** person.

The mortgage company has a **lien** on their house.

may be   *v.* to be allowed or permitted to

maybe   *adv.* perhaps; possibly

We **may be** able to tour downtown Chicago tomorrow.

Maybe we should send her an e-mail.

personal *adj.* private; pertaining to a particular person

personnel *n.* people employed; staff of a company

They made a **personal** choice not to attend.

All **personnel** arrived at 9:30 a.m.

• **Proofread technical material and legal descriptions in pairs.**

• **When proofreading a lengthy report, proofread all similar parts as a separate step. For example, check the format of all side headings; then check all paragraph headings. Check separately the continuity and sequence of all numbered pages, tables, and figures.**

• **When preparing a multipage document, prepare a style sheet to show how unusual features, such as names, titles, or terminology, will be handled.**

PROOFREADING APPLICATIONS

Exercise 13-2 PARAGRAPHS FROM A REPORT

Proofread the following paragraphs from a report, and mark all format errors using the appropriate proofreaders' marks. If the line is correct, write **C** to the left of the number.

1. **Germany**

2. History

3. Germany was immersed in two devastating World Wars in the first

4. half of the twentieth century and was occupied by the victorious

5. Allied powers of the United States, the United Kingdom, France, and

6. the Soviet Union in 1945. With the start of the Cold War, two

7. German states were formed in1949: the Federal Republic of

8. Germany (FRG) and the German Democratic Republic (GDR).

9. Geography

10. Germany is located in Central Europe and borders the Baltic Sea

11. and the North Sea. The total land area is 349,223 square kilometers.

12. Government

13. Germany is a federal republic with its capital located in Berlin.

14. Germany has 16 states. Unification of East Germany and West

15. Germany took place on October 3, 1990.

Exercise 13-3 SPELLING AND WORD USAGE CHECK

Compare the words in Column A with the corresponding words in Column B. Use the appropriate proofreaders' marks to correct the misspelled or misused words. If both columns are correct, write **C** to the left of the number.

Column A	Column B
1. commission	comission
2. quantity	quanity
3. tomorrow	tomorrow
4. financial	finantial
5. preperation	preparation
6. offerred	offered
7. permissable	permissible
8. approximately	approximatly
9. disatisfied	dissatisfied
10. guarantee	guarentee
11. knowledgeable	knowledgeable
12. counselor	counseler
13. Dodd Associates has experienced some lien years.	The marker leans to the south.
14. Josh maybe able to help us.	May be the time is right!
15. Let's not make this personal.	Our company has hired personal for the new Macon plant.

Exercise 13-4 INTERNATIONAL VOCABULARY

Compare the Spanish words in Column A with the corresponding words in Column B. If the word in Column B is different from the word in Column A, use the appropriate proofreaders' marks to correct Column B. If the words in both columns are the same, write **C** to the left of the number.

Column A	Column B
1. acantilado	acantilado
2. coleccionista	colecionitsa
3. entusiasmar	entusasmar
4. llamamiento	llamemiento
5. telegrama	telegrama

Exercise 13-5 REPORT

Proofread the following report; and correct all formatting, grammar, and spelling errors using the appropriate proofreaders' marks.

WALES

One part of Great Britain that is not too well known is the country of Wales. Wales is located on a peninsula directly across the Irish Sea from Ireland. The peninsula is approximately 130 miles long from north to south and approximitely 95 miles from east to west at its widest point. Wales is part of Great Britain, as is Scotland and England. England lies to the east of Wales, and Scotland lies to the northeast of Wales (and to the north of England).

Geography

Wales is a very mountainous country, with Mount Snowdon at 3,500 feet in northern Wales being the highest point in England and Wales. Slate quarrying was a major source of employment in northern Wales for many years. In recent years other types of building materials has replaced slate, and it is no longer as prominent in the Welsh economy.

Some of the world's finest coalfields for steam coal are located in the mountainous part of southern Wales. Many people have gained an impression of Welsh coal minors and their way of life from scenes in the movie *How Green Was My Valley*. The movie, based on the book by the same name by Richard Llewellyn, was set in the Rhondda Valley of southern Wales. Over the years, as alternate forms of energy were developed, the demand for steam coal decreased. Today very few mines are still open.

Language

One of the distinctive features of Wales is its language—Welsh. Many people consider it to be a difficult language to learn until they find out that *w* and *y* are considered vowels. Some of the sounds of Welsh letters are different from those in English. For example, an *f* is pronounced like a *v*. The word *Gymanfa* is pronounced "gih-MAHN-vah."

Some other unique sounds in the Welsh language is the ones for *dd* and *ll*. The *dd* is pronounced like "th" in the English word *the*. Therefore, in the Welsh word *Eisteddfod,* the middle syllable is pronounced "teth" rather than "ted."

The *ll* sound requires that the speaker place the tip of his or her tongue at the top of the back side of the front teeth and then carefully blow out each side. This technique is used twice in pronounceing the name of the city Llangollen and the author Llewellyn.

Conclusion

Much more could be written about this small country and its contribution to music, the arts, politics, the economy, etc. It is a "region of great . . . beauty."[1]

_____

[1]The Encyclopedia Americana, International Edition, S.V. "Wales."

Exercise 13-6 APPLICATION LETTER

Proofread the following letter; and correct all formatting, grammar, and spelling errors using the appropriate proofreaders' marks.

433 Spring Street
Idaho Falls, ID 83403-9044
June 15, 200-

Mr. Lamont Herbert
Personnel Division
CAS Financial Services
1005 Underwood Avenue
Idaho Falls, ID 83403-4980

Dear Mr. Herbert:

Mr. Mario Guzman, counselor at Lexington High School, has informed me that you have an opening for an assistant bank teller. Because I am very interested in working in the finantial services industry, please consider me a candidate for the position.

As you will see from the enclosed resume, I have a lot of related work experience. I worked for Wells Fargo Bank on a part-time basis for approximatly two years. I also worked as a telemarketing representative where I offered warranties/guarantees to prospective customers. In this position I learn the importance of accuracy, dependability, and efficiency. None of my past employers has been dissatisfied with my work.

I would appreciate the opportunity to meet with you the first week of July to discuss how I can contribute to your companys success. I will call your office next week to inquire about setting up an appointment. If you would like to contact me before then, you may use the address and telephone number listed at the top of my resume.

Sincerely,

Micaela Roush

Enclosure

Exercise 13-7   RESUME

Proofread the following resume; and correct all formatting, abbreviation, capitalization, and spelling errors using the appropriate proofreaders' marks.

MICAELA Roush
433 Spring Street
Idaho Falls, ID 83403-9044
804.555.0140
micaelaroush@express.com

Education

Lexington High School, Idaho Falls, Idaho, 2001–2005
Received high school diploma, May 2005
Graduated with highest honors (3.99 on 4.00 scale)

Special Courses:
Desktop Publishing, Business Communications, Business Law, and Economics

COMPUTER Experience

Familiar with the following software applications: PageMaker, Microsoft Word, Microsoft Access, and PowerPoint

SCHOOL Activities

Varsity Basketball, 2003–2005; Captain, 2004–2005
Spanish Club, 2001–2005; Vice President, 2004–2005
Lexington Business Club, 2002–2004

WORK EXPEREINCE

Northwest Bank, Idaho Falls, Idaho
Assistant Teller, Worked 20 hours per week, 2003–2005
Responsibilities:
• Served customers
• Balanced night deposits
• Completed application forms

Brickhof Telemarketing Communications, Idaho Falls, ID
Customer Service Representative, 2004–2005
Responsibilities:
• Answered customer questions
• Sold warranties and guarentees

PROOFREADING AT THE COMPUTER

Exercise 13-8 APPLICATION LETTER

1. Open 13-08 from the Chapter 13 folder on the Student CD. (This is a computer copy of Application 13-6.)

2. Proofread and correct all errors on the screen copy that you indicated with proofreaders' marks in Application 13-6. Use the spelling checker.

3. Produce the letter in block format following the standard procedures described in the previous chapters.

Exercise 13-9 RESUME

1. Open 13-09 from the Chapter 13 folder on the Student CD.

2. Proofread the resume on the screen. Correct all errors.

3. Produce the resume following the standard procedures.

Exercise 13-10 E-MAIL MESSAGE

1. Open 13-10 from the Chapter 13 folder on the Student CD.

2. Proofread the e-mail message on the screen. Correct all errors.

3. Produce the e-mail message following the standard procedures.

CUMULATIVE APPLICATION

Exercise 13-11 UNBOUND REPORT

Proofread the following two-page unbound report, and correct all errors using the appropriate proofreaders' marks.

THE VALUE OF BUSINESS COMMUNICATION SKILLS

The world in which we work has seen an explosion of changes in the ways we communicate in a global society. No longer must we rely entirely on a hard copy of a business document to be sent by mail from one location to another. Instead, information may be send electronically by satellite, by computer, by electronic mail, etc. Depending on the channel used, messages that are critical in making a decision may be received within seconds of the time they are sent.

Regardless of the channel used to send a business message, the writer of a message must have a basic understanding of language skills. These basic skill include excellent grammar, spelling, and punctuation skills. They include the ability to analyze an audience an to determine the purpose of a message. They also include the ability to edit and revise a document. Without basic language skills, the technology used in preparing a business document is of little value.

A business writer must also be an excellent proofreaders and catch errors in format, word use, spelling, and punctuation. Perhaps an even more important concept is that the writer must understand some of the complexities of writing business documents. "Quantity" in writing is not important, but "quality is important.

Sequence of Ideas

One basic fact that writers must understand is the importance of using the right sequence of ideas in a business document to provide the the greatest impact on the reader. When a person decides to write a business document, one of the first questions to be answered are "What will be the impact on the reader? Will he or she be pleased with the content? Will he or she be disappointed? Will he or she be neutral in his or her reaction?" The answers to those questions provide a clue as to the sequence the writer should use in creating the communication.

Deductive Sequence. If the writer assumes that the readers reaction will be neutral or pleasant, the correct sequence of ideas is to use a deductive approach. With a deductive approach, the writer starts with the main idea in the first sentence. This is then followed with details that elaborate on the main idea.

Inductive Sequence. If the writer assumes that the reader will be disappointed with the message or must be persuaded to do something he or she may not ordinarily do, the writer should use an indirect approach. The direct approach starts with a neutral beginning and is followed by a detailed explanation of details. To further lesson the impact on the reader, the negative answer should be placed somewhere in the middle paragraphs.

Careful attention to the sequence of ideas in a business document will make the message even more effective, and the communication will have it's maximum impact. As Guffey states, "The most successful players in this new world of work will be those with highly developed communication skills."[1]

Do you have what it takes to be a successful player? Let's hope so!

---

[1]Mary Ellen Guffey, <u>Essentials of Business Communication</u>, 6th Edition (Cincinnati: Thomson/South-Western, 2004), 4.

CHAPTER

14

Editing for Content, Clarity, and Conciseness

Spotlight on ACCURACY

Like the letter of application in the job search, a resume briefly summarizes your qualifications for the job for which you are applying. This document, too, must be perfect—without *any* errors. How do you think a prospective employer might react to the following statements in your resume?

- Attended the University of Ohio from 1892–1997.

- Graduated Magna Cum Loud.

- A position that allows me to use my superior commuter skills.

- My GPA at night is 3.2 (4.0).

Objectives

- Edit a message for completeness, correctness, and consistency in content.

- Edit a message for conciseness by avoiding redundancy and eliminating unnecessary modifiers.

- Edit a message for clarity by using simple words; avoiding trite, overused expressions; and presenting ideas logically.

- Distinguish between active and passive voice.

- Spell correctly 12 frequently misspelled words.

- Use correctly three sets of commonly confused and misused words.

WHAT IS EDITING?

As you know, **proofreading** is the process of locating mechanical errors that may occur because of incorrect keying, spelling, capitalization, grammar, punctuation, abbreviation, word division, number usage, and formatting. **Editing** involves checking copy to see that every aspect of the content is correct and that the message is clear, concise, and complete. Editing may also require changing words, correcting errors, and rewriting parts of the document.

Editing and proofreading are two distinct activities that must be performed separately. The objectives of both, however, are the same—to improve the quality of the final copy and to make the intended message clear so that no possibility of misunderstanding or misinterpretation exists. Once copy is edited, however, it must be proofread a second time for accuracy. It is impossible to edit the content of a message and proofread for mechanical errors at the same time.

EDITING FOR CONTENT

Editing for content involves checking to see that the message is accurate. All facts, figures, and calculations must be correct. If errors in content exist, the reader may lose confidence in the writer. Correctness shows competence and regard for the reader.

The best way to locate content errors is to read the document carefully, at a natural, unhurried rate, and concentrate on what you are reading. As you read, be alert for:

• Incomplete information (omission of essential information).

• Incorrect facts (names, dates, addresses, numbers, etc.).

• Inconsistency in the way material is written (style and format).

• Incorrect usage of words, especially **homophones** (words that sound alike but differ in spelling and meaning). Examples: cite, site, sight; right, rite, wright, write; sell, cell; sail, sale.

It is important to realize that the editing changes may vary due to the proofreader's understanding and interpretation of the material. Therefore, the proofreader must make sure that the editing changes retain the message the writer intended to convey.

Complete Information

Editing a message for completeness means checking to see that all necessary information is included. How puzzling it is to discover that the enclosures mentioned in a letter have not been included. How frustrating it is not to be able to make a business decision because important information has been omitted. When possible, answer the "who, what, when, where, and why" information in bulleted items rather than in long, drawn-out sentences.

To assure completeness, reread the message and check to see that dates, addresses, times, and other factual information are included. Make sure that any enclosures mentioned in the letter are indeed enclosed.

Check for omissions of copy by comparing the final copy with the rough draft or the original document source. Reading the wrong column or the wrong line results in material being omitted, especially in long or complex documents. Skipping a word or a whole line also leads to omissions. Likewise, if information has been transferred from one document to another, double-check to make sure that nothing has been omitted.

To avoid omissions in tables and lists, use a helpful device such as a card, a ruler, or a piece of paper. Laying the straight edge of the card, the ruler, or the paper under the line you are reading helps focus your attention.

Correct Facts

"The meeting will be held from Wednesday through Friday, September 15–18." This statement is confusing. Since *Wednesday* is *September 15*, *Friday* is definitely not *September 18*. Did the writer intend to say *Wednesday through Saturday*, *Tuesday through Friday*, *September 15–17*, or *September 16–18*?

Incorrect facts may appear in numerical data (dates, amounts, ZIP Codes, social security numbers, serial numbers, identification numbers, stock numbers, and addresses).

Unusual, unfamiliar, and foreign names (*Papadopulos*, *Teutschel*, *Shimabukuro*) as well as similar sounding names (*Johnson/Johnston*) must be checked for accuracy. Names are easily misspelled, especially because they can be spelled in so many different ways. Note the various ways the following names can be spelled:

Andersen, Anderson

Brown, Browne, Broune, Braun

Cain, Caine, Cayne, Kane, Kaine, Kayne

Carol, Carole, Carrol, Carroll

Hernandes, Hernandez

Smith, Smithe, Smythe

Schmid, Schmidt, Schmit, Schmitt

Schneider, Schneiter, Snider, Snyder

Tomson, Thomson, Thompson

Never assume you know how to spell a name; always check to see that the spelling used in the original document source is correct. In a business letter, for example, check the addressee's name in the letter address, in the salutation, within the body, and on the mailing envelope.

Locating incorrect facts is not easy. It requires concentration and attention to detail. Whenever possible, you should check the document against the rough draft or the source document. If you are not sure about the accuracy of a statement, write a question mark next to the copy to alert the writer that the message is unclear and that the statement should be revised.

Consistency

Consistency means that all similar ideas are handled the same way. Related ideas should be expressed in the same grammatical form (parallel structure). Likewise, format within a document should be consistent. Although enumerations may be blocked at the left margin or indented, all enumerations within a document should be formatted in one style.

© GETTY IMAGES/PHOTODISC

Correct Word Usage

The proficient proofreader should be able to determine whether the correct words are used so that the reader will understand the writer's message. **Word usage** refers to how language is used to best convey the intended meaning. Words that sound alike but are spelled differently and have different meanings (homophones) must be checked carefully. Study these sentences, and notice how the italicized words are used.

There is no solution in *sight*.

The *sights* of London are breathtaking.

The *site* of the new building is convenient to public transportation.

He was *cited* for speeding.

Note: Answers to the exercises in this chapter will vary because there is often more than one acceptable answer. Remember that you must retain the meaning intended by the writer.

Exercise 14-1 PROOFREAD AND MARK

Using the factual information in the table as a reference, edit the message for content errors. Correct the message using the appropriate proofreaders' marks. Write the revised message on the blank lines.

Speaker	Dr. Elayne Rachut, Pembroke Graduate School of Business
Topic	"Preparing for Global Literacy"
Location	Foust College, Johnston City
Date	Thursday–Friday, March 21–22, 200-
Time	2:30 p.m. to 5:30 p.m., Thursday 4 p.m. to 6:30 p.m., Friday
Completion	Certificate awarded for two-day attendance
Fee	$25 for one day; $40 for two days

The three-day conference, "Preparing for Global Literacy," is scheduled for Friday–Saturday, March 14–15, at Foust College in Johnson City. Friday's session will be from 4:30 to 6:30 p.m.; Saturday's session, from 3:00 to 5:30 p.m. The workshop will be conducted by Miss Elayne Rachute, noted professor at Pembroke Business School.

_____

_____

_____

_____

_____

_____

_____

_____

Exercise 14-2 PROOFREAD AND MARK

Edit the following message for completeness. On the blank lines, list any important but missing information that you believe would make the message clearer.

Here are your travel arrangements for the three-day meeting at Foust College on March 21–22. You will fly Liberty Airlines and earn frequent flyer miles. I know you like to stay at the Royal Court Hotel. Let me know if these arrangements are satisfactory.

_____

_____

_____

EDITING FOR CLARITY

It is important to check that the words used to write messages do not confuse the reader and that ideas are presented in a clear, logical manner.

Clear and Simple Words

Clear and simple words are not only easier to write, but also easier to read. Such words help the writer say exactly what he or she means. When writing, use the same words that you would use when talking to that person face-to-face. Clear messages are more likely to be understood as they were intended. When proofreading a document, follow these guidelines to correct unclear messages.

◆ Use Familiar Words

Familiar words increase understanding. Difficult words annoy the reader and distract him or her from concentrating on the message. To achieve clarity, substitute a simpler word for a more difficult one. Compare the more difficult words in the first column with the simpler words in the second column.

DIFFICULT WORDS	SIMPLER WORDS
alternative	choice
germane	appropriate, fitting
optimum	best
oblivious	unaware

DIFFICULT WORDS	SIMPLER WORDS
provincial	unsophisticated, narrow
remuneration	pay
sagacious	keen, shrewd
substantiate	prove
verbose	wordy

◆ Use Precise Words

Words have different meanings for different people. For example, to one person, *average* may mean "mediocre"; to another person, it may mean "normal." To a customer waiting to receive an order, the word *soon* may mean "tomorrow"; to the retailer who must first obtain the merchandise from a supplier, *soon* may mean "within ten days." When editing a message for clarity, use words that help convey the exact meaning.

Appropriate Words

Some words and expressions are outdated or overused. Inappropriate words and expressions do not impress a reader. They imply that the writer did not try hard enough to express ideas in a simple-to-understand manner. Apply the following guidelines to help make a message clear.

◆ Avoid Cliches

Cliches are ready-made expressions. They are dull, overused, sometimes old-fashioned, and trite. Avoid cliches and use language that is more appropriate. Cliches are especially confusing to people whose first language is not English. Here are some examples of cliches.

a stick-in-the-mud
barking up the wrong tree
bite off more than you can chew
jump on the bandwagon
keep your head above water
keep your nose to the grindstone
the bottom line
the head honcho or the big enchilada
the tip of the iceberg
throw in the towel
turn over a new leaf
a day late and a dollar short

◆ Eliminate Overused Words and Expressions

Replace overused words and expressions with exact words. In the following examples, notice that the words in the second column are more direct and clearer than the words in the first column.

OVERUSED EXPRESSIONS	EXACT EXPRESSIONS
acknowledge receipt of	received
at your earliest convenience	immediately, tomorrow, Friday
due to the fact that	because
enclosed herewith	here is
enclosed please find	enclosed is
in spite of the fact that	although
in the near future	within __ days
in the event that	should, if
pursuant to your request	as requested, you asked
thanking you in advance	thank you
under separate cover	in another package, separately
would like to recommend	recommend

Logical Organization

Well-organized messages are easy to read and understand. All ideas within a business letter, for example, should generally support one primary purpose. Likewise, each sentence within a paragraph should focus on one central idea or concept. When editing for clarity, ask yourself these questions:

- Is the main idea or purpose of the message clear to the reader?

- Does each paragraph express one idea?

- Do all of the paragraphs support the main idea of the message?

- Is there a logical relationship that binds all of the parts of the message together?

- Does one idea flow easily into another?

Exercise 14-3 PROOFREAD AND MARK

Edit the following message for clarity using the appropriate proofreaders' marks. Write the revised message on the blank lines.

Enclosed herewith is the information pursuant to your request of February 10. In the event that you find these accommodations germane for your business trip next month, I would like to recommend the optimum hotels in the city.

_____

_____

_____

_____

_____

_____

Exercise 14-4 PROOFREAD AND MARK

Edit the following message for clarity using the appropriate proofreaders' marks. Write the revised message on the blank lines.

So that you won't be barking up the wrong tree, I have listed two lodging alternatives where you will be comfortable. Remember to obtain receipts for your expenses to substantiate business expenses to the head honcho so that you can be remunerated for out-of-pocket expenses.

_____

_____

_____

_____

_____

_____

Exercise 14-5 PROOFREAD AND MARK

Edit the following message for clarity using the appropriate proofreaders' marks. Write the revised message on the blank lines.

Due to the fact that fiscal budget preparations will begin in the near future, the bottom line is that we must have all of the essential facts regarding operations before the first meeting.

_____

_____

_____

_____

_____

_____

EDITING FOR CONCISENESS

Conciseness means saying only what is necessary to send the intended message to a reader. Conciseness requires eliminating unnecessary words or repetitious ideas. Businesspeople appreciate messages that make each word count. Concise messages have impact.

Unnecessary Words and Modifiers

Follow these guidelines to achieve conciseness:

- **Delete** phrases such as *I believe* or *in my opinion*. Generally, what is stated is the writer's belief. However, such expressions can serve the purpose of conciliation or diplomacy. They can soften criticism too.

- Revise sentences that begin with *There is/are* or *Here is/are* whenever possible.

- Avoid using unnecessary modifiers; say *unique*, not *absolutely unique*, or *perfect* instead of *almost perfect* or *nearly perfect*.

Note in the table on the next page how the words in the right column have greater impact than those in the left column.

WORDY	CONCISE
as a matter of fact	in fact, indeed
at the present time	now
basic fundamentals	basics
come to the conclusion	conclude
consensus of opinion	consensus
during the time that	while
each and every	each, every (do not use both)
end result	result
feel free to	please
for the amount of $250	for $250
free gift	gift
in spite of the fact that	even though
in the amount of	for (give exact amount)
in the near future	soon, on (exact date)
past history	history
true facts	facts

Active Versus Passive Voice

Voice indicates whether the subject is performing the action or receiving the action of the verb. The **active voice** portrays the subject as performing the action and assigns responsibility to someone or something. For example, in the sentence "The accountant wrote the report," the subject *accountant* is performing the action of the verb.

The **passive voice** portrays the subject as receiving the action of the verb. "The report was written by the accountant" is expressed in the passive voice and shows the subject *report* receiving the action of the verb. The passive voice is also used to de-emphasize a negative message. Generally, business messages are written in the active voice. As the examples on the following page illustrate, the active voice is forceful and concise.

ACTIVE VOICE	PASSIVE VOICE
The instructor selected the software for the course.	The software for the course has been selected by the instructor.
Verify the facts before writing the report.	The facts should be verified before the report is written.
You did not submit your report on time.	Your report was not submitted on time. (de-emphasizes the negative message)

© GETTY IMAGES/PHOTODISC

Active voice: The council members reached an agreement on Thursday.

Passive voice: An agreement was reached by the council members on Thursday.

Exercise 14-6 PROOFREAD AND MARK

Edit these sentences to make them more concise. Rewrite each sentence on the blank lines. Convert sentences written in the passive voice to the active voice.

1. There are several ideas that I would very much like to introduce at the staff meeting.

   _____

   _____

   _____

2. In my opinion, this report lacks the basic fundamentals needed to come to the conclusion that the budget be increased.

   _____

   _____

   _____

3. As a result of last week's increase in sales, all sales staff may anticipate receiving bonuses in the near future.

   _____

   _____

   _____

4. The past history indicates that the agents are always late whenever they must submit their reports.

   _____

   _____

   _____

5. It is my personal opinion that we should continue on with the project.

   _____

   _____

   _____

CONFUSED AND MISUSED WORDS

quiet	*adj.* calm; opposite of noisy
quit	*v.* to stop; to resign
quite	*adv.* completely; considerably

You must be **quiet** when working in the library.

I may **quit** my job.

Kirk didn't **quite** understand your directions.

recent	*adj.* occurring at a time immediately prior to the present; modern or new
resent	*v.* to feel anger from a sense of being injured or offended
re-sent	*v.* (past tense of *resend*) sent again

Jolene's **recent** haircut looks great!

Will you **resent** not being asked to run the meeting?

Dell **re-sent** the statement last week.

seas	*n. pl.* continuous bodies of salt water
sees	*v.* (third-person form of *see*) to perceive with the eye; to observe; to view
seize	*v.* to grasp suddenly and forcibly; to take or grab

Cruise ships sail the seven **seas**.

Lynda always **sees** the best in people.

The government can **seize** your assets if you don't pay your taxes.

PEP Tip

- **Read the document at a normal, unhurried pace when editing so that you can concentrate on what you are reading.**

- **Wait a few minutes before you edit your own writing. You may find mistakes that you would have otherwise overlooked.**

- **Edit the document for one specific purpose at a time. For example, first check the accuracy of facts. Then check for completeness, conciseness, and clarity.**

- **Proofread for mechanical errors after you have edited the document.**

PROOFREADING APPLICATIONS

Exercise 14-7 MESSAGES

Edit the following messages for completeness and clarity using the appropriate proofreaders' marks. Write your revision on the blank lines. Convert sentences in the passive voice to the active voice.

1. Enclosed please find your travel arrangements for the two-day conference at Reedley College on October 20–22. Attendees will be staying in the campus dorms. I would like to recommend that you take time to visit the Gourmet Garden for lunch or dinner while in town.

   _____

   _____

   _____

   _____

2. Due to the fact that the board meeting is in the near future, a decision needs to be made on what to order in for lunch. We must make these arrangements early in spite of the fact that the restaurant is very accommodating.

   _____

   _____

   _____

   _____

3. As a result of last week's study session, Mark's and Lucy's test grades are up.

   _____

   _____

4. In my opinion, this is the most successful fund-raiser we have ever had; and I think a decision should be made to have it again next year.

   _____

   _____

   _____

5. There are some issues that I want to be sure to discuss with each and every student at the next student council meeting.

   _____

   _____

Exercise 14-8 SPELLING AND WORD USAGE CHECK

Compare the words in Column A with the corresponding words in Column B. Use the appropriate proofreaders' marks to correct the misspelled or misused words. If both columns are correct, write **C** to the left of the number.

Column A	Column B
1. adequate	adquate
2. admissable	admissible
3. capacity	capacity
4. continueing	continuing
5. dependant	dependent
6. familiar	familar
7. miscellaneous	miscellanous
8. practise	practice
9. referrence	reference
10. resturant	restaurant
11. accessable	accessible
12. immediately	immedaitely
13. The audit went quite well.	We had quiet a scare.
14. Bring a resent photo.	I re-sent the bill.
15. Dr. Orozco sees only babies.	Our motto is "Seas the Day!"

Exercise 14-9 INTERNATIONAL VOCABULARY

Compare the Spanish words in Column A with the corresponding words in Column B. If the word in Column B is different from the word in Column A, use the appropriate proofreaders' marks to correct Column B. If the words in both columns are the same, write **C** to the left of the number.

1. saludable	saludabel
2. sopa	soap
3. sorprender	sorrprender
4. suelo	suelo
5. teletrabajo	teletrarbajo

Exercise 14-10   BUSINESS LETTER

Work with a partner to edit the following letter for correctness, conciseness, and clarity in content. Supply additional information, if necessary, to make the message more complete and clearer. Facts: Letter was addressed to Ms. Nereyda Garza-Lozano, 1101 East University, Fresno, CA 93741-0765, in block style with open punctuation. The correct information is printed in the table on page 239.

Teamwork

STATE CENTER COMMUNITY COLLEGE DISTRICT
1525 East Weldon Avenue, Fresno, CA 93741-2312
(509) 555-0110 Fax: (509) 555-0170
Email: sccd@brakenet.com

September 8, 200-

Ms. Nereyda Garza-Lozano
1101 East University
Fresno, CA 93741-0765

Dear Ms. Garza-Lozano

Congratulations are in order! Your proposal for a study abroad program to Salamanca, Spain, was approved by the board of trustees during the time that they met last night. You are authorized to move forward with plans at the present time.

In spite of the fact that the budget is tight, the board believes that a trip such as this is one that each and every one of our students should have the opportunity to experience. Our office staff will prepare a flyer for you pursuant to your request. We will print copies in the amount of 500 for distribution to students. If you require more, feel free to request them. Due to the fact that there are so many details, please check the following information for accuracy.

Academic Courses

Spanish 1	Beginning	4 units
Spanish 2	High Beginning	4 units
Spanish 3	Intermediate or Spanish 3NS (for native speakers)	3 units
Spanish 4	Intermediate or Spanish 4NS (for native speakers)	4 units
Spanish 5	The Short Story (Spain)	3 units
Spanish 6	The Short Story (Latin America)	3 units
Spanish 7	Advanced Grammar and Composition	3 units
Spanish 8	Advanced Conversation	3 units

Ms. Nereyda Garza-Lozano
Page 2
September 28, 200-

Flights
Departure from Fresno to Madrid: June 2, 200-. Our flight is scheduled to leave at
7:15 a.m. Be at the airport by 5:15 a.m.

Return from Madrid to Fresno; July 20, 2000-. We are scheduled to arrive in Fresno at
8:45 p.m.

Passports
Because this is an international flight, you will be required to carry a passport. If you do
not have a current passport, please apply for one immediately. The process can take up to
two months. You can obtain an application form at any post office (or online at
http://www.usps.com) or at many public libraries.

Payment Information
Program fee is $4,500, which includes round-trip air and ground transportation from Fresno
to Salamanca and housing with a Spanish family (including breakfast and lunch and
dinner). Application deadline is March 1, 200-, with a deposit of $550; balance of $3,900 is
due by March 24, 200-. Deposit is nonrefundable. Students are enrolled on a first-come,
first-served basis.

Please notify me immediately of any necessary corrections. Keep up the good work—this is
a wonderful opportunity for our students. Thank you for your service.

Sincerely

Mr. Kim Quesada
Administrator

rrh

Academic Courses		
Spanish 1	Beginning	4 units
Spanish 2	High Beginning	4 units
Spanish 3	Intermediate or Spanish 3NS (for native speakers)	4 units
Spanish 4	High Intermediate or Spanish 4NS (for native speakers)	4 units
Spanish 5	The Short Story (Spain)	3 units
Spanish 6	The Short Story (Latin America)	3 units
Spanish 7	Advanced Grammar and Composition	3 units
Spanish 8	Advanced Conversation	3 units
Flights		
June 2, 200-: Fresno to Madrid; 7:15 a.m. departure		
July 2, 200-: Madrid to Fresno; 8:45 p.m. arrival		
Payment Information		
Program fee is $4,500, which includes round-trip air and ground transportation from Fresno to Salamanca and housing with a Spanish family (including breakfast and lunch or dinner). Application deadline is March 1, 200-, with a deposit of $550; balance of $3,950 is due by March 24, 200-. Deposit is nonrefundable. Students are enrolled on a first-come, first-served basis.		

Exercise 14-11 BROCHURE

Edit the following brochure text for correctness, clarity, and conciseness. Then proofread for mechanical errors.

SENSIBLE EATING ON THE ROAD

Don't be a stick-in-the-mud about your eating habits while you are traveling. It is easy to follow a sensible diet while you're at home where everything is familiar. When you travel, however, you must practice a different discipline. Try these healthy, easy-to-follow rules for eating on a plane or in a restaurant.

Eat a good, healthy breakfast. A healthy breakfast includes whole wheat toast, cereal (hot or cold with skimmed milk), and fresh fruit—not canned. Special dietetic menus are sometimes available pursuant to your request on flights, so check on this before the departure date.

If you are eating later than usual, counting lunch as dinner and keeping the entree on the lean side is a good idea. The amount of food served in restaurants at lunch is usually smaller than what is served at dinner—and it costs less too. Use salad dressing sparingly. If you are dining buffet style, take only one small serving. Don't go back for seconds in spite of the fact that you may want to.

Develop a habit of eating healthful snacks, such as fresh fruits and vegetables, and keep them handy. You can use them to keep your head above water between meals. Another good habit is to drink a lot of water; it fills you up. The fact of the matter is that you should drink eight cups of water each day. Water is a great substitute for sweet, syrupy soft drinks. If possible, avoid caffeine; it stimulates your appetite and may cause nervousness and insomnia.

Use these tips whenever you travel, never throw in the towel. Eat right and stay healthy!

PROOFREADING AT THE COMPUTER

Exercise 14-12   MANUSCRIPT

1. Open 14-12 from the Chapter 14 folder on the Student CD. (This is a computer copy of Application 14-11.)

2. Edit the text for correctness, conciseness, and clarity, using the marked copy for Application 14-11. Use the spelling checker.

3. Produce the manuscript following the standard procedures described in the previous chapters.

Exercise 14-13   EXCERPT FROM NEWSPAPER COLUMN

1. Open 14-13 from the Chapter 14 folder on the Student CD.

2. Edit the text for correctness, conciseness, and clarity. Use the spelling checker.

3. Produce the document following the standard procedures.

Exercise 14-14   E-MAIL MESSAGE

1. Open 14-14 from the Chapter 14 folder on the Student CD.

2. Edit the text for correctness, conciseness, and clarity. Use the spelling checker.

3. Produce the document following the standard procedures.

CUMULATIVE APPLICATION

> **Exercise 14-15** BUSINESS LETTER

Proofread and correct all errors using the appropriate proofreaders' marks. Facts: Letter was addressed to Mr. Alfonso Farentino, 4098 Bellflower Road, Aiken, SC 29808-8616, in block style with mixed punctuation.

TWENTIETH CENTURY BUSINESS COLLEGE
400 Broadway • Aiken, SC 29802-1532
(803) 555-0122 Fax: (803) 555-0123
E-mail: century@sccom.com

Mr. Alfonso Farentino

4098 Bellflower Road

Aiken, SC 29808-8616

Dear Mr. Farentino

Dean Stephanie Quiring informed me that you have completed all of the requirements for the advanced course in Business Administration. I understand that you are now submitting your application for employment to a number of inter-national companies recommended by our Placement Department.

Congratulations! I am confident that you will be successful in obtaining employment within a very short time.

While obtaining employment is your primary concern now, I strongly encourage you to take the long view and to consider your career in relation to other factors that will come into play as you advance in your profession—your work, your family, you continuing education, and your social life.

Your work. Because work will be a major part of your life, you must be prepared to make adjustments, if not sacrifices, to accommodate yourself to the urgencies and requirements of your chosen field. You may be asked to work a few hours of uncompensated

Mr. Alfonso Farentino

Page 2

(current date)

overtime, you may have to come in early and leave late when the workload is heavy, or you may be forced to postpone a vacation during the busy season. This is the name of the game, and it may well be the pattern for many years—at least until you establish yourself in your career. Don't be stubborn; accept it graciously.

<u>Your family</u>. Your family must come first. But there's no denying the fact that there will be times when you must make a difficult decision concerning the little League game you promise to attend but can't, the school play starring your daughter that gets lost in your're busy schedule, and the class reunion your wife is looking forward to attending but can't because of an unexpected visit by your company president.

Your continuing education. Education is an invaluable tool in your career path. It prepares you for greater responsibility and keeps you up to date on the changes and developments in your chosen field. Take advantage of this opportunity because education has an impact on your future.

<u>Your social life</u>. Socializing is important in many businesses. Train yourself to be not only an interesting dinner partner but also a desirable one. Learn how to initiate or hold a conversation, take time to learn, if not master, the basic dance steps; and develop an interest in art and music and painting. Besides being enjoyable in and of themselves, these skills can also be a factor in your career development as well as position advancement.

Before excepting any job offer, ask yourself if the company is a good fit for you. You should also stay organized; the interviews

Mr. Alfonso Farentino

Page 3

(current date)

can come quickly, and the follow-up process is important in your job search. Don't underestimate the importance of thank-you letters.

Remember that a career is more than an occupation; it is a way of life that has a bearing on the lives of everyone with who you come in contact. You will have choices to make; and if you make them wisely, they will sustain you throughout your lifetime.

Again, congratulations! I wish you the very best in what, I am confident, will be a very successful career.

Sincerely,

Eldon R. Goodsen, Ph.d.

President

tcp

CHAPTER

15

Proofreading and Editing on Computer

© STOCKBYTE GOLD

Spotlight on ACCURACY

Technology is changing the way people work, both personally and professionally. Spelling checkers, grammar checkers, online dictionaries, and voice recognition technology all work to make tasks easier. But is the technology always right? How accurate was the spelling checker in the following?

- Isn't technology grate!!

- Know won knows better than me what a difference it makes. Me own spelling checker tells my that my righting is perfect. I've maid know errors!

- This whey I don't have too rely on some won else proof reading me work for me.

- So you sea, bee smart and play the game.

- Let you spelling checker due you work for you!

Objectives

- Understand and apply the principles of on-screen proofreading.

- Increase your productivity level in preparing written business documents.

- Improve the quality of your written business documents.

- Spell correctly 12 frequently misspelled words.

- Use correctly three sets of commonly confused and misused words.

245

INTRODUCTION

The increased use of computers and information processing programs has made the task of creating written materials easier and faster. However, the speed with which information is processed through computers and printers has placed a heavy responsibility for accuracy upon the operators of such equipment. The need for proficient proofreading and editing skills is critical when using a computer.

Most word processing programs have a feature that can merge addresses with a "shell" document to instantaneously create personalized sales letters for distribution to hundreds or even thousands of people. If errors exist in the shell document, all of the merged letters will have the same errors. Consequently, customers receiving those letters will have a poor impression of the company. The result may be fewer sales; or, in some cases, the company may have to send out corrected copies of the letter, which would increase the cost of the mailing substantially.

ON-SCREEN PROOFREADING

The types of errors found in on-screen copy are the same as hard copy errors, so the same proofreading skills are applied. However, there is a major difference between hard copy proofreading and on-screen proofreading. In hard copy proofreading, proofreaders' marks are written on the hard copy to identify the errors. In on-screen proofreading, when an error is located on the computer screen, the proofreader corrects the error immediately, saving time that would otherwise be spent rekeying. The diligent proofreader who detects and corrects all of the errors in the on-screen copy will produce a printed hard copy that is free of errors. Several tools and tips can simplify on-screen proofreading.

Spelling Checker

The **spelling checker**, found in most information processing software programs, should be used first—after saving the document. With this feature, the program compares the spelling of each on-screen word with the words in a dictionary stored within the computer's memory. If the on-screen word matches the stored dictionary word, the computer moves to the next word. If it does not, the on-screen word is highlighted. At this point the operator must either purposely ignore the highlighted word and continue with the spelling checker or correct the misspelled word by selecting one of the suggested choices listed in the memory dictionary. The computer will not automatically correct the misspelled word; the operator must choose the correct word.

The spelling checker is an extremely valuable tool for the proofreader. However, the spelling checker will not locate inappropriately used but correctly spelled words, such as homophones. For example, in the following paragraph, the spelling checker would identify only one incorrectly spelled word. However, seven incorrect words appear in this copy. Can you find the errors?

> At the meering held last weak, the members decided that their should bee a committee too prepare a proposal four expansion of the west central office located inn Los Angeles, California.

Grammar Checker

The grammar checker is a feature of some software programs that allows proofreaders to identify and correct grammar errors in their written documents. The grammar checker may be employed after the spelling checker is used. Depending on the specific program, a grammar checker program analyzes the material on the screen for various aspects of writing, including correctness of grammar, sentence structure, punctuation, and spelling.

Grammar checker software lets you select the checking style that is best for your writing style. In addition, German, French, and Spanish versions are available from some companies.

Cursor Movement Check

A third step in on-screen proofreading is to use the cursor. When reading on-screen copy, the proofreader should use the cursor and the directional arrow keys to move through the copy. A simple technique is to proofread on-screen material by moving the cursor down one line at a time. When the cursor is at the bottom of the screen, continuing to move it down will bring a new line to the bottom of the screen. A line at the bottom of the screen is easier to proofread because there are no words below the line (see Figure 15-1).

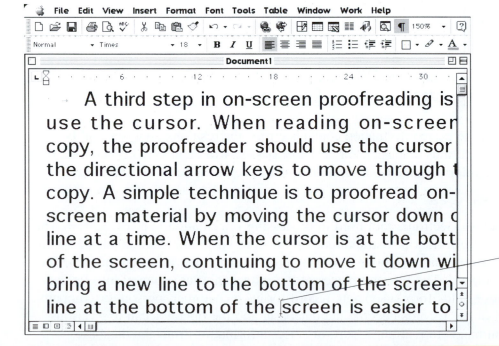

Figure 15-1

On-Screen Editing in Word Processing Program

Cursor

Print Preview

Most word processors have a feature you can use to preview the document before it's printed. By using **print preview**, you can see if the margins, formatting, spacing, etc. are correct. You can also see if the document fits on one page; if not, you must make adjustments to fit the document on one page or create a second-page header (for a letter or memo) or footer (for a report). Using Print Preview before printing a document saves time and paper.

INFORMATION PROCESSING TOOLS

When proofreading on- or offscreen, you will work with information processed in a variety of software programs. Familiarizing yourself with formats such as the spreadsheet and database will help you proofread more effectively.

Spreadsheet

An important tool used in business management is the **spreadsheet**. Basic information is entered into columns and rows. The spreadsheet program processes the information through a variety of calculations; and additional data is generated in other columns and rows, as shown in Figure 15-2.

Figure 15-2

Sample Spreadsheet

	A	B	C	D	E	F	G	H	I	J	K	L
1	1	Acct. No.		Title	Budget		Used/Sep		Bal. 9/30		Used/Oct	
2	2	3721		Supplies	1500		250		1250		150	
3	3	3722		Phone	100		10		90		15	
4	4	3723		Travel	1000		0		1000		0	
5	5	3724		Mags.	150		50		100		0	
6	6	3725		Lecturer	500		0		500		0	
7	7	3726		Film	125		25		100		20	
8	8	3727		Misc	100		0		100		0	

If the basic information contains errors, the resulting analyses will be incorrect; thus, management decision making will be affected. Therefore, the basic information entered into the spreadsheet must be proofread carefully.

Database

Another electronic tool used in processing information is a **database**. The database format is a structured way to store basic information such as names, addresses, and telephone numbers; product data; and information on services performed. The bits and pieces of the information are entered into fields. These fields form a separate record for each customer, person, or company. All of the records become the database; and the operator can use various commands to rearrange, sort, or select information from the database.

A crucial step in the preparation of a database is keying the initial information. Uncorrected errors will result in incorrect data. Each record should be carefully checked against the original information and all errors corrected.

Voice Recognition Software

Voice recognition software gives you the ability to transfer your spoken words directly into text. As you speak into a microphone connected to your computer, the sound card transfers your speech into written form.

Since each person has a unique voice profile, the software must learn your voice pattern. Most programs first ask you to speak a sample list of words or sentences into the microphone. As you practice your speech skills, the software learns your voice and your unique way of speaking. The success rate for the software depends on your computer's speed, but it's not unusual to have an accuracy rate of 95 percent or higher.

ELECTRONIC MAIL (E-MAIL)

Electronic mail, or e-mail, is the most widely used Internet service. E-mail is convenient and easy to use as it allows you to electronically send, receive, and store written messages. Anyone with Internet access can send and receive messages 24 hours a day, almost instantaneously.

To use e-mail, you need special software and an e-mail account. You must also know your receiver's e-mail address. E-mail addresses are similar to a postal address in that the e-mail address enables the computer to deliver your message to the right person. Everyone has a unique e-mail address. The first part is the receiver's individual name; the second part comes after the @ sign and is called the site or domain name. The domain name identifies the name of the Internet service provider (ISP).

It is important to remember that e-mail is not private. Numerous court cases have determined that company e-mail messages belong to the company, not the individual. If a subpoena is issued to your ISP, everything you have done or said can be traced.

Although e-mail generally uses a more conversational tone than other traditional forms of communication, you still need to use good communication skills to prevent misunderstandings. When writing an e-mail message, consider the following:

- Understand that your e-mail messages represent you and that first impressions are important.
- Use correct spelling, grammar, and punctuation, as they are still important.
- Write descriptive subject lines.
- Use short paragraphs, and keep your message short.
- Consider carefully what you write because it is a permanent record that can be forwarded to others.

- Do not use all capital letters (often perceived as *shouting*).
- Do not attach large files (perhaps over 500K) without first receiving permission from your recipient.
- When forwarding messages, key your comments at the top.
- Do not overuse acronyms such as BTW (by the way), IMHO (in my humble opinion), and ROFL (rolling on floor laughing).
- Do not use e-mail for highly sensitive or confidential information.
- Be aware of format.

CONFUSED AND MISUSED WORDS

principal	*adj.* main; *n.* money that earns interest; *n.* head official of a school; chief
principle	*n.* a basic truth; a rule or standard

The **principal** met with the Student Council members on Thursday.

This is an important ethical **principle**.

raise	*v.* to lift; to move upward; to bring up or rear; to grow things; *n.* an increase in pay
rise	*v.* to get up; to move upward by itself; to increase in intensity, volume, or speed

Mona appreciated the **raise** she received after her last performance appraisal.

The noise level continued to **rise** during my presentation.

right	*adj.* correct, truth, proper; opposite of left
rite	*n.* religious or solemn ceremony
write	*v.* to form letters of the alphabet on a surface with a tool such as a pen or pencil

Santana moved to his **right**.

The **rite** of baptism is a solemn ceremony.

Please **write** a three-page report describing your experience.

- Use the cursor; and proofread the bottom line of on-screen copy, advancing only one line at a time.
- Do not rely solely on spelling and grammar checkers to find and correct errors in your electronic communications. Remember to check for misused words that are spelled correctly.
- Proofread and edit your e-mail messages as you would any other written correspondence.

Exercise 15-1 SPELLING AND WORD USAGE CHECK

Compare the words in Column A with the corresponding words in Column B. Use the appropriate proofreaders' marks to correct the misspelled or misused words. If both columns are correct, write **C** to the left of the number.

Column A	Column B
1. exceed	exceede
2. phenomenen	phenomenon
3. sufficeint	sufficient
4. negotiable	negotible
5. consceous	conscious
6. guidence	guidance
7. advantagious	advantageous
8. extraordinary	extraordenary
9. precedent	precident
10. occurrence	occurrence
11. extention	extension
12. unique	unikue
13. Do you understand the principle?	I earn 8 percent on the principle.
14. They raise two kinds of goats.	You need to raise and get dressed.
15. Your answer was rite.	I should write a letter to my congressperson.

Exercise 15-2 INTERNATIONAL VOCABULARY

Compare the Spanish words in Column A with the corresponding words in Column B. If the word in Column B is different from the word in Column A, use the appropriate proofreaders' marks to correct Column B. If the words in both columns are the same, write **C** to the left of the number.

Column A	Column B
1. propuesta	propuista
2. encomienda	encomienda
3. talentoso	talentiso
4. asoleado	asolaedo
5. hondonada	hondoneda

PROOFREADING AT THE COMPUTER

In this chapter the exercises will give you an opportunity to proofread on-screen documents. In some cases you will proofread the on-screen copy against a hard copy draft. Proofread the on-screen copy very carefully. Your goal should be to print an error-free document the first time.

Exercise 15-3 BUSINESS LETTER

Open 15-03 from the Chapter 15 folder on the Student CD. Proofread the letter on the screen, and make all corrections before printing the hard copy. Follow the standard procedures for proofreading the hard copy—revising, resaving, and reprinting.

Exercise 15-4 MEMORANDUM

Open 15-04 from the Chapter 15 folder on the Student CD. Proofread the memo on the screen, and make all corrections before printing the hard copy. Follow the standard procedures for proofreading the hard copy.

Exercise 15-5 SHORT REPORT

Open 15-05 from the Chapter 15 folder on the Student CD. Proofread the report on the screen, and make all corrections before printing the hard copy. Follow the standard procedures for proofreading the hard copy.

Teamwork

Exercise 15-6 STATISTICAL REPORT

Open 15-06 from the Chapter 15 folder on the Student CD. Work with a partner to proofread this document. Your partner should read from the correct handwritten document on page 253 while you make all corrections to the computer file before printing the hard copy.

OFFICE FURNITURE AND EQUIPMENT COMPARISON

Central City Competitors

Model No.	Description	Our Price	Store A	Diff +/-%	Store B	Diff +/-%	Store C	Diff. +/-%
DC-10	Desk Chair	$ 75	$ 90	+20%	$ 95	+26%	$ 70	-07%
DT-21	Desk	320	410	+28%	580	+81%	300	-06%
CT-28	Computer Table	250	220	-12%	340	+36%	250	None
CR-42	Calculator	15	20	+33%	28	+87%	20	+33%
FC-58	File Cabinet	75	65	-13%	90	+20%	70	-07%
ET-61	End Table	90	90	None	120	+33%	75	-17%
DL-36	Desk Lamp	45	50	+11%	75	+67%	45	None
TR-32	Desk Tray	10	12	+20%	15	+50%	9	-10%
FM-15	Floor Mat	70	75	+07%	90	+28%	65	-07%
FC-62	File Cabinet	90	85	-06%	110	+22%	85	-06%

Exercise 15-7 NEWS ARTICLES

When using desktop publishing programs, the writer and/or the editor often creates separate articles that are imported to specific locations on the newsletter page. Open 15-07 from the Chapter 15 folder on the Student CD. Proofread the two articles, and make all corrections on the screen before printing the hard copy. Follow the standard procedures for proofreading the hard copy.

Exercise 15-8 EDITED MEMORANDUM

Open 15-08 from the Chapter 15 folder on the Student CD. Using the following list of changes, make corrections and changes in the document. Proofread the material, and make any additional corrections on the screen before printing the hard copy. Follow the standard procedures for proofreading the hard copy.

CHANGES IN MEMO:	
Subject line:	Insert "Proposed" between "for" and "Denver."
New paragraph 1:	Insert the following as the first paragraph: On May 1 the Management Council asked for information about the sales potential in the Denver metropolitan area. Contacts were made to conduct a survey.
Old paragraph 1 becomes new paragraph 2:	In line 2 add "representatives of" between "by" and "City." In line 3 change "3" to "four." In line 3 add "eastside" between "the" and "shopping." Also change "survey instruments" to "questionnaires."
Old paragraph 3 becomes new paragraph 4:	Start paragraph with "Because of national radio and television advertising." In line 1 insert "the names of" between "with" and "several." In line 2 delete "However."
Last paragraph:	In line 1 insert "major" between "A" and "conclusion." In line 1 insert "viable" between "a" and "market." In line 2 delete "the process of opening" and replace it with "determining the feasibility of establishing."

Exercise 15-9 MERGED DOCUMENTS

Open 15-09A from the Chapter 15 folder on the Student CD; you will merge the names and addresses in this list with the shell document in 15-09B. Then open 15-09B, proofread the shell document, and make all corrections. Merge and print the letters.

Exercise 15-10 SPREADSHEET

Open 15-10 from the Chapter 15 on the Student CD. Proofread the spreadsheet against the basic data that follows. Make corrections on the screen, and print a hard copy. Follow the standard procedures for proofreading the hard copy.

Data for Spreadsheet:

Grayer: January–1348; February–1235; March–1436; April–1371; May–1368; June–1384

Burnes: January–932; February–742; March–991; April–1122; May–973; June–873

Abeyta: January–562; February–491; March–590; April–530; May–492; June–503

Weston: January–1732; February–1622; March–1978; April–1368; May–1567; June–1473

Milton: January–1436; February–1288; March–1222; April–1250; May–1242; June–1303

CD

Exercise 15-11 DATABASE

Open 15-11 from the Chapter 15 folder on the Student CD. Proofread each record in the database against the information given on the registration cards that follow. Make corrections on the screen, and print a hard copy. Follow the standard procedures for proofreading the hard copy.

ANNUAL ARTS RECOGNITION DINNER RESERVATION

TO: AARD Chairperson, 357 Armstrong Avenue, Minneapolis, MN 55418-1833

Please make ___*1*___ (No.) reservation(s) for the AARD on May 8.

A check for ___*$18*___ ($18 per person) is enclosed.

Meal choices are as follows:

Reservation No. 1: Chicken _____ Fish ___✓___ Vegetarian _____

Reservation No. 2: Chicken _____ Fish _____ Vegetarian _____

Name: ___*Julia West*___

Address: ___*4783 Dell Street*___

City, State, ZIP: ___*Hopkins, Minnesota 55343-1862*___

ANNUAL ARTS RECOGNITION DINNER RESERVATION

TO: AARD Chairperson, 357 Armstrong Avenue, Minneapolis, MN 55418-1833

Please make ___*2*___ (No.) reservation(s) for the AARD on May 8.

A check for ___*$36*___ ($18 per person) is enclosed.

Meal choices are as follows:

Reservation No. 1: Chicken ___✓___ Fish _____ Vegetarian _____

Reservation No. 2: Chicken _____ Fish ___✓___ Vegetarian _____

Name: ___*Dwight Fern*___

Address: ___*27624 7th St.*___

City, State, ZIP: ___*Edina, MN 55424-2388*___

ANNUAL ARTS RECOGNITION DINNER RESERVATION

TO: AARD Chairperson, 357 Armstrong Avenue, Minneapolis, MN 55418-1833

Please make ___2___ (No.) reservation(s) for the AARD on May 8.

A check for ___$36___ ($18 per person) is enclosed.

Meal choices are as follows:

Reservation No. 1: Chicken _____   Fish ___✓___   Vegetarian _____

Reservation No. 2: Chicken _____   Fish _____   Vegetarian ___✓___

Name: ___Walter Gappa___

Address: ___18321 Fairmont___

City, State, ZIP: ___Crystal, MN 55428-1381___

ANNUAL ARTS RECOGNITION DINNER RESERVATION

TO: AARD Chairperson, 357 Armstrong Avenue, Minneapolis, MN 55418-1833

Please make ___2___ (No.) reservation(s) for the AARD on May 8.

A check for ___$36___ ($18 per person) is enclosed.

Meal choices are as follows:

Reservation No. 1: Chicken ___✓___   Fish _____   Vegetarian _____

Reservation No. 2: Chicken ___✓___   Fish _____   Vegetarian _____

Name: ___Felipe Baca___

Address: ___832 Chestnut St.___

City, State, ZIP: ___St. Paul, Minnesota   55125-2162___

ANNUAL ARTS RECOGNITION DINNER RESERVATION

TO: AARD Chairperson, 357 Armstrong Avenue, Minneapolis, MN 55418-1833

Please make ___2___ (No.) reservation(s) for the AARD on May 8.

A check for ___$36.00___ ($18 per person) is enclosed.

Meal choices are as follows:

Reservation No. 1: Chicken ___✓___   Fish _____   Vegetarian _____

Reservation No. 2: Chicken ___✓___   Fish _____   Vegetarian _____

Name: ___Esther Birr___

Address: ___Box 83___

City, State, ZIP: ___Byron, Minnesota   55920-0083___

ANNUAL ARTS RECOGNITION DINNER RESERVATION

TO: AARD Chairperson, 357 Armstrong Avenue, Minneapolis, MN 55418-1833

Please make ___1___ (No.) reservation(s) for the AARD on May 8.

A check for ___$18___ ($18 per person) is enclosed.

Meal choices are as follows:

Reservation No. 1: Chicken _____ Fish _____ Vegetarian ___✓___

Reservation No. 2: Chicken _____ Fish _____ Vegetarian _____

Name: _Senjen Vilaysing_

Address: _11362 Mill_

_____

City, State, ZIP: _Mound, MN 55364-2183_

ANNUAL ARTS RECOGNITION DINNER RESERVATION

TO: AARD Chairperson, 357 Armstrong Avenue, Minneapolis, MN 55418-1833

Please make ___1___ (No.) reservation(s) for the AARD on May 8.

A check for ___$18___ ($18 per person) is enclosed.

Meal choices are as follows:

Reservation No. 1: Chicken ___✓___ Fish _____ Vegetarian _____

Reservation No. 2: Chicken _____ Fish _____ Vegetarian _____

Name: _Tara Mead_

Address: _628 Point Street_

_____

City, State, ZIP: _Barrow, Wisconsin 54812-1371_

ANNUAL ARTS RECOGNITION DINNER RESERVATION

TO: AARD Chairperson, 357 Armstrong Avenue, Minneapolis, MN 55418-1833

Please make ___2___ (No.) reservation(s) for the AARD on May 8.

A check for ___$36___ ($18 per person) is enclosed.

Meal choices are as follows:

Reservation No. 1: Chicken _____ Fish ___✓___ Vegetarian _____

Reservation No. 2: Chicken _____ Fish _____ Vegetarian ___✓___

Name: _Ruby Palo_

Address: _34 N. 8th_

_____

City, State, ZIP: _Durand, WI 54736-8034_

ANNUAL ARTS RECOGNITION DINNER RESERVATION

TO: AARD Chairperson, 357 Armstrong Avenue, Minneapolis, MN 55418-1833

Please make __2__ (No.) reservation(s) for the AARD on May 8.

A check for __$36.00__ ($18 per person) is enclosed.

Meal choices are as follows:

Reservation No. 1: Chicken _____ Fish _____ Vegetarian __✓__

Reservation No. 2: Chicken _____ Fish _____ Vegetarian __✓__

Name: __Gordon Maas__

Address: __Box 135__

_____

City, State, ZIP: __Aitkin, MN 56431-0135__

ANNUAL ARTS RECOGNITION DINNER RESERVATION

TO: AARD Chairperson, 357 Armstrong Avenue, Minneapolis, MN 55418-1833

Please make __2__ (No.) reservation(s) for the AARD on May 8.

A check for __$36__ ($18 per person) is enclosed.

Meal choices are as follows:

Reservation No. 1: Chicken __✓__ Fish _____ Vegetarian _____

Reservation No. 2: Chicken __✓__ Fish _____ Vegetarian _____

Name: __Meg Reskin__

Address: __Box 322__

_____

City, State, ZIP: __Baldwin, WI 54002-0322__

ANNUAL ARTS RECOGNITION DINNER RESERVATION

TO: AARD Chairperson, 357 Armstrong Avenue, Minneapolis, MN 55418-1833

Please make __2__ (No.) reservation(s) for the AARD on May 8.

A check for __$36__ ($18 per person) is enclosed.

Meal choices are as follows:

Reservation No. 1: Chicken _____ Fish _____ Vegetarian __x__

Reservation No. 2: Chicken _____ Fish _____ Vegetarian __x__

Name: __Dorian Wu__

Address: __Rt. 3__

_____

City, State, ZIP: __Hudson, Wisconsin 54016-0329__

Exercise 15-12 ORDER CONFIRMATION

CD

Open 15-12 from the Chapter 15 folder on the Student CD. Proofread the order confirmation against the basic data that follows. Make corrections on the screen, and print a hard copy. Follow the standard procedures for proofreading the hard copy.

Data for Order Confirmation:

Bill to: Levi McCormick
396 Chickasaw Street
Sand Creek, MI 49279

Customer Number: 377972797XY
Order Number: 498719

Trumpet Vine; Item 388973; Quantity 3; Unit Price $19.95; Total $59.85
Lasting Love Rose; Item 455235; Quantity 1; Unit Price $22.95; Total $22.95
Cardiocrinum Giganteum; Item 844734; Quantity 2; Unit Price $31.95; Total $63.90

Astilbe Collection; Item 424485; Quantity 1; Unit Price $25.95; Total $25.95
Blue Jaye Hosta; Item 497792; Quantity 4; Unit Price $15.95; Total $63.80
Casa Blanca Oriental Lily; Item 774903; Quantity 5; Unit Price $4.95; Total $24.75

Merchandise Total: $261.20
Shipping and Handling: 26.12
Grand Total: $287.32

THE EDITOR
ONLINE

Computerized Minisimulation

Objectives

- Demonstrate an understanding of the importance of accurate proofreading through the careful review of typical business documents.

- Identify a variety of proofreading errors.

- Use appropriate proofreaders' marks to show what corrections should be made.

the Editor Online

Instructions: You work in the main office of The Editor Online, an organization that edits and publishes books and then promotes them through Internet web sites and bookstores. The company is based in Columbus, Ohio, but works with staff across the nation via computer. Your responsibilities include proofreading internal and external company documents. This simulation includes a group of these documents prepared by the staff at The Editor Online:

- Edgar Aponte, Project Manager

- Barbara Conti, Editor

Use the appropriate proofreaders' marks to show what corrections should be made. Each document is identified by number.

Document 1 WEB PAGE

Netscape: The Editor Online

Back Forward Reload Home Search Netscape Images Print Security Stop

Go To: http://www.TheEditorOnline.com/index.html

Authors, let me introduce The Editor Online! New technology is changing the publishing industry. We have the capability of producing one book at a time, on demand, which allows retailers to carry smaller inventories and still meet their customers' needs. Publishers can now offer the works of many authors with no cost to the publishers—opening the door for numerous would-be authors.

The Editor Online has formed partnersihps with online bookstores, making your book available to a wide range of customers, which results in more sales for you. Our affiliations include the following:

• **_Great Books.com_**, the fourmost source for online books
• **_Books-4-You_**, one of the nation's leading bookstores
• **_Reading Experts, Inc._**, the world's largest book wholesaler and distributor

Perhaps you're not ready to publish but would like more information. We offer **_chat rooms_** where you can talk with other authors. In addition, we offer subscriptshons to our **_newsletter_**, which updates you on industry trends.

Submissions

Our staff reveiws each manuscript to determine whether it is ready for publication. Within two weeks of submitting your manuscript, you will be notified about the status of your work. For a small **_fee_**, our editorial staff can help you improve a weak manuscript, if necessary.

Our basic cost for publication is $375. This includes a professionally designed cover for your book. You are charged only if your book is published. Submisssions require the three components below. Click on the links to view or download the documents.

1. A signed **_Publishing contract_** (Download, sign, and mail it to us; or indicate your agreement with the contract terms online and submit.)

2. a completed **_submission form_** (Download, complete, and mail the form; or complete it online and submit.)

3. **_Payment_** (If you are mailing your submission, send a check for the $37 fee. If you are e-mailing your submission, enter your credit card number on our secure line. Payment will be processed only if work is is selected for publication.)

Document 2   E-MAIL CONFIRMATION TO POLLY VALCKE

Directions: Proofread the e-mail message against the completed form below. Correct any errors you find.

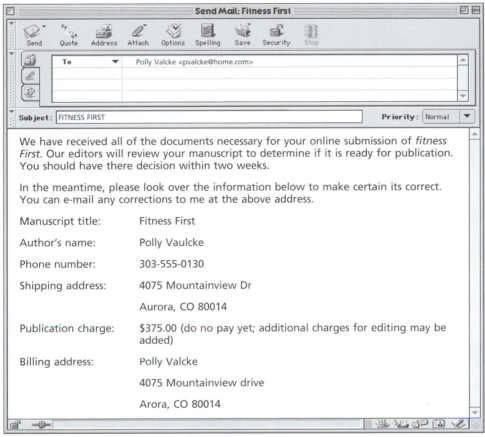

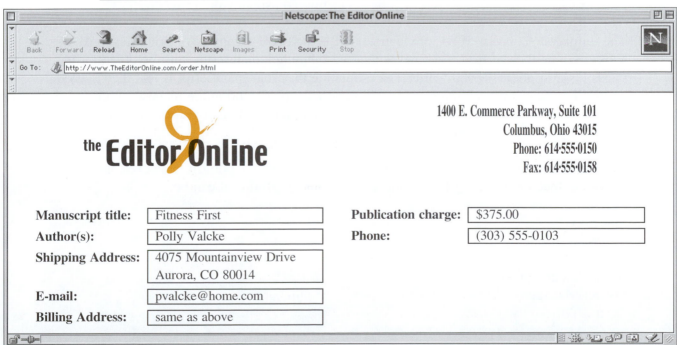

Document 3 ACCEPTANCE LETTER TO POLLY VALCKE

1400 E. Commerce Parkway, Suite 101
Columbus, Ohio 43015
Phone: 614·555·0150
Fax: 614·555·0158

March 11, 200-

Ms. Polly Valcke
4075 Mountainview Drive
Aurora, CO 80014

Ms. Valcke:

Thank you again for submitting you manuscript to The Editor Online. We are pleased to tell you that *Fitness First* has been excepted for publication. Please see my initial comments on the enclosed sheet. Your editor will be Barbara Conti, whom has been with The Editor Online since it began. She will be contacting you soon with her feedback.

The immediate concern of our production staff is the book's length. We print our books in a six- by nine-inch format. This means that the submitted manuscript must be at least 108 pages long, or about 40,000 words. I'm estimating that your manuscript is less then 30,000 words. The best approach might be to add more examples to bring the manuscript up to 40,000 words. Of course you can also add more diagrams and photographs. Barbara will talk with you to get your input.

Our authors are generally very pleased with the books that we publish. However, its important that we work together to make your book as good as it can be.

Sincerely,

Edgar Aponte, ph.D.
Project Manager

Initial Evaluation: _Fitness First_   **Date:** <u>March 10, 200-</u>

Organization

☒ smooth, logcial presentation

☒ titles and subtitles follow table of contants

☒ detailed appendix

☐ needs more work

Book Elements

☒ interesting opening

☒ periodic summarys or reviews

☐ appropriate graphics

☐ one or more elements needs more work

Content

☐ geared to intended readers

☐ to detailed

☒ too few examples

☐ in appropriate examples

☐ needs more work

Writing Style

☒ consistant use of active voice

☐ too much passive voice

☐ Needs more work

Grammar

☐ few errors

☒ moderate number of errors

☐ needs more work

Sales Prediction

☐ should appeel to a wide audience

☒ somewhat narrow market:
   younger audience

Recommendations

☒ excepted to be published

☒ will need some auther revisions (See above comments.)

☐ rework and resubmit, following above comments

☐ does not meet The Editor Online standards

Document 4 MEMO TO BARBARA CONTI

 the **Editor**Online

INTEROFFICE
MEMORANDUM

TO: Barbara Conti, Editor

FROM: Edgar Aponte, Project Manager

DATE: March 14, 200-

SUBJECT: NEW MANUSCRIPT: *FITNESS FIRST*

Please review my initial evaluation of Polly Valckes new manuscript, which I am enclosing. I believe that *Fitness First* is well-written and is based on solid principles. The author, however needs to provide additional examples to help explain her main points. Many of these examples could be incorporate as graphics.

First, I recommend that you suggest that Holly evaluate other fitness books and note their use of examples and graphics. Excellent sources include the following books on physical fitness: *Jump into Fitness* by Thaddeus Jackowski, *Complete Guide to Navy Seal Fitness* by Steward Shepherd, and *The Mars & Venus Diet and Exercise Solution* by Jillian Gleason. I high recommend any of those books.

Second, the author needs to show how her fitness recommendations will help readers meet there own needs. It would be helpful if she could explain how a series of exercises for ex-ample will benefit the readers in his or her daily lives. I'm confident that Polly will benefit from your recommendations. You might ask her to revise the 1st chapter and submit it to you to make sure she's on the track right.

As I noted on my evaluation, Pollys' manuscript contains too many grammatical errors. Many of these errors would be caught by a grammer checker, so you might recommend that she use one.

Please let me know, Barbara, if I can provide further assistance with this manuscript. I look forward to reading Polly's second draft.

Enclosure

Document 5   LETTER AND EDITED MANUSCRIPT TO POLLY VALCKE

Directions: Proofread and edit Barbara's letter and the one-page manuscript that follows.

the **Editor Online**

1400 E. Commerce Parkway, Suite 101
Columbus, Ohio 43015
Phone: 614·555·0150
Fax: 614·555·0158

march 18, 200-

Ms. Polly Valcke
4075 Mountainview Drive
Aurora, Co 80014

Dear Ms. Valcke,

The project manager and me are both quite pleased with your 1st draft. I would like to recommend some changes that will farther strengthen your manuscript.

I have enclosed a hard copy of your manuscript with a number of place marked where you might add examples. For additional help, you might read *Jump into Fitness* by Thaddeus Jackowski, *Complete Guide to Navy Seal Fitness* by Steward Shepherd, or *The Mars & Venus Diet and Exercise Solution* by Jillian Gleason These sources show how you can incorporate specific examples and graphics in your manuscript.

Enclosed herewith you will also find one page that I have edited to make the writing clearer and less verbose. Please review these changes and continuing on to make the same kinds of changes in the rest of the manuscript. Do not hesitate for a second to call me if you have any questions about my changes.

Due to the fact that this manuscript must be ready for production by July 1, I need to have your 2nd draft by May 15. We may need the rest of May and june for other revisions.

I look forward to receiving your next draft.

Sincerely,

Barbara Conti, Editor

Enclosures

Getting Started

When it comes to exercise some people bite off more than they can chew. They are soon ready to throw in the towel and retreat to the couch. Exercising should be relaxing, not stressful.

You are a unique and special individual, and No one can choose the perfect exercise program for you. People must choose forms of exercise that suit their lifestyles so they will continue doing them. Also remember that exercise spread throughout the week are more healthful then exhausting workouts on each and every weekend.

Here are four reasons why people give up exercising and ways to overcome them.

1. They don't have enough time. If this sounds familiar, try exercising for short periods several times a day. For example, three 10-minute walks.

2. They are embarrassed about their bodies, or they feel awkward about their coordination. These people can start by exercising at home, following an exercise routine on DVD. Many of these products are available for beginning exercisers. Soon they may may feel confident enough to join a class.

2. They are to tired to exercise. The result of exercise is more energy. You will experience this yourself soon after you begin to exercise regularly.

3. The weather is bad. either too hot or too cold. Regular exercisers learn to be flexible about where they exercise. Even a brisk walk through the Mall can provide exercise if the whether is bad on a particular day.

4. Exercising costs to much. You might wonder what to do if you can't afford a membership to a fitness club? Your city may have a community center that offers free or low-cost exercise programs. You also might consider also walking some places instead of driving.

Document 6 E-MAIL ANSWERING POLLY VALCKE'S QUESTIONS

Directions: Use Barbara's notes below to proofread her e-mail message to
Polly Valcke on the next page.

Polly's questions:

<u>When will my book be published?</u>

It should be ready for sale online within 60 days. Of course,
this time period depends on how long you take to check the
proofs that we send to you.

<u>How much will my book cost?</u>

Soft-cover books such as yours usually range between $5.99
and $7.99.

<u>Will my book be sold in the Books-4-You stores?</u>

There is no guarantee of this, but Books-4-You does choose
several books each month to promote in its stores. Your book
might be one of them. Your book would also be available online
at Books-4-You.

<u>Will my book be carried by bookstores besides Books-4-You?</u>

More than 4,500 bookstores nationwide will be able to order
your book through the Reading Experts, Inc., listings.

<u>Where is The Editor Online located?</u>

We have offices in Columbus, Ohio; San Diego, California;
Minneapolis, Minnesota; and Oklahoma City, Oklahoma.

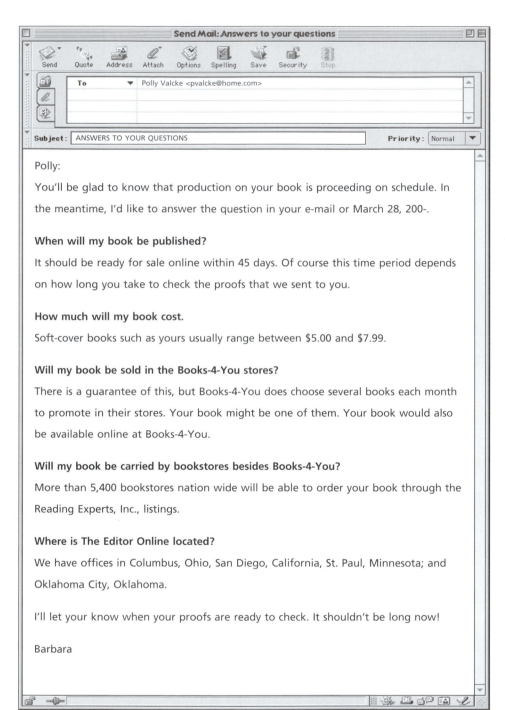

Send Mail: Answers to your questions

Send　Quote　Address　Attach　Options　Spelling　Save　Security　Stop

To　▼　Polly Valcke <pvalcke@home.com>

Subject: ANSWERS TO YOUR QUESTIONS　　　　Priority: Normal ▼

Polly:

You'll be glad to know that production on your book is proceeding on schedule. In the meantime, I'd like to answer the question in your e-mail or March 28, 200-.

When will my book be published?

It should be ready for sale online within 45 days. Of course this time period depends on how long you take to check the proofs that we sent to you.

How much will my book cost.

Soft-cover books such as yours usually range between $5.00 and $7.99.

Will my book be sold in the Books-4-You stores?

There is a guarantee of this, but Books-4-You does choose several books each month to promote in their stores. Your book might be one of them. Your book would also be available online at Books-4-You.

Will my book be carried by bookstores besides Books-4-You?

More than 5,400 bookstores nation wide will be able to order your book through the Reading Experts, Inc., listings.

Where is The Editor Online located?

We have offices in Columbus, Ohio, San Diego, California, St. Paul, Minnesota; and Oklahoma City, Oklahoma.

I'll let your know when your proofs are ready to check. It shouldn't be long now!

Barbara

PROOFREADING AT THE COMPUTER

SIM-1 WEB PAGE

Alternate instructions:

1. Open SIM-1 from the Simulation folder on the Student CD. (This is a computer file of Document 1.)

2. Correct any errors in the web page. Follow your proofreaders' marks on Document 1.

3. Proofread the document on the screen. Use the spelling checker.

4. Save as SIM-1R and print.

5. Proofread the hard copy. If you find additional mistakes, correct the errors, resave, and reprint.

SIM-2 E-MAIL CONFIRMATION TO POLLY VALCKE

Alternate instructions:

1. Open SIM-2 from the Simulation folder on the Student CD. (This is a computer file of Document 2.)

2. Revise the e-mail message, correcting any errors you indicated with proofreaders' marks. Make sure you check the information against the printed form that Polly completed.

3. Proofread the document on the screen. Use the spelling checker.

4. Save as SIM-2R and print.

5. Proofread the hard copy. If you find additional mistakes, correct the errors, resave, and reprint.

SIM-3 ACCEPTANCE LETTER TO POLLY VALCKE

Alternate instructions:

1. Open SIM-3 from the Simulation folder on the Student CD. (This is a computer file of Document 3.)

2. Revise the letter and initial evaluation, correcting any errors you indicated with proofreaders' marks.

3. Proofread the documents on the screen. Use the spelling checker.

4. Save as SIM-3R and print both pages.

5. Proofread the hard copy. If you find additional mistakes, correct the errors, resave, and reprint.

SIM-4 MEMO TO BARBARA CONTI

Alternate instructions:

1. Open SIM-4 from the Simulation folder on the Student CD. (This is a computer file of Document 4.)

2. Revise the memorandum, making the corrections you indicated with proofreaders' marks.

3. Proofread the document on the screen. Use the spelling checker.

4. Save as SIM-4R and print.

5. Proofread the hard copy. If you find additional mistakes, correct the errors, resave, and reprint.

SIM-5 LETTER AND EDITED MANUSCRIPT TO POLLY VALCKE

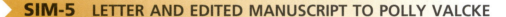

Alternate instructions:

1. Open SIM-5 from the Simulation folder on the Student CD. (This is a computer file of Document 5.)

2. Revise the letter and one-page manuscript, correcting any errors you indicated with proofreaders' marks.

3. Proofread the two documents on the screen. Use the spelling checker.

4. Save as SIM-5R and print both pages.

5. Proofread the hard copy. If you find additional mistakes, correct the errors, resave, and reprint.

SIM-6 E-MAIL ANSWERING POLLY VALCKE'S QUESTIONS

Alternate instructions:

1. Open SIM-6 from the Simulation folder on the Student CD. (This is a computer file of Document 6.)

2. Revise the e-mail message, correcting any errors you indicated with proofreaders' marks.

3. Proofread the e-mail message on the screen. Use the spelling checker.

4. Save as SIM-6R and print.

5. Proofread the hard copy. If you find additional mistakes, correct the errors, resave, and reprint.

Appendix

COMMONLY CONFUSED WORDS

accept *v.* to agree to; to receive
except *prep.* but; other than

addition *n.* process of summing; an added part
edition *n.* copies of a published book

advice *n.* recommendation
advise *v.* to give advice; to inform

affect *v.* to influence
effect *v.* to bring about; *n.* result

all ready *adj.* (two words) completely ready
already *adv.* before now or a specified time

all right *adj.* (two words) all correct or appropriate
alright unacceptable spelling of *all right*

all together *adv.* (two words) gathered into a single unit or group; collected in one place
altogether *adv.* entirely, completely, utterly

allude *v.* to make an indirect reference to something
elude *v.* to avoid or escape notice

allot *v.* to allocate or distribute
a lot *n.* (two words) a large amount; many
alot unacceptable spelling of *a lot*

among *prep.* comparison of three or more persons or things
between *prep.* comparison of only two persons or things

any one *adj./pron.* (two words) certain person; use when the pronoun is followed by an *of* phrase
anyone *pron.* anybody; any person at all

assistance *n.* help
assistants *n.* helpers

assure *v.* to give confidence to; to feel sure; to convince
ensure *v.* to make sure, certain
insure *v.* to cover with insurance; to guarantee; to secure from harm

can *v.* to be able to do something
may *v.* to be possible; to give permission

capital *n.* official seat of government; money to invest
capitol *n.* a building in which a legislature meets

cent *n.* 1/100; penny
scent *n.* a distinctive odor; perfume; a sense of smell
sent *v.* past tense and past participle of *send*

cite *v.* to quote; to acknowledge
sight *n.* a vision; *v.* to see or observe
site *n.* a location

complement *n.* something that adds to or completes a whole; *v.* to complete or make perfect
compliment *n.* an expression of praise; *v.* to praise

cooperation *n.* working together
corporation *n.* a legal entity

correspondence *n.* a communication by exchange of letters
correspondents *n.* those who write letters

council *n.* an assembly of people
counsel *v.* to give advice or guidance; *n.* a lawyer or group of lawyers; *n.* advice received

currant *n.* small, seedless raisin
current *adj.* up-to-date; *n.* electricity

dairy *n.* a commercial firm that processes and/or sells milk and milk products
diary *n.* a daily personal record of events, experiences, and observations

device *n.* a machine or gadget
devise *v.* to invent or to plan

envelop *v.* to cover with a wrapping
envelope *n.* a paper container for correspondence

farther *adv.* more distant
further *adj.* to a greater degree; additional

foreword *n.* an introduction; a preface
forward *adj.* at or near the front; *v.* to send mail

its *adj.* possessive form of *it*
it's contraction of *it is* or *it has*

later *adv.* after
latter *adj.* the second of two

lay *v.* to place or set down an object
lie *v.* to rest; to recline

lean *adj.* thin; not fat; meager; *v.* to slant away from a vertical position
lien *n.* the right to sell property of a debtor

loose *adj.* not fastened; free
lose *v.* unable to find; to fail to win
loss *n.* a person or thing lost; a defeat

may be *v.* to be allowed or permitted to
maybe *adv.* perhaps; possibly

moral *adj.* concerned with goodness or badness of human action and character; *n.* lesson contained in a story or an event
morale *n.* attitude of an individual

personal *adj.* private; pertaining to a particular person
personnel *n.* people employed; staff of a company

precede *v.* to come before in time or rank
proceed *v.* to go forward

principal *adj.* main; *n.* money that earns interest; *n.* head official of a school; chief
principle *n.* a basic truth; a rule or standard

quiet *adj.* calm; opposite of noisy
quit *v.* to stop; to resign
quite *adv.* completely; considerably

raise *v.* to lift; to move upward; to bring up or rear; to grow things; *n.* an increase in pay
rise *v.* to get up; to move upward by itself; to increase in intensity, volume, or speed

recent *adj.* occurring at a time immediately prior to the present; modern or new
resent *v.* to feel anger from a sense of being injured or offended
re-sent *v.* (past tense of *resend*) sent again

right *adj.* correct, truth, proper; opposite of left
rite *n.* religious or solemn ceremony
write *v.* to form letters of the alphabet on a surface with a tool such as a pen or pencil

seas *n. pl.* continuous bodies of salt water
sees *v.* (third-person form of *see*) to perceive with the eye; to observe; to view
seize *v.* to grasp suddenly and forcibly; to take or grab

stationary *adj.* immovable; fixed
stationery *n.* writing materials

than *conj.* used in comparison
then *adv.* at that time

their *adj.* possessive form of *they*
there *adv.* in or at that place
they're contraction of *they are*

to *prep.* toward; for the purpose of
too *adv.* also; more than enough
two *n.* one more than one

vain *adj.* without success; not resulting in the desired outcome; conceited
vane *n.* a rotating device that indicates the direction of the wind
vein *n.* a blood vessel

weather *n.* conditions in the atmosphere; *v.* to endure
whether *conj.* if

who's contraction of *who is*
whose possessive form of *who* and *which*

your possessive form of *you*
you're contraction of *you are*

FREQUENTLY MISSPELLED WORDS

accessible
accommodate
achieve
acknowledge
acknowledgment
adequate
admissible
advantageous
already
analyze
anxiety
anxious
appropriate
approximately
arrangements
assessment

beginning
believe
benefit
brochure
business

canceled
cannot
capabilities
capacity
categories
cautious
censor
changeable
clientele
commission
commitment
committee
communication
compel
compelled
compliance
conceited
conference
congratulations

conscientious
conscious
consensus
consistent
consultant
continuing
controlling
convenience
cooperate
corporate
correspondence
counseling
courteous
criteria
curriculum
customer

decision
defendant
dependent
description
design
desirable
development
dissatisfied

efficient
eligible
eliminate
embarrassed
emergency
emphasis
enclosing
equipment
especially
evaluate
exceed
excellent
existence
extension
extraordinary

facilities
faculty
familiar
financial
foreign

government
grievance
guarantee
guidance

harassed
hierarchy

illegible
immediately
impatient
implement
indispensable
installation
institution
interfere
interference
interrupt
irate

jealousy
judgment

knowledgeable

leisure
liability
library
likelihood

maintenance
manageable
mathematics
maximum
mediocre
miscellaneous

misspell
mortgage

necessary
negotiable
noticeable

obvious
occasionally
occurred
occurrence
offered
offering
omitted
opportunity

palette
parallel
partial
participation
particular
pastime
pedestrian
percent
permissible
perseverance
pertinent
phenomenon
plagiarism
plagiarize
possibility
potential
practice
precede
precedent
preferable
preference
preferential
preferred
prejudice
preparation
prior

privilege
proceed
processing
proficiency
proficient
pursue

questionnaire

receipt
receive
recognize
recommendations
reference
referred
regard
responsibility
restaurant

salary
schedule
self-confident
separate
session
similar
situation
submitted
substantially
succeed
sufficient

transferred
truly

unanimous
unique
usable
usually

vacuum
vague
vendor
vengeance

COMMONLY MISSPELLED U.S. CITIES

Abilene, TX	Decatur, GA or AL	Honolulu, HI	San Bernardino, CA
Albuquerque, NM	Des Moines, IA	Indianapolis, IN	San Francisco, CA
Berkeley, CA	Dubuque, IA	Milwaukee, WI	Savannah, GA
Bismarck, ND	Durham, NC	Pasadena, CA or TX	Schenectady, NY
Boise, ID	Everett, WA	Philadelphia, PA	Shreveport, LA
Butte, MT	Fayetteville, NC or AR	Phoenix, AZ	Sioux City, IA
Charlotte, NC	Fremont, CA, NE,	Pittsburg, CA or KS	Sioux Falls, SD
Chattanooga, TN	or OH	Pittsburgh, PA	Tallahassee, FL
Cincinnati, OH	Gainesville, FL or GA	Raleigh, NC	Tucson, AZ
Cleveland, OH	Hialeah, FL	Roanoke, VA	Worcester, MA

SPELLINGS AND ABBREVIATIONS OF STATES AND U.S. TERRITORIES

Alabama	AL	Illinois	IL	Nebraska	NE	South Carolina	SC
Alaska	AK	Indiana	IN	Nevada	NV	South Dakota	SD
Arizona	AZ	Iowa	IA	New Hampshire	NH	Tennessee	TN
Arkansas	AR	Kansas	KS	New Jersey	NJ	Texas	TX
California	CA	Kentucky	KY	New Mexico	NM	Utah	UT
Colorado	CO	Louisiana	LA	New York	NY	Vermont	VT
Connecticut	CT	Maine	ME	North Carolina	NC	Virgin Islands	VI
Delaware	DE	Maryland	MD	North Dakota	ND	Virginia	VA
District of	DC	Massachusetts	MA	Ohio	OH	Washington	WA
Columbia		Michigan	MI	Oklahoma	OK	West Virginia	WV
Florida	FL	Minnesota	MN	Oregon	OR	Wisconsin	WI
Georgia	GA	Mississippi	MS	Pennsylvania	PA	Wyoming	WY
Hawaii	HI	Missouri	MO	Puerto Rico	PR		
Idaho	ID	Montana	MT	Rhode Island	RI		

Index

Index

nonrestrictive elements, 148

nouns
    collective, 99–100
    singular and plural, 97

number expression errors, 16–17, 75–83
    dividing numbers, 31
    numbers expressed as figures, 78–79
    numbers expressed as words, 76–78
    ZIP Codes, 80–81

number in pronouns, 110

O

object of the preposition, pronouns as, 115

objective case of pronouns, 114–15

omitted copy errors, 14–16

on-screen proofreading method, 6–7, 246

open punctuation in letters, 185, 186, 191

organizations, abbreviations in, 60

P

paragraph headings, 202

parallel structure in sentences, 127–28

parenthetical expressions, 148

periods, 163

person in pronouns, 110

personal section of resume, 206

personal titles. *See* titles of people

phrases in sentences, 95, 126

plural nouns, 97

possessive case of pronouns, 117

predicate pronouns, 113–14

prepositions, pronouns as objects of, 115

print preview, 248

professional titles. *See* titles of people

pronouns
    agreement of indefinite, 112–13

and antecedent agreement, 110–11

case of, 113–17

direct object of the verb, 114

indefinite, 100–101

indirect object, 115

and infinitive phrases, 115

nominative case, 113–14

object of the preposition, 115

objective case, 114–15

possessive case, 117

predicate pronouns, 113–14

subject pronouns, 113

than or *as,* 117

who and *whom,* 116–17

proofreaders, 3
    see also proofreaders' marks; proofreading

proofreaders' marks, 3
    capitalize, 42
    change copy as indicated, 94
    change letter, 13
    close up space, 12, 58
    delete a comma, 144
    delete or omit copy, 12
    delete period, 58
    double-space, 64
    express as figures, 76
    format marks, 180–81
    insert a comma, 144
    insert copy, 15
    insert diagonal mark, 30
    insert diagonal mark and hyphen, 30
    insert hyphen, 27
    insert period, 58
    insert space, 15
    lowercase, 42
    move, 64
    for punctuation, 162
    question the author, 94
    single-space, 64
    spell out, 58, 76
    stet (keep as is), 64
    transpose, 11

proofreading
    comparative proofreading method, 6
    on computer, 245–50
    definition, 3, 222
    importance of, 2–3
    on-screen proofreading method, 6–7, 246
    reference sources for, 5
    reports, 204, 211
    team method of proofreading, 7
    see also computer proofreading and editing; errors; proofreaders' marks

proper nouns, dividing, 31

punctuation marks, 154, 161–72
    apostrophes, 167–69
    colons, 166–67
    exclamation marks, 163
    importance of, 144
    internal, 144, 164–67
    periods, 163
    question marks, 163
    quotation marks, 170–71
    semicolons, 164–65
    terminal, 144, 163
    underscoring and italics, 170
    see also commas

Q

question marks, 163

questions, 163

quotation marks, 170–71

R

race and ethnic group bias, 133

reference initials in letters, 187

reference section of resume, 207

reference sources for proofreading, 5

references in reports, 203, 204

related activities section of resume, 206

religion bias, 134

PROOFREADERS' MARKS

SYMBOL	MEANING	MARKED COPY	CORRECTED COPY
‖	Align copy.	‖112,416 105,000	112,416 105,000
¶	Begin a new para- graph at this point.	this course.¶Come and join us.	this course. Come and join us.
≡	Capitalize letter or word(s).	southwest The Examiner	Southwest THE EXAMINER
‾ or /	Change copy as indicated.	*invoice* The bill was send.	The invoice was sent.
/	Change to lowercase letter(s).	TALK of The Town	Talk of the Town
‿	Close up extra horizontal space.	Please make two photo copies.	Please make two photocopies.
ℓ	Delete copy.	They passed the the motion.	They passed the motion.
ℓ	Delete copy and close up the space.	harrassed	harassed
DS >	Double-space copy.	of the meeting. The committee <DS	of the meeting. The committee
stet or	Ignore the previous correction.	*stet* Send the reply card as soon as you can.	Send the reply card as soon as you can.
⌄! or ↑!	Insert an exclama- tion mark.	We won Hurrah	We won! Hurrah!
=/ or ∧	Insert a hyphen.	up to date report email message	up-to-date report e-mail message
∧	Insert a letter here.	*m* Accomodations at the hotel are good.	Accommodations at the hotel are good.
⊙	Insert a period.	Meet me at the office⊙	Meet me at the office.
∧ ⌄	Insert a punctuation mark.	Ron's car a blue convertible, is new.	Ron's car, a blue convertible, is new.
⌄? or ?⌢	Insert a question mark.	What time is it	What time is it?

PROOFREADERS' MARKS

SYMBOL	MEANING	MARKED COPY	CORRECTED COPY
#/	Insert a space.	It is all right.	It is all right.
~~	Make bold.	**Caution!**	**Caution!**
⊔ ⊓ ⊏ ⊐	Move copy in direction of closed side of bracket.	the of ⊔ session Ballots were Hand ⊓ the copy in ⊏ However, the	of the session Ballots were Hand in the copy However, the
] [	Center copy.	Grove Office Products] New York [	Grove Office Products New York
/?	Question the writer.	the next meeting. ? no ¶ The speakers will allow questions and answers.	the next meeting. The speakers will allow questions and answers.
no ¶	Do not begin a paragraph here. Join with previous paragraph.		
SS<	Single-space copy.	The next event SS< will be on May 5.	The next event will be on May 5.
(sp)	Spell out word or number.	sp ①Fifth Ave. sp	One Fifth Avenue
∽	Transpose or turn around copy.	reveiw the agenda (the for) next meeting	review the agenda for the next meeting
or ital	Underscore or italicize copy.	You <u>cannot</u> be late. ital <u>The Tribune</u>	You <u>cannot</u> be late. *The Tribune*